SOCIAL SCIENCE INFORMATION IN INDIA

CONCEPTS IN COMMUNICATION
INFORMATICS & LIBRARIANSHIP
(CICIL)

For a list of titles in this series,
see pp. 277-280 at the end of the book

ABOUT THE AUTHOR

DR. S.D. VYAS (*b.* 1945) at present University Librarian of Banasthali Vidyapith (a deemed university institution), Rajasthan, received his M.A. (Geography) degree from the University of Udaipur in 1966, B.Lib.Sc. in 1967 and M.Lib.Sc. in 1971 from the University of Delhi. He is a recipient of the Das Gupta Memorial Gold Medal for M.Lib.Sc. examination. He earned his Ph.D. Degree from the University of Rajasthan in 1989. He has taught Library Science at the University of Rajasthan (1971), the University of Delhi (1971-72) and P.G. Diploma in Library Science course run by the Delhi Library Association (1972-78). He has given special lectures at the Dakshin Bharat Hindi Pracharini Sabha, Hyderabad (1989-90). He is a life member of Indian Library Association, Delhi Library Association and Academy of Library Science and Documentation, Hyderabad.

Dr. Vyas was Librarian of Hindu College, Delhi (1972-80). He then joined the American Studies Research Centre, Hyderabad, as Deputy Librarian (1980-89) and Banasthali Vidyapith, Rajasthan, as University Librarian in 1989.

He has to his credit three books, twenty- five articles, two monographs, eight reviews and has presented five papers in the ILA, IASLIC and local conferences. He has participated in 50 national and international conferences held in the country, and has given special lectures.

Concepts in Communication
Informatics & Librarianship-41

General Editor: **S.P. Agrawal**

SOCIAL SCIENCE INFORMATION IN INDIA

Effort Towards Bibliographical Control

S.D. VYAS
University Librarian,
Banasthali Vidyapith, Banasthali

CONCEPT PUBLISHING COMPANY, NEW DELHI 110059

ISBN 81-7022-445-4

First Published 1992

Published and Printed by
Ashok Kumar Mittal
Concept Publishing Company
A/15-16, Commercial Block, Mohan Garden
NEW DELHI 110059 (India)

Lasertypeset by
Microtech Advance Printing Systems (Pvt.) Ltd.
H-13, Bali Nagar
NEW DELHI 110015

Dedicated

To

C.D. Sharma

Director
Rajasthan University Library
Jaipur

GENERAL EDITOR'S INTRODUCTION

In today's world, bibliographic control should relate not only to documents containing macro- and micro-thought but rightfully extend to other forms and formats conveying information.

Libraries need to exercise bibliographic control in order to serve their clientele well. Undertaken on a national scale, it registers a country's intellectual output.

Even when we think only of social sciences in India, is a single agency better suited for the purpose? Are private commercial ventures better or are professional organizations to be preferred? Should there be transliteration in one uniform script? Is it not advisable to have it on a regular continuing basis and not as a once-for-all project?

Latent in the word "control" is the concept of proper management. Again, an idea allied to bibliographic control is availability of needed item of information.

Looking at the scene presented by Dr. Vyas in this CICIL title, one may not be tempted to end up with the remark, "Situation normal, all fouled up".

S.P. AGRAWAL

PREFACE

When India attained Independence in 1947, she witnessed political, social, cultural and educational upheavals and economic problems of varying magnitudes. These compelled the National Government to adopt the principle of planned development for the efficient and effective growth, especially economic of the country. Social scientists had acted as analysts and significantly helped in shaping the development of the nation, framing national policies and involving themselves in decision-making. The importance attached to social sciences led to the development of large-scale production of literature by various government agencies (departments), universities, research organizations and professional bodies. This posed a severe problem of bibliographical control. In the absence of such control proper and effective use of already existing knowledge was not possible. It also caused avoidable duplication of effort.

On the basis of literature search, it was presumed that literature explosion in social sciences in India is a post-Independence phenomenon. There were few libraries directly dealing with social sciences, and their literature was limited. Surprisingly social science literature has exponentially grown after Independence. Therefore, bibliographical control as a measure against literature explosion is also a post-Independent phenomenon. This presumption has come true as has been amply proved in the book on the basis of available literature and field surveys.

Social science in itself is a vast area. Thus concentration of study is confined to social sciences alone. Further the coverage is limited to social science literature published in English language only.

No scientific study of social science would be complete without obtaining factual data based upon observations, surveys and field studies. To collect necessary data, two surveys at national level were undertaken, and the data analysed and/or presented in the book.

The book is based on my Ph.D. work done on *Bibliographical Control of Social Science Literature in Post-Independent India*.

S.D. VYAS

CONTENTS

LIST OF TABLES

LIST OF MAPS & FIGURE

MAPS

FIGURE

LIST OF ABBREVIATIONS AND ACRONYMS USED

AGRIS – Agricultural Research Information System
AIU – Association of Indian Universities
ALA – American Library Association
APINESS – Asian Pacific Information Network in Social Sciences
ASLIB – Association of Special Libraries and Information Bureaux
ASRC – American Studies Research Centre
CAS – Current Awareness Service
CLOSS – Checklist of Social Sciences Serials
DEVINSA – Development Information Network for SAARC Countries
DEVSIS – Development Science Information System
DISISS – Designs of Information System in the Social Sciences
DRTC – Documentation Research Training Centre
DST – Department of Science and Technology
FID – International Federation for Information and Documentation
GIPL – Guide to Indian Periodical Literature
IASLIC – Indian Association of Special Libraries and Information Centres
ICSSR – Indian Council of Social Science Research
ICSU – International Council of Scientific Unions
ICWA – Indian Council of World Affairs
IFLA – International Federation of Library Associations and Institutions
IIPS – International Institute for Population Sciences
ILA – Indian Library Association
ILRC – Inter Library Resources Centre
INB – Indian National Bibliography
INFLIBNET – Information Library Network
INFROSS – Investigation into the Information Requirements of Social Sciences
INSDOC – Indian National Scientific Documentation Centre

INSSDOC – Indian National Social Science Documentation Centre
IPI – Indian Press Index
IULNET – Indian University Library Network
JNU – Jawaharlal Nehru University
NABARD – National Bank for Agriculture and Rural Development
NASSDOC – National Social Science Documentation Centre
NATIS – National Information System
NCAER – National Council of Applied Economic Research
NCST – National Committee on Science and Technology
NICD – National Institute of Community Development
NIEPA – National Institute of Education Planning and Administration
NIHFW – National Institute of Health and Family Welfare
NIRD – National Institute of Rural Development
NISIET – National Information of Small Industries and Extension Training
NISSAT – National Information System for Science and Technology
NISSS – National Information System for Social Sciences
NSSL – National Social Science Library
PAIS – Public Affairs Information Service
PRECIS – Preserved Context Indexing System
RPC – Research Programmes Committee
RTL – Ratan Tata Library
SAARC – South Asian Association for Regional Cooperation
SDI – Selective Dissemination of Information
SENDOC – Small Enterprises National Documentation Centre
SSDA – Social Science Data Archives
SSDC – Social Science Documentation Centre
UAP – Universal Availability of Publications
UBC – Universal Bibliography Control
UGC – University Grants Commission
UNESCO – United Nations Educational, Scientific and Cultural Organization
UNISIST – World Science Information System
USEFI – United States Educational Foundation in India
USIS – United States Information Service

1

BIBLIOGRAPHICAL CONTROL

Definitions

The term "Bibliographical Control" can be defined as mastery over written records in different forms like books, periodicals, microforms, theses and dissertations, conference proceedings and unpublished reports, etc. The literature produced in these records is controlled bibliographically by means of producing subject bibliographies, indexing, abstracting tools, etc. In fact, bibliographical control is also a means to know the different kinds of bibliographical tools in order to find out what development have taken place in different subject fields and what remedies have been suggested in the past to meet the problems in their development. Bibliographical control does not mean simply an adequate recording of all materials, but gearing up the machine as a whole to answer specific queries relating to the literature on a subject. Stokes defines bibliographical control as the process of knowing various kinds of bibliographical tools.[1] Davinson describes it as various kinds of bibliographical measures that were taken in the past and that should be taken in future in order to achieve full bibliographical control.[2] Unesco defines if as "the development and maintenance of a system of adequate recording of all forms of materials, published and unpublished, printed, audio-visual or otherwise, which add to the sum of human knowledge and information.[3] The American Library Association defines it as:

> "a term which covers a range of bibliographic activities; complete bibliographic records of all bibliographic description; provision of physical access through consortia, networks, or other cooperative endeavours; and provision of bibliographic access through the compilation and distribution of union lists and subject bibliographies and through bibliographic centres."[4]

Robert B. Downs believes that there comes a stage when one feels the literature being produced is under full control. That stage of utopia will never come.[5] Stiles projects two aims of bibliographical control: One, to locate information or material, and the other to do so in quickest possible time, i.e. how much time is needed to satisfy a request.[6]

Herbert Coblans feels that the previous generation has quite successfully coped with the literature explosion and feels optimistic in regard to the future generations as well. However, he looks at bibliographical control in a different way. He claimed that 90 per cent of the world's most significant scientific information is contained in between 10 per cent and 20 per cent of the literature. On the basis of his investigations he suggested to limit the growth of the literature by tougher editorial measures so as to eliminate second-rate material. This course of action was also advocated by many writers in the past. And it serves as a reminder that the term "bibliographical control" at one time meant to imply the need for limiting the growth of literature.[7] Davinson points out,

> "It is a matter of historical fact that bibliographers over the centuries have constantly exercised the functions of evaluation and selection in compiling their works. In this sense the 'Control' element of bibliographic control could, indeed, be defined as a censoring and repression role, since the items left out in bibliographies are surely lost and dead."[8]

2. The Need

The problem of bibliographical control is as ancient as the beginning of writing itself. With the invention of typography in the 15th century, the problems of bibliographers vastly increased. While stating the proliferation of literature, Robert B. Downs says

> "the proliferation of literature has taken various forms. For over two centuries after Gutenberg's invention, publication was restricted almost entirely to the book, the monograph. Then in 1665, with the inauguration of Royal Society's *Philosophical Transactions,* the floodgates were opened to a vast and steadily expanding sea of periodical literature. Subsequently, the books and the journals were joined by the tremendous output of

government publications, by great collections of historical sources and texts, and other varied types of records pouring into libraries".[9]

It is interesting to note that the rate of book production has been accelerating year after year and specially during the present century it has taken a serious turn. Though the statistics of world book production are incomplete, it is estimated that the world book production of the last eight decades has crossed the total number of books published during the last four centuries — 1500 to 1900. Similarly, there has been a fast growth in periodicals and other forms of publications. The second edition of *Union List of Serials in the United States and Canada* recorded approximately 120,000 titles of which 43 per cent are still current and the third edition of *World List of Scientific Periodicals* includes no less than 50,000 titles in science alone. To have a reliable record of such a vast literature, systematic bibliographical control is absolutely essential.

Bibliographical control is also necessary for a systematic acquisition of material. Merely listing of documents in an order is not enough. It is also necessary to know the whereabouts of the material. Therefore, to indicate location is an important step to obtain a sound bibliographical control. National union catalogues and current national bibliographies are needed to answer this aspect of bibliographical control. Concrete measures are also necessary in respect of unpublished and non-book materials such documents are the documents of vital importance in research libraries. Emphasising the real need of bibliographical control, H.A. Lorentz says,

> "the end to be attained is that, no book or manuscript should be out of reach that we should be able to know where any book is to be found, and how it may be made accessible as early as possible. You may think that it is a little thing, but in reality it is a great thing".[10]

3. Attempts Towards Bibliographical Control

Attempts towards bibliographical control have been made at both national and international levels.

3.1. *At International Level*

Unesco and IFLA (International Federation of Library Associations) have given considerable importance to the cause of universal bibliographical control. Under the Universal Bibliographic Control (UBC), IFLA proposed to Unesco to adopt a major policy objective for the promotion of a worldwide system for the control and exchange of bibliographic information. The purpose of this system is to promptly make available a universal bibliographic data of all publications issued in all countries in the internationaly acceptable form.

3.1.1 *Unisist: World Science Information System*

At the Eleventh General Conference of the International Council of Scientific Unions (ICSU) held in Bombay in January, 1966, a proposal was adopted to create a committee to examine the feasibility of a world scientific information system aimed of achieving compatibility among existing and prospective programmes related to the storage and retrieval of science information. Two organizations — Unesco and ICSU — came together and created a Unesco-ICSU Central Committee in January, 1967, to carry out a feasibility study for a world science information system. After three years of study, the committee submitted a report in October, 1970, for the establishment of UNISIST.[11]

Unisist as a system is a reaffirmation of the traditional principles for the unrestricted interchange of scientific information in terms of modern communication technology. It is also the expression of the result of observable economic forces towards increased co-operation among the information systems serving science in all countries. In the action programme, Unisist represents a combined potential effort of governments and scientists to guide the evaluation of scientific information systems in a period of rapid technical developments so that they can provide optimal satisfaction to the needs of scientists at a cost which society is prepared to pay through governments. Unisist had also decided to extend its programme to the social sciences before the decision of Unesco to sponsor National Information System (NATIS). Science and Technology are closely linked to social sciences because of there impact on society.[11a]

Unisist is, therefore, a name which stands for a number of

concepts. As a feasibility study, its life expired with the publication of the study report. As a philosophy and conceptualization, it reaffirms long-standing traditions of the sciences in a time of change. As a movement, it represents an informed and purposive response to economic forces which impel sharing of the costs of information systems, and as a programme it represents the organizational requirements to stimulate positive cooperative action among the world's scientific information services.[12]

3.1.2. *UAP (Universal Availability of Publications)*

Another step towards bibliographical control was the development of Universal Availability of Publications Programme guided by a Steering Committee of the International Federation of Library Associations (IFLA). In June, 1979, Stephen Vickers was appointed to work full-time on the UAP Programme at the office. The functions, staffing and financing of the programme were then clearly separated from those of the Office for International Lending which continues to be supported wholly by the British Library. The Programmes Management Committee decided in December, 1980, that henceforth the focus for the UAP programme should be formally designated as International Office for UAP, in line with the International Office for UBC in London. Finance for the programme is expected to come from individual agencies which would take care of the salary, administrative expenses, research and travel costs. Such contributors will be centrally managed by the Programme Management Committee. The allocation of these contributors will be decided by the Programme Management Committee.[13]

3.2 *At National Level*

the latest thinking developed at the international level is to strengthen the noting to developed their own national bibliographics on the formal designed by Unesco/IFLA. In view of this, at national level, each country should undertake the task of recording its own publications in the form of national current bibliography. Unesco has to far held three regional seminars to discuss the problem of bibliographical control. Funds have been provided for seminars, workshops and congresses. It has brought out useful manuals, guidelines and standards for preparing national bibliographical output and held the following seminars in different parts of the third world.

First Unesco Regional Seminar on Bibliographical Control in African Countries, Lagos, Nigeria (1978).
Second Unesco Regional Seminar on Bibliographical Control in African Countries, Daker, Senegal (979).
Third Unesco Regional Seminar on Bibliographical Control in African Countries, Banjul, The Gambia (1981).[14]

The aim of Unesco and IFLA is to turn the world bibliographical control into a reality. But, to be practical, it was made clear that the ambition could be achieved through national bibliographical control. The whole idea behind bringing out national bibliographical tools is to prevent duplication of effort in cataloguing and bibliographic recording which is based on the following two simple convictions.

(i) that each country is best qualified to identify and record the publications of its own authors, and
(ii) that all countries are willing to record their national publications following the international bibliographic standards.[15]

Based on the above two convictions, there is a practical possibility of developing a universal bibliographical system which "presupposes the creation of a network made up of component national parts, each of which covers a wide range of publishing and library activities, all integrated at the national level of form the total system".[16]

India was a member of the Steering Committee of Unisist, and has been actively participating in its programmes right from the beginning. A. Neelameghan (DRTC, Bangalore) was chairman of the Unisist Advisory Committee. India has hosted, the second Unisist Meeting of Experts on Regional Information Policy and Planning in South and Central Asia in New Delhi from March 18 to 20 1976.[17]

4. Current National Bibliography

The term "National Bibliography" appears to have been first used about a century ago. As already indicated, bibliographies of this type were in existence even four hundred years ago. National bibliography is a type of enumerative bibliography. It is difficult to specifically define national bibliography. In 1896, Frank Campbell proposed for England a national system of bibliography comprising the listing of the national libraries which would be ideal copyright depositories, supplemented by the list of government documents issued by the government printers. Shortly after Campbell's pioneering efforts, French librarian C.V. Langlois defined national bibliographies as repertories of books on all subjects which have the common characteristic of being published within the territory of a given nation. Langlois indicated that a national bibliography is called retrospective if it is devoted to material formerly published in a country. And it is called periodic or current if it is periodically issued and lists new publications as and when they appear.

K. O. Murra stated the concept of current complete national bibliography as which "embraces the means to produce complete bibliographical control, currently by nations". Shores defined national bibliography as "limited to the records of a single nation or language". Traditional distinction is made between retrospective and current bibliographies. L. H. Linder has given the exact and full definition of a current complete national bibliography. "Current complete national bibliography is a complete or nearly complete listing in one or more parts of the records of a nation, about a nation, copyrighted in a nation, or in a single language issued serially at appropriate intervals as the records appear."[18]

5. **Retrospective National Bibliography**

Today's current bibliography is tomorrow's retrospective bibliography. But the difficulty of establishing a current national bibliography should not be underestimated. However, once established it is an enterprise which yields results immediately. Providing a retrospective record is much more difficult. Thus there is a satisfactory current national bibliography, it will automatically take care of the past record.

The problem is worse in the Third World countries which earlier were colonies, but are now independent nations. Their earlier records are lying in their master countries. Such countries also lacked indigenous book trade because in the colonial days most of their needs were met from the ruler country. There are many examples of a best library collection relating to a particular country being now held in the libraries of the former imperial powers than in the emerging nation itself.[19]

If one has to study the development of a complete national bibliography it is convenient to begin with retrospective bibliography, and then look at the current records. Retrospective bibliography is regarded as most reliable when one of the following two basic preconditions is fulfilled:

1. That the retrospective record was originally compiled as a current bibliography.
2. That though not originally compiled as a current record, all items embodied in the retrospective record have been compared with the actual text they represent.[20]

Because making or compiling bibliography then was not considered a well-organized crafts as now, many early retrospective bibliographies are regarded unsatisfactory by contemporary users. The bulk of current national bibliographies emanate from government agencies or other quasi-national institutions; most retrospective bibliographies are the result of individuals or non-official institutional activity.

The concept of Universal Bibliographical Control (UBC) getting importance has led to the development of current national bibliographies during the past 10 years. These now exist in more than 100 countries. During its Medium-Term Programme 1981-85, IFLA's Section on Bibliography has concentrated on the development of current bibliographies and the study and preparation of retrospective bibliographies. The recommendations maintain that unlike current national bibliography whose primary function is information, the main function of retrospective national bibliography is the identification of all the documents which constitute the national production for monographs.[21]

6. Bibliographical Control of Social Science Literature

The following areas/sectors are considered as the major social science information generating agencies:

(a) State agencies such as the legislature, executive and judiciary. In addition temporary organs of the States, such as commissions, panels and working groups, are constitute from time to time to advise the government on matters where it is considered advisable to seek such advice;

(b) Institutions, for example, universities, college departments, research and documentation centres, organisations of the trade, industry and labour, associations of professional persons, etc.;

(c) Individual research and resource personnel and the corporation/ company;

(d) International agencies such as the U.N. and its allied agencies, the World Bank and its associates and transnational corporation; and

(e) Foreign countries, organizations and individual research workers working on socio-economic and political problems of the countries other than their own.[22]

The information generated by the above-listed agencies is contained in files, data documents, reports, trade and institutional publications, Ph.D. dissertations, etc. It is clear from statistics that the social science monograph production is increasing year after year although compared to science and technology, monograph production is not that high.

If we look at the social science monograph production of 1970, two points are clear: (1) the USSR ranks first in monograph production having produced 19.278 titles (18.3%) of the world output as against 8,373 titles (7.9%) produced by the USA; (2) in social science periodical publications, the USA ranks first whereas the USSR ranks eighth. Now let us have a look at India's position. India's monograph production during 1970 was 4,979 titles, 4.6 per cent of the world total, and it ranks seventh. Surprisingly, India also ranks seventh in serial publications.

It is estimated that about 100,000 documents are produced annually by the U.N. and its affiliated agencies alone. There has been remarkable growth in the serial production dealing with social sciences. Also Ulrich and Unesco estimated the number of social science serials at between 20,000 and 27,000 current titles in 1970.

According to the Checklist of Social Sciences Serials (CLOSS) there were nearly 4,000 current titles in 1974. This includes academic titles only. In 1820, the number of current serials was just 22. In 1920 the number rose to 694. In 1950, it rose to 1806, in 1961 to 2251 and in 1970 rose to 3490. This surely shows tremendous growth of social science current serials.[23, 24]

Social science research is equally important to administrators and planners is equally important to administrators and planners for the formulation of government policies. Government agencies are not only important generating agencies for social science information, but are potential users of such information appearing in various monographs, research reports, surveys and other documents. Therefore, for an effective utilization of social science information, bibliographical control is necessary. Also in-order to bring discipline in the prevailing chaotic state of affairs.

7. Conclusion

Bibliographical control is a concept as well as a system of adequate recording of published/unpublished and audio-visual material through which one knows about their existence. It is necessary to have a check over the tremendous proliferation of publications so as to know their whereabouts and make its effective use. Various attempts have been made at the national and international level. Most significant of these are by Unesco and IFLA. The Unisist programme inquired into the feasibility of a world science information system including social sciences. The UPA programme was meant for improving national and international provisions for supply of documents and was jointly launched by Unesco and IFLA. Current national bibliographies have been in vogue for long, as a system of copyright publications by national governments. Retrospective national bibliographies have also been found useful for evaluating the rich national literacy heritage.

The last few decades have witnessed in explosion of knowledge. A large number of social science information generating agencies became active and this has resulted in an exponential growth of literature necessitating its bibliographical control.

REFERENCES

1. Roy Stokes, *Bibliographical Control and Services* (London: Andre Deutsh, 1965), pp. 13-16, 38-40.
2. Donald Davinson, *Bibliographic Control* (London: Clive Bingley, 1975), pp. 10-53.
3. Unesco, *Manual on Bibliographic Control,* Compiled by the IFLA

International Office for UBC, 1983, p. 2.

4. Heartsill Young, *The ALA Glossary of Library and Information Science,* (Chicago: American Library Association,1983), p.21.
5. Robert B. Downs, Problems of Bibliographic Control. In *Essays on Bibliography,* ed. Vito J. Brenni, (Metuchen: N.J., Scarecrow Press, 1975), pp. 124-132.
6. H.E. Stiles. Identification of the Conditions for Valid Applications of Machines to Bibliographical Control. In *Essays on Bibliography,* ed. Vito J. Brenni (Metuchen: N.J. Scarecrow Press, 1975), pp. 145-154.
7. Donald Davinson, p.10.
8. Ibid, p.10.
9. Robert B. Downs. p.124.
10. Ibid, pp.125-132.
11. P.S.G. Kumar, *Computerization of Indian Libraries* (Delhi: B.R. Publishing Corporation, 1987), p.35.

11a. Chandlev George, *International and National Library and Information Services: A Review of some Recent Developments 1970-80* (Oxford: Pergamon Press, 1982), p. 12.

12. Unesco, *Manual on Bibliographic Control,* Complied by the IFLA International Office for UBC, 1983, pp. 1-2.
13. M.B. Line, "Universal Availability of Publications", *IFLA Journal,* 7, 2 (1980), pp. 166-171.
14. Unesco, *Manual on Bibliographic Control,* p.6.
15. Unesco, *Unisist : Synopsis of the Feasibility Study on a World Science Information System,* (Paris: Unesco, 1971), pp.vi-vii, 19-21.
16. Ibid, pp.19-21.
17. P.S.G Kumar, *Computerization of Indian Libraries,* p.35.
18. Le Roy Harold Linder, *The Rise of Current Complete National Bibliography* (New York: Scarecrow Press, 1959), pp.13-18.
19. Donald Davinson, pp. 31-33.
20. Ibid, p. 33.
21. Franze George Kaltwasser. Universal Bibliographic Control. In *Essays on Bibliography,* ed. Vito J. Brenni (Metuchen : N.J. Scarecrow Press, 1975), pp.157-165.
22. N.K. Goil, p. 73.
23. Harsha Parekh. "Social Science Literature; Size, Use-patterns and Bibliographical Services," *Economic and Political Weekly,* 17, 35 (August 28, 1982), pp. 1423-28.
24. N.K. Goil, "Need for a Social Science Information System: Guidelines for a Model for India", *Library Herald,* 17, 1-4 (April 1975 — March 1979), pp. 70-93.

2

DEVELOPMENT OF SOCIAL SCIENCES IN INDIA

Introduction

Scholarship and libraries have been in existence in India since time immemorial. Indian civilization is one of the oldest in the world, dating back to 3000 B.C. In ancient times, India was the centre of institutions of higher learning and libraries. Libraries were a part of the Indus Valley civilization which flourished in India from 2000-1500 B.C They were called *Pustakalayas* and the collection in these libraries consisted of inscribed cylinder seals and clay tablets. Confirming the tradition of learning and teaching in India during ancient times, Dr. S. Radhakrishnan once said : "In the old days teachers of India were themselves librarians and they were held in very high esteem".[1] It is believed that knowledge passed from one generation to another by way of oral teaching. The handwritten books were few and were considered a rare entity worth preserving for future generations. Social sciences were claimed to be a part of India's heritage.

History of social sciences can be traced back to the beginnings of the 20th century. Among different social science disciplines, economic and political sciences were the first to gain recognition as independent or autonomous disciplines. The disciplines of sociology, psychology and anthropology were latecomers on the scene and are still in the adolescence.

During the British rule, development of social sciences in India was slow because the system of higher education was narrowly conceived and was not conducive to serious academic work. Also social science studies during this period were narrowly confined to the decennial censuses and surveys started by the British Government in the seventies of the 19th century, and ethnographic studies of Christian Missionaries who did missionary work in the tribal areas. Slow growth of social sciences during the colonial rule could also be attributed to the fact that many Indian universities did not offer facilities for doctoral work. But the dawn of independence and the expansion of the university system have greatly stimulated the growth of social sciences.

Social sciences are supposed to be an authentic body of classified knowledge of human society formulated with the objective of discovering general truths or the operation of general laws. Within the scope of definition, the social sciences can justly lay claim to being called sciences.

New Century Dictionary defines "social science or sciences as the science or group of sciences concerned with all that relates to the social condition of man, or to his existence and well-being as a member of an organised community".

Macmillan Modern Dictionary defines social sciences as "science which treats the structure and development of society; sociology, also any group of studies dealing with man in his relating to his fellows and his environment, as geography, civics, economics and history".

Encyclopaedia Britannica defines "the social sciences are concerned with orderly investigation of the behaviour of man in society with the aim of cumulating a body of relevant theory. Theories concerning group behaviour, whether economic, political, social are legion. They are implicit in men's actions, transmitted in customary beliefs and elaborated in literature".

Webster's Third New International Dictionary defines social sciences "as the branches of knowledge that deal with the institutions and functioning of human society, and with the interpersonal relationship of individuals as members of society".

According to Charles A. Beard,

> "a social science is a body of knowledge and thought pertaining to human affairs as distinguished from sticks, stones, stars and physical objects". He further continues "with what, in more detail, are the social sciences concerned? They are concerned with the actualities of human societies in development with thought and with methods of acquiring knowledge respecting their actualities of human societies in development.[2]

According to E.S.R.A. Seligman, "social sciences be defined as those mental or cultural sciences which deal with activities of the individual as a member of group".[3]

Thus social sciences are concerned with the disciplines that deal with human behaviour in its social and cultural aspects — economics, political science, sociology, social and cultural anthropology, social psychology, social and economic geography.

White's *Sources of Information in the Social Sciences* includes history, geography, economics and business administration, sociology, anthropology, psychology, education and political science as the main subjects of social sciences. These subjects have, in common, a concern for the behaviour of man in relation to his fellows and to the environment they share.[4]

The Indian Council of Social Science Research (ICSSR) has laid down, for the purpose of research support, the following subjects as constituting social sciences: anthropology, commerce, demography, economics, education, geography, law, management, political science (including international affairs), psychology, public administration, sociology, statistics, town and country planning, etc.[5] History is excluded as this is covered by humanities. Indian Council of Historical Research takes care of historical studies. However, White considers history as a part of social sciences in his *Sources of Information in the Social Sciences*. Social history could be considered a social science as it studies the social aspect of the human history.

Social sciences in their development are viewed as relatively young in comparison to the natural sciences despite being more than 200 years old. The ideas of social sciences developed from philosophy as did many other branches of knowledge. Now they have an independent status of their own and after a long period of neglect, they have gained recognition.

Systematic study of various aspects of human society which began in the 19th century has expanded further in the 20th century, and vast piles of information have accumulated in each of the disciplines of social sciences. As a consequence of this accelerated activity, the subject matter of social sciences is divided, and divided again, forming new, more specialized sub-disciplines.

Among the subjects which formed social sciences, two main tendencies dominated: first was to drive towards unification, i.e. towards a single master social science, the second was to drive towards diversification. The latter triumphed with the result that highly specialized disciplines have emerged.

1. Role and Need of Social Sciences in India

Social sciences are a major contemporary influence, but their growth has followed a slow and tortuous path. They are often considered as some kind of luxury, a status symbol, whose relevance and applicability are still vague and undemonstrated. Nevertheless, social sciences are a recognized stream of knowledge and their practitioners must be viewed essentially as men of knowledge. The functions of social sciences are well defined. A noted Indian social scientist, S. C. Dube, defines the functions of social sciences as follows:

(i) Discovery of facts and their interpretation,
(ii) Discovery of problems,
(iii) Systematization of knowledge,
(iv) Systematization of existing body of knowledge,
(v) Dissemination of knowledge, and
(vi) Fighting for truth, i.e. for establishing the logical validity of an approach.[6]

The above functions describe the role of a social scientist in society. Facts, problems and techniques of investigation become meaningful by demonstrating their capacity to generate significant ideas that can be tested and proved and have some applicability. To be socially useful these ideas are systematically organized and analyzed facts which require wide diffusion. These useful ideas should percolate atleast to the decision-making and moulders of public opinion to make an impact on the society.

Meaningful social science research involves asking the right questions and fashioning tools that can elicit answers to them with economy and precision social sciences are equally relevant to the rich and poor nations. The developing societies have a set of special problems ranging from their viability and survival as independent nations to technological transformation and economic progress.

India as a developing nation has all the well-identified problems of a developing society, i.e. an urgency of creating a cohesive, viable and durable nation; the need for rapid economic growth; and to persevere for meeting the persistent demand for distributive justice. After independence, India has gone through a wide range of experiences and moods from hope to despair, from fear of disruption to evidence of unanticipated reserves of strength and unity, and from threats of economic collapse to signs of recovery.

India has a wider range of relatively dependable statistics. Its social morphology is understood in a broad outline. Much of the research exercise has little contemporary relevance as it has touched only the surface. A great deal of research engages itself in the pursuit of the trivial. There is considerable reluctance to take up major issues of investigation, in developing appropriate research tools for them, and in making analyses that throw up significant ideas. The potential of social science research to provide an insight into the key issues and critical areas remains largely unutilized. According to Dube social science research is not a substitute for national development. In many instances it would not even indicate a policy line. Social science practitioners are essentially analysts. Further, he has listed the following major possibilities of utilization of social science research towards national development:

1. Social science research throws up valuable background data from which the planner can make his own assessment of the prevailing situation, especially of the magnitude, complexity and ramifications of the problems he has to handle.
2. Carefully designed analytical studies can illuminate critical areas of policy. The overt and covert dimensions of a given problem emerging in such studies provide the planner with a measure of foresight to deal with them effectively and efficiently.
3. The studies open up the possibility of testing the validity of the assumptions that must, of necessity, be made by the planner in setting his proximate and ultimate objectives.
4. They enable the planner to foresee the possible consequences and the cost of the different choices available to him in determining the path for the attainment of his goals.
5. Diagnostic studies suggest where and why a particular project went wrong. The unexpected consequences are also brought to light.
6. Wide dissemination of social science research findings increases general awareness about the situation to be met as well as the policy designed for this purpose. This may enhance the credibility of particular policies and prepare the people for them. It may also help towards building up popular pressures

for reformulation of particular policies or weeding them out altogether.[7]

According to the Review Committee of the ICSSR Report (1973) the following statement makes explicitly clear the needs and purposes of social science research in India:

1. In the social transformation of Indian society, therefore, social sciences are an essential input. This particular role calls for a sustained appreciation by the administrators as well as the academic community of their possible contribution and can in turn lead to an action-role for the social scientists in the formulation, implementation and evaluation of policies and programmes. There is indeed some confusion, if not conflict, in the minds of many social scientists, between basic and applied research and the primacy of one over the other. That two types of research interact with each other leading to the enrichment of theories, the sharpening of research methodology and validation of social action calls for a depth of understanding which does not necessarily obtain at all levels. The social relevance of research will admittedly entail polemical considerations but the issues remain relevant for all that.
2. In order to participate effectively in the task of building a new India, social sciences will aim at performing a basic function in studying and shedding a new light on the contemporary social situation. There is a need to ask relevant questions, fashion analytical tools and work out conceptual frameworks which can elicit adequate responses to real-life challenges.
3. Economic growth, the development and application of science and technology, social change, inequality and the war against poverty and other social crises together with their solutions are the dominant concerns of India today. Social sciences may only ignore them at their peril.
4. *Economic Development*: Social sciences are of particular significance to planned economic growth which is recognizably a prior concern in India. They can define and clarify the economic goals, concrete objectives of development and supply of requisite models for dynamics of economic development. The planning process as it does rational choices

calls for an application of scientific knowledge and techniques. In addition, the success of planning involves the appraisal of resources, the ensuring of the adequacy and reliability of organization and administrative structures and procedures, the calling forth of a certain quality of leadership, political interest and socio-cultural moves that help to set a motivation in people and foster the right attitudes . . . social sciences can directly contribute to a resolution of problems in these areas. To carry the fruits of development to millions of people is yet another task in which social sciences can be pressed into service.

5. *Social Chance*: India is caught up in a change of many dimensions. Traditional socio-political structures, economic bases, family patterns and community moorings have all been affected as a result. The traditional authority structure is loosing its foothold under the influence of change caused by science, technology and urbanization. Evidently, the old order is changing. In this context, the social scientists are required to provide an understanding of the process of contemporary social change and to provide therefore knowledge and skills that can guide and control the change mechanism.
6. *Science and Technology*: India is deeply concerned with scientific knowledge and the application of the resultant technology to create conditions of material prosperity. The successful diffusion of a scientific and technological culture calls for insights that serve to identify socio-cultural values that favour science and technology as distinct from those that do not. In addition social scientists must define the framework that can nurture a scientific culture.
7. *Poverty and Inequality*: Poverty is an acknowledged reality in India today. Nearly a quarter of our population, i.e. over 130 million, is estimated to be living below the poverty line defined in terms of the per capita intake of food at 2,200 calories per day. These people are illiterate for the most part and many are school dropouts living in urban slums and rural settings have been denied the basic health requirements.
8. The causes and consequences of poverty are both enmeshed in the all too familiar social and economic inequality that have reinforced each other. Disparity exists between the urban and rural communities just as it exists within the rural and urban

groups. Wide disparities exist moreover as between the primary, secondary and tertiary sectors of the economy. The average per capita annual income varied from Rs. 428 in the primary sector to Rs. 933 in the secondary sector and to Rs. 1,117 in the tertiary sector during 1970 to 1971 at contemporary prices.

9. Poverty is a scourge and social justice demands that such blatant inequality be transformed through decent standards of living and that a sense of human dignity be established in every human being. Caste is dysfunctional both to the growth of science and the abolition of poverty and the socio-economic inferiority of the untouchables deserves consideration as a priority. Social science can no longer ignore these live issues. As it has a definite role in developing a strategy of economic development so it must confront and face the economic issues of concentration of property and wealth to good purpose.
10. *Social Crises*: Socio-cultural issues, such as the generation gap, the authority relation in a kinship setting, social brasses, stereotype tensions, violence and aggression, socio-economic phenomena associated with corrupt practices are more lively today than before. Social Sciences can illafford to take an oversimplified stance in dealing with them. Indeed, their casual roots as also their ramifications and implications must be studies that an effective guideline can be devised to give more meaning and content to public policy.
11. Against this backdrop, social sciences can no longer remain an instrument for the generation of knowledge which involve commitment in the education of the policy-maker and in the policy-making processes themselves. Therefore, social sciences must, above all, constantly strive for new meanings of human existence and of social purpose. Social relevance must become their central and definite objective.[8]

Social science research in India lacks a national focus and is not relevant to the major concerns of the day. The right questions are not asked, and if asked, they are not pursued vigorously and seriously. There is no evidence of vigorous methodological innovation. Unfortunately, there is excessive reliance on concepts established abroad and much uncritical use of borrowed methodology.[9]

Since the inception of ICSSR in 1969, funds have been made

available to support social science research on selected themes. A considerable amount of data was gathered through these sponsored projects. These data are useful in planning. The government's sponsorship did provide an impetus to social science research. But one wonders how much they have enriched the research tradition. Some of the problems are of cost benefit analysis. We have to consider whether the gains are commensurate with what the taxpayer is paying for. This is applied to almost all national research organizations irrespective of subject specialization. Thus there is need to find out and correct if there are any organizational incompatibilities and contradictions in government-run research institutions.

Many universities have in adequate funds earmarked for research. But UGC has now offered to every university a grant for development of research. The number of scholarships and fellowships have also increased over the years, and it is likely to increase further. This is to be welcomed. These are often distributed equitably among the different departments and within the department of students on the basis of marks, but without any consideration of the quality of the research proposal or of the ability of the scholar to carry it out. Pre-Ph.D training either does not exist, and if it does, it is not very effectively organized and pursued.

Social sciences are mainly explanatory. Only under certain conditions they can be diagnostic. They cannot project a definite course of social action, at best they can only suggest policy alternatives. A social scientist will be judged by the quality of his product and his success in communicating it to the community in general and to the policy planning in particular.

Social sciences have a dual function — contribute to policy processes and extend the frontiers of knowledge. Both functions are relevant in the Indian context today. In policy-making the role of social sciences is increasingly recognized. The centres of higher learning, the government and the world of business do recognize this role which is manifested in a growing number of social scientists being engaged as administrators, research officers, advisers, consultants, professional evaluators, personnel managers, social workers and planers in government and industrial organizations and other agencies. The conviction that social science research can contribute to the growth of industry and material prosperity of the country has steadily gained ground. Development and growth of social sciences in India can be assessed by a number of indicators which are as follows:

2. Growth of Social Science Research in India

2.1 *Rapid Increase in the Number of Universities After Independence*

In 1947, there were about 70 universities. In 1975-76 the number of universities rose to 101. Today there are more than 150 universities and are deemed to be university institutions in the country. In 1971, 91 universities had 823 post-graduate departments in social science subjects out of which 397 were located in universities and 426 in colleges affiliated to the universities. The number of such departments has been growing with qualified and competent faculty, which have been responsible for the growth of social science literature.

2.2 *Growth of Research Institutions in Social Sciences*

Social science research is not the monopoly of universities and research institutions alone. A survey of research institutions undertaken by ICSSR indicates that in 1971 there were 95 research institutions which operated outside the university system. They were either wholly government institutions or autonomous, but were entirely financed by the government. However, there were some autonomous institutions which were independent of any government support. Central and State Governments also carry on research which is policy oriented. The research and development wing is increasingly becoming an essential part of every government organization. The fields in which there is noticeable contribution by the governmental institutions include anthropology, agricultural economics, population studies, criminology, economic planning, etc. Many worthwhile reports, surveys, etc., have been added to the existing literature of social sciences as a result of the activities of these research institutions.

2.3 *Emergence of Funding Agencies for Research in Social Sciences*

Prior to independence, development of social science research was inexorably linked with the growth of universities and research institutions only. The government did not play any active role in the propagation of social science research. But the establishment of the Planning Commission in 1950 gave impetus for the involvement of the government in social science research. The Planning Commission after its creation realized the need for social science research on the topics of relevance and significance for national development. The Research Programmes Committee (RPC) formed in 1953 was established to work out and administer suitable schemes of research investigation into social, economic and administrative problems relating to national development in consultation with universities and other institutions. In the First Five Year Plan, Rs. 50 lakhs were spent on promoting the above objectives. In 1953-69, RPC financed 400 research studies on socio-economic problems having a bearing on the planning process. With the establishment of ICSSR, 45 on-going research projects of RPC were transferred to ICSSR and RPC's role was the problems having a direct bearing on the Plan formulation and implementation.

During 1963-64 UGC initiated a scheme of financial assistance to university/collage teachers for undertaking short-term minor research projects, in humanities and social sciences with a view to enabling individual teachers — more particularly college teachers and young lecturers in the universities — to engage themselves in research work. The scheme was intended to provide facilities which would help research projects and give minimum support by way of books, field work, etc. Further UGC started a teacher fellowship scheme in 1975-76 enabling teachers from affiliated colleges offering instruction in social sciences, to work for either an M.Phil. or a Ph.D. Degree. Besides this, UGC has been promoting research activities in the field of social sciences along with other fields through various schemes.

The Planning Commission had set up a committee on social science research in August 1965, under the Chairmanship of Dr. V.K.R.V. Rao. The Committee in its report (1967) recommended establishment of Indian Council of Social Science Research (ICSSR) for promoting research in social sciences. ICSSR was set up by the Government of India on April 15, 1969, with promotion of research as its central activity.

ICSSR research programme includes:

1. Financial support to research proposals received from social scientists and institutions.
2. Grant of fellowships.

Out of the total budget of Rs. 162.83 lakhs of ICSSR in 1976-77,

Rs. 31.20 lakhs (i.e., 19.28%) was spent on research grants, Rs. 16.48 lakhs (10.18%) on research fellowships and Rs. 54.13 lakhs (33.57%) on research institutions. These three activities most extensively used instrument of ICSSR — accounted for nearly two-thirds of the budget of ICSSR. A total of 708 research projects were sanctioned between 1969-70 and 1976-77. A classification by discipline indicates that two-thirds of all approved proposals belong to the three major social science disciplines, viz. economics, political science and sociology, and between the three they are equally divided. But the need for a few research institutes in social sciences outside the university system was also recognised. In 1975-76, ICSSR supported 15 research institutes and spared a sum of Rs. 50.58 lakhs for this purpose.[10] The Second Review Committee (1978) acclaimed the contribution of ICSSR in the followed words:

> " . . . clearly, one of the important landmarks in the development of social science in India. Its work in the past nine years has fully justified its establishment. . . ." "It has made a significant contribution to the development of social research in the country".[11]

Among the foreign agencies, the United States Educational Foundation in India (USEFI), the Ford Foundation and the Rockefeller Foundation have been providing financial assistance for social science research. Among the private Indian foundations, mention may be made of the Tatas, Birlas and other industrial and business families and companies. But the government is the main funding agency for social science research. In the distribution of funds for research, however, social sciences are given a low priority. In 1973, India spent about Rs. 250 crores per year on research and development in natural, technological, agricultural and medical sciences, and only Rs. 2.5 crores on research in the social sciences which is one-hundredth of what is being spent on natural sciences. However, within the next 10 years, in 1983-84, the expenditure on scientific research and development was estimated to be Rs. 1,427.8 crores.[12] *ICSSR Annual Report 1984-85* claims that Rs. 363.07 lakhs were spent on social science research.[13]

Let us compare our social science research expenditure with the USA — in 1951, out of 217 million dollars, six million dollars were spent on social science research. In 1971, this expenditure rose to

5,150 million dollars out of which 421 million dollars were spent on social science research. This accounts for 6.85 per cent of the total research expenditure as compared to 2.80 per cent in 1951. Thus there is a perceptible increase in the expenditure. This reflects the importance the US government assigns to social science research for formulating their government policies.

3. Growth of Social Science Literature

Social Science : A Bibliography of Doctoral Dissertations Accepted by Indian Universities 1857-1970 brought out by the Inter-University Board of India indicates the course of development of the respective disciplines of social sciences. The publication presents the history of their growth in India. From this point of view, the bibliography fills an important lacuna. Indeed a rigorous analysis of the trends of research carried out by the subject specialists on the basis of information provided therein would prove immensely helpful. The bibliography lists 2,810 theses accepted by the Indian universities for doctoral degrees in social sciences. It includes sociology, political science, law, public administration, economics, commerce, management education, library science, journalism and psychology. This bibliography indicates that the first Ph.D. degree in social sciences was awarded by Allahabad University in 1901. It is a coincidence that a research degree in social sciences was awarded with the beginning of the 20th century. In economics the first Ph.D. degree was awarded by Calcutta University in 1911.

Another important bibliography that covered the Indian subcontinent is Patterson's *South Asian Civilization : A Bibliographic Synthesis* (Chicago : The University of Chicago, 1981). This bibliography covers almost all historical periods and disciplines of social sciences and humanities. According to Patterson a serious study of all aspects of South Asia is a phenomenon of the period following Second World War and the consequent achievement of independence in the subcontinent. This bibliography charts or maps an intellectual field or area, both by defining its limit and by placement of references to pertinent books and other written materials within these limits. Though foreign the bibliography is yet the best bibliographical tool available on India. In Patterson's own words:

"For those who would venture into the vast, almost limitless, area of Indian civilization, this book presents charts — some detailed, some sketchy — of material showing highways, broad avenues, lanes, and paths that the scholar may take on his travels in this domain".[14]

3.1 *Research Activities*

Table 2.1 indicates the development of research in social sciences in India. Another indicator which shows the growth is the number of doctoral degrees awarded. In social sciences 1849 degrees were awarded till 1967. In the succeeding years, 266 doctoral degrees were awarded in 1968 alone, 265 in 1969, 349 in 1970, and 452 in 1975-76. However, 846 Ph.D. degrees were awarded in 1984. This shows intensification of research work leading to almost doubling of Ph.D. degrees. The major subject areas are history, economics, education, commerce, political science, psychology and geography as shown in the Table 2.2.

TABLE 2.1: Subject and year-wise distribution of dissertations in Social Sciences accepted by Indian universities, 1857-1970

Subject	Up to 1920	1921 1930	1931-1940	1941-1950	1951-1960	1961-1970	Total
Commerce	—		2	7	35	78	122
Economics	3	4	17	71	293	647	1036 *
Education	—	—	—	10	79	233	322
Journalism	—	—	—	2	2	3	7
Law	7	3	1	3	11	42	67
Library Science	—	—	—	1	1	2	4
Management	—	—	—	2	15	65	82
Political Science	—	3	5	13	83	285	392 *
Psychology	—	1	2	3	36	169	211
Public Administration	—	—	1	12	34	103	150
Sociology	—	1	5	39	98	282	426 *
Total	10	12	33	163	687	1909	2819 *

* Year of award of degree is not available for the following number of scholars of Lucknow University:

Economics — 1
Political Science — 3
Sociology — 1

Source: Inter University Board of India. *Social Science : A Bibliography of Doctoral Dissertations Accepted by Indian Universities 1857-1970*, 1974, p. iii.

TABLE 2.2: Doctoral theses accepted by Indian universities in 1984

Subject	Number of Doctoral Theses
Commerce	92
Economics	134
Education	110
Geography	62
History	151
Home Science	10
Law	8
Library Science	8
Management	26
Military Science	4
Political Science	93
Psychology	79
Public Administration	7
Social Anthropology	11
Social Work	3
Sociology	48
Total	846

Source: University News, 1984.

Social science research is essential for the formulation of policies which is evident from the increasing support and involvement of the government. Rapidly increasing investments in social science scholarships and research have led to the production of enormous bodies of reports, articles, papers and other information carriers. Further, imprecision of social science vocabularies, proliferation of specialized terminologies and marked cultural and ideological contrasts in approaches to social, political, and economic problems have also led to the growth of social science literatures.

Most of the social science research is undertaken by the social scientists in the universities and colleges. Therefore, an idea of their number would be of great significance. According to UGC, 2,582 social science teachers were employed in university departments in 1969-70. They were engaged in the various social science disciplines. It is estimated that, at present, there are about 7,000 social scientists working in India. They are making significant contributions to the growth of social science literature. According to the latest figures available there are 9,500 social science teachers engaged in universities and colleges.[15]

ICSSR statistics show 60 professional associations existed in the year 1971, out of which 33, were all-India and 27 of regional level. The earliest professional organization was in the field of history (1919), anthropology (1921), geography (1926), linguistics (1928) and economics (1929). A gradual increase in the number of professional associations since independence is shown in Table 2.3.

TABLE 2.3: Growth of professional associations

Year	No. of Associations
1947	16
1951-59	25
1967	47
1970	60

The largest number of associations is in the field of geography (10), anthropology (8), economics (7) and political science (7) and the rest represent the remaining disciplines. These have also been promoting research and publication activities.

3.2 *Development of Various Social Science Journals in India*

Any discipline grows with the volume of research, and therefore, the need for journals to publish the research findings is increasingly felt. The number of research journals in a discipline is an indicator of its status and growth. An ICSSR survey indicates that there were 863 social science journals in 1973. The volume of publications in this field has been steadily increasing since than. It has been noted that 16,729 research publications were published in India during 1925-65. Thus, on an average, 418 research publications were published every year.[16]

Another research study conducted by R.P. Kumar shows that 106 journals were published before 1947 in the area of social sciences and allied subjects. Such periodicals have seen ups and downs as most of them had undergone a change of titles. Table 2.4 shows the subjectwise number of journals originated in India during 1780-1947.[17]

TABLE 2.4: Social Science journals in pre-independence period

Subjects	No. of Journals
Economics	13
Education	10
Government and Politics	8
History	15
Law	15
Indological Studies	45
Total	106

Source: R.P. Kumar: *Research Periodicals of Colonial India 1780-1947*, Delhi, Academic Publications, 1985.

Journals which originated prior to the beginning of the 20th century have been discontinued because of the problems peculiar to periodicals. It is difficult to keep them updated. Despite many journals published prior to 1947 which collected a lot of social science data, no planned and systematic bibliographical attempts were made by any single institution.

According to M.H. Gopal only those Indian social science journals could be considered as learned journals which have had a fairly long life. According to him, a periodical should have run for a few years in order to claim professional status. Normally, an academic research is published either in an article or a book. The measure of the standard of an article should be the journal wherein it has been published. Any good journal should have the following checks. First, the help of senior faculty members in the concerned discipline. Secondly, the professional utilization of the periodical as evidenced by citations of its articles. Finally, wherever available the choice made by standard publications in indexing articles. Applying the foregoing qualifications the following Indian periodicals in different social science subjects emerge as the standard bearer for scrutinizing the research output in India.

3.2.1 *Economics*

The main economic problem of the country is the slow rate of economic growth which has been baffling most economists of the country. After independence the role of economists in India has radically changed. They were associated with economic policies, and they compelled to take constructive stands on important economic questions. Economics has grown by leaps and bounds in post-independence India.[18] The following journals are considered as the best Indian journals in the field of economics.

1. *Arthaniti* (a relatively new quarterly but indexed in full in AEA Index).
2. *Arthavijnana* (Gokhale Institute of Politics and Economics, Pune).
3. *Indian Economic Journal* (Organ of the Indian Economic Association).
4. *Indian Economic Review* (Delhi School of Economics, University of Delhi).
5. *Indian Journal of Agricultural Economics* (Organ of the Indian Agricultural Economics Society).
6. *Indian Journal of Economics* (the oldest economic quarterly and once the Organ of the Indian Economic Association).

3.2.2 *Political Science*

Research in political science including public administration and international affairs is still in its infancy despite researchable problems being plentiful and research funds generous. Because of their infancy, Indian journals are not of a high order of scholarship, and certainly not of an exacting international standard. This could be proved by the fact that the Indian journals are not cited in international journals. Because of the lower scholarly reputation of the faculty, fewer articles are published in foreign journals by Indian academics. Given these considerations, the following journals may be taken as indicators of quality in political science:

1. *India Quarterly* (Indian Council of World Affairs).
2. *Indian Journal of Political Science* (Organ of the Indian Political Science Association).
3. *Indian Journal of Public Administration* (Organ of the Indian Institute of Public Administration).
4. *Indian Political Science Review* (Delhi University).
5. *International Studies* (Jawaharlal Nehru University).

3.2.3 *Sociology*

Sociology, including social work and anthropology, is comparatively an old discipline of study in Indian universities. But, its growth in terms of research output and its spread among universities have been slow. M.H. Gopal is critical of Indian sociological research. He feels that there are hardly a couple of Indian sociologists of international repute and hardly a dozen of national standing. As a consequence of all this, there are a few periodicals in India of international scholarly standing. The following are the best journals:[19]

1. *Eastern Anthropologist* (Ethnographic and Folklore Culture Society, Lucknow, U.P.).
2. *Indian Journal of Social Work* (Tata School of Social Sciences, Bombay).
3. *Man in India* (Edited by Dr. Surjit Sinha, Ranchi).
4. *Sociological Bulletin* (Organ of the Indian Sociological Society).

The first journal of sociology was started in January, 1920. Named *Indian Journal of Sociology* it was edited by Alban G. Widegery of the Baroda College, Baroda, with the sanction and support of the government of His Highness the Maharaja Gaikwar of Baroda. The journal published articles on such themes as nature of sociology, child welfare, religious organization in Indian cities, education, politics, civics and town planning. It contained a review section, and also published notes on sociology in Indian universities written by Patrick Geddes. The Indian Sociological Society was founded in 1952, under the leadership of G.S. Ghurye. It started *Sociological Bulletin* in the same year, which became the main forum for the publication of research papers in the field. The Indian Sociological Conference, an all-India body, got merged with the Indian Sociological Society. At present there is only one all-India body, namely, Indian Sociological Society. In addition to *Sociological Bulletin*, *Indian Journal of Sociology* and *Social Science Research Journal* also publish research papers in the field of sociology.

The Indian Association of Trained Social Workers was started by J.M. Kumarappa, founder Director of the Tata Institute of Social Sciences. One of the achievements of the Association was the starting of a quarterly journal, *Social Work Forum*, in 1964. Other journals dealing with social work are: *Social Work Review*, a yearly publication of the Faculty of Social Work, M.S. University, Baroda; *Social Action*, a bi-annual review of social trends started by the Indian Social Institute, Delhi, 1951; *Kurukshetra*, a monthly open forum on community development started by the Ministry of Community Development and Cooperation in 1952; and *Social Welfare*, a monthly started in 1954 by the Central Social Welfare Board.[20]

It is important to note that establishment of several scholarly journals during the late 18th, 19th, and early 20th centuries gave a forum for publishing the results of researches. Some of these journals were:

1. *Journals of the Asiatic Society of Bengal* (1784).
2. *Indian Antiquary* (1872).
3. *Journal of the Anthropological Society of Bombay* (1886).
4. *The Quarterly Journal of the Mythic Society, Bangalore* (1909).
5. *Man in India* (1921).

Anthropology was included as a section of the Indian Science Congress in 1912. It is important to note that no clear-cut division between social anthropology and sociology was maintained. The Asiatic Society of Bengal also promoted research in Indology under the leadership of Sir William Jones.[21]

3.2.4 *Psychology*

One of the rapidly growing disciplines of social sciences which is also branching out into many specialities is psychology. However, compared to its growth in the USA the discipline in Indian universities is still in infancy. Consequently, the Indian periodicals are few in number and the research articles in them have still to touch international standards. However, the following could be considered as few good journals in psychology.

1. *Indian Journal of Psychology* (Indian Psychological Association).
2. *Journal of Psychological Researches* (University of Madras).
3. *Psychological Studies* (Department of Psychology, University of Calicut, Calicut).

Some of the psychological journals published regularly are *Indian Journal of Applied Psychology, Indian Journal of Experimental Psychology, Indian Journal of Psychology, Indian Psychological Review, Journal of Psychological Researches, Manas* and *Psychological Studies*. Many good articles of psychological research done by Indians are published in foreign journals, and in journals of education, social work and university journals.

It was only after 1947 that the real growth of social science emerged for which steps towards bibliographical control became necessary. According to S.P. Agrawal only 24 new Indian social science journals were begun in the first 50 years of the 20th century as compared to 241 which appeared between 1950-1980. Thus the rate of growth of social science journals is quite phenomenal, and by the turn of this century many new journals will emerge. NASSDOC and its other coordinating agencies will have to have an effective bibliographical control. This will necessitate provision of proper funds to NASSDOC to bring out indexing and abstracting tools and other bibliographical tools to have full coverage of what is produced in social science subjects.[22]

4. Indian Social Scientists and Their Contribution

Social sciences in India suffer from paucity of creative contributions. The state of the social sciences in India is protracted barrenness. Despite social sciences having been taught in Indian universities for a fairly long time to an increasingly large number of students, fundamental contributions have been rather rare.

Modern social sciences did not originate in India. Their roots are in modern Western Society, and has been shaped in their spirit and content by the ethos and processes of that society. Social sciences grown in the West were transplanted to the Indian soil and cultural climate. But they have failed to grow and yield fruit. It is understandable, therefore, that even if an Indian teacher or a student was able to understand and remember theories imported from the West, he could seldom contribute to their fundamental growth. Indra Dev has pointed out the following drawbacks as the main causes of lack of creativity among Indian social scientists:

1. Most academics were busy in nationalistic movement, and they did not bother much about what they have to teach.

2. Intellectual creativity was in the foreign medium.

Use of English as a language medium by the Indian intelligentsia tends to become a barrier in easy communication with the masses. This becomes a serious drawback for the development of social sciences.[23]

Again social scientists in India, as elsewhere, began their career with hybrid vigour. The pioneers drawn from distinct fields such as economics, anthropology, Indology and social philosophy had worked hard to establish the claim of this discipline through their own research and subtle infiltration of sociological orientation in the course taught by them. Their students contributed the first pressure group for the recognition of sociology as a separate discipline by the Indian Universities. Bombay and Lucknow were the only two bold universities to grant a status to social science subjects.[24]

P.C. Joshi recognises Radhakamal Mukherji and D.P. Mukherji as founders of the Lucknow School of Social Sciences. The School made a major contribution to the development of an Indian perspective on social sciences and specially to the evolution of an Indian School of Economics closely related to Indian Sociology. The term Lucknow School is deliberately being used here as Radhakamal Mukherji very explicitly and consciously viewed his intellectual efforts and those of his colleagues in terms of building up an Indian School of Economics and Sociology. Social sciences have not yet assimilated the vital elements of the contributions by the pioneers who were not only gifted social scientists individually, but were also collectively the builders and promoters of a school of thought.

Social sciences grow under the stimulus and shocks provided by the problems thrown up by the changing objective social reality. In the evolution of social sciences there is a complementarity between the roles and functions of social scientists as sages, as theoreticians and as technicians. The sages provide the broad philosophical approach of social sciences in the context of transition from a religious to a secular world. The founders of the Lucknow School acquired the structure of sages in the history of social sciences in India by their writing as social scientists and by their teaching, but also by pursuing a way of life which was sage like in every sense of the term. The creative and innovative clan of pioneers of Indian social science is eroded by an initiative approach, by surrender to intellectual fashion waves from the West by large sections of the

Indian social science community.

P.C. Joshi laments:

> "It is a paradox that during the fifties and sixties when Western social scientists were emphasizing the inter-disciplinary orientation and institutional approach and were reinterpreting the concept of development, in India the issues pioneered by the Lucknow School suffered and eclipsed. In Indian social science institutions, the craze for narrow specialization and technical sophistication seemed to overshadow the concern for bridge building between disciplines. Even if attempts were made to bring the social science disciplines together at some centres (e.g. at Indian Statistical Institute and at the Delhi School of Economics), these could not be sustained for long and the practitioners of each of the disciplines soon restricted within their narrow shells".[25]

The new wave of delimiting the boundaries of economics, sociology and political science relegated into oblivion the rich legacy of the pioneers of the School of Indian Economics, Sociology and Politics which had grown in the pre-Independence period at Lucknow, Bombay, Poona and Calcutta. The new generation of post-Independence economists, sociologists and political scientists had perhaps not much familiarity, understanding or sympathy with the work of the pre-Independence pioneers of social science in India.

4.1 *Radhakamal Mukherji*

Radhakamal Mukherji was a well-known Professor of Sociology in Lucknow University. During his academic career, he lectured at different universities of the country. He stressed the need for an institutional approach and observed that "the principles of Western economics could not be applied to Indian conditions in the same way as the rules of grammar and syntax of one language". In one of his lectures at St. Stephen's College, Delhi, Mahatma Gandhi observed that the subjects should be studied out of doors, in the fields, cottages and workshops, in relation to actual facts and conditions instead of cramming Western economics as heedless and forgetful of the phenomena around them. Radhakamal Mukherji stressed that the social scientist should be connected with the people through social work and social service, if social sciences are not to get dehumanized.

The following are Radhakamal Mukherji's contributions towards the growth of Indian social sciences.

1. *Principles of Comparative Economics* 2 Vols. (1921)
2. *Borderland of Economics* (1925)
3. *The Rural Economy of India* (1926)
4. *Fields and Farmers of Oudh* (1929)
5. *Land Problems of India* (1933)
6. *The Regional Balance of Man* (1938)
7. *Food Planning for Four Hundred Millions* (1939)
8. *Institutional Theory of Economics* (1941)
9. *Ground Work of Economics* (1942)
10. *Man and His Habitation* (1940, 1968)
11. *The Social Structure of Values* (1950)
12. *The Dynamics of Meals* (1951)
13. *The Indian Working Class* (1951).

Radhakamal Mukherji was also associated with the teaching of sociology at Calcutta University for five years (1917-21). He came from Lahore to Calcutta University and taught economics, sociology and political philosophy.

Mukherji's contribution will be remembered as a path-breaking thinker and social scientist of the era of India's freedom struggle and first phase of national consolidation. He will also be remembered as one who trained generations of students in the methods of social science inquiry and investigation specially into Indian problems. Mukherji also served as a guide to research students in most of the social science branches for their Ph.D. dissertations for about four decades. Karl Manheim's commendatory comment about Mukherji was that prior to Mukherji's work there was no systematic work on the sociology of values in India.

Radhakamal Mukherji well known for his sociological researches on regionalism and social ecology was appointed professor of both economics and sociology in the Department of Economics in 1921. In those days teaching of sociology was done by the Department of Economics.

4.2 *D.P. Mukherji*

Another brilliant social scientist of Radhakamal's time was D.P.

Mukherji, a contemporary of R.K. Mukherji. His major essays are: "Indian Tradition and Social Change" and "On the Present State of Economic Theory". The following are his significant works in the field of social sciences:

1. *Modern Indian Culture* (1928)
2. *Notes of Indian Culture* (1951)
3. *Diversities* (1958).

D.P. Mukherji was for the unity of social sciences. He was a missionary-type social scientist. He was R.K. Mukherji's senior colleague in Lucknow University. D.P. Mukherji influenced more with his voice than with his pen. He was an intellectual colossus, a renaissance figure. Both R.K. and D.P. could be considered as the founding fathers of the Indian social science. D.P. Mukherji joined Lucknow University in 1922 and gave emphasis to sociology of culture.[26]

4.3 *G.S. Ghurye*

G.S. Ghurye made significant efforts in developing Indian sociology. He not only encouraged his students to study tribes, but also himself dealt with the tribal problems in his *The Aborigines* (1943) which created a sensation as it controverted Verrier Elvin's notions of tribal isolationism. He emphasized the fact that, in the Indian social context, the distinction between anthropology and sociology was artificial.[27]

4.4 *B.S. Guha*

B.S. Guha was one of the few scholars in sociology of this period who were trained in the USA. He obtained his Ph.D. from Harvard in 1924 for his thesis on *The Racial Basis of the Caste System in India*. On his return, he joined the University of Calcutta in 1926. After a year's service in the University he joined the Zoological Survey of India as an anthropologist, a post which was newly created. Most of his contributions have been in the field of physical anthropology.[28]

4.5 *D.N. Majumdar*

A separate Department of Anthropology was created in Lucknow

University in 1951 under the supervision of D.N. Majumdar. He founded the Ethnographic and Folk Culture Society (U.P.) in 1945 which started publishing a journal, *Eastern Anthropologist*. He built up a strong Department of Anthropology and his interest ranged from physical anthropology to culture change among the tribes to urban studies.[29]

It is important to note that a sharp distinction between anthropology and sociology did not emerge. G.S. Ghurye, K.P. Chattopadhyay and D.N. Majumdar were trained in anthropology, they did researches both among the tribes and the castes, and in the rural and the urban settings. Similarly, the Department of Sociology in Bombay, Mysore and Lucknow included courses in anthropology. Ghurye once remarked that in Bombay, sociology included social anthropology and in Calcutta social anthropology was extended to include sociology.

Another university to introduce sociology was Calcutta, and Asutosh Mukherjee established the postgraduate councils of Arts and Science in the middle of the first decade of the 20th century. Sociology was taught at the M.A. level along with economics and political science.

4.6 *A.R. Wadia*

In 1917-18, Mysore University started teaching sociology at the undergraduate level, and it was first to do so. A.R. Wadia, who was responsible for the introduction of sociology and its teaching, looked upon sociology as applied philosophy. He had his education at Bombay, Cambridge, Oxford and London. However, research in sociology was not announced as in other universities in the early years.

The above social scientists were the social scientists in true sense of the word. Man like Radhakamal Mukherji guided research not only in sociology and economics, but also in other subjects like geography, anthropology, etc. Such social scientists were against compartmentalization of social science disciplines and always wanted that social sciences should grow as a one unified subject.

Patterson's observation about the Indian situation particularly after 1947 is relevant. It is also important to know how a foreign bibliographer views the Indian bibliographical situation. In Patterson's words:

". . . there are some systematic, planned approaches to social science and historical research in modern India. The Census organization has throughout its hundred-year history asked a series of questions and presented the resultant descriptors attempts to look at broad areas of research, note trends, and pin-point lacunae, Indian government bodies are producing multivolume surveys of research by academic disciplines (Indian Council of Social Science Research) drawing up plans for historical research in fields deemed neglected, and producing "nationalistic" histories to counter socalled imperialist interpretations of the past century (Indian Council of Historical Research)."[30]

5. ICSSR Surveys of Social Sciences in India

Late D.R. Gadgil, first chairman of ICSSR, put forward the idea of conducting surveys in all the branches of social sciences to formulate priorities and significant programmes in promoting social science research in India. He argued that this task would be greatly facilitated if a survey of all research conducted so far in social sciences is quickly carried out.

Under this scheme, the entire area of social sciences was divided into the following seven major fields:

1. Economics, Commerce and Demography.
2. Political Science including International Relations.
3. Public Administration.
4. Management.
5. Sociology, Anthropology, Social Work and Criminology.
6. Psychology.
7. Economics, Human and Political Geography.

Focus of the survey was on research carried out by Indians on Indian problems and a trend report in each of the fields was to be accompanied by a select bibliography.

5.1 *Economics*

Till independence there was no scope for practical experimentation, there were neither pressures for right revision, nor scope for improvement. After independence, the role of economists in India underwent a radical change. They were increasingly associated with economic policies, and were thus compelled to take constructive stands on important economic questions. The thinking they gained was sharp, precise and relevant. Economic research was sponsored significantly by the Research Programmes Committee of the Planning Commission, UGC, Ministry of Food and Agriculture and other Government Departments. Economic dailies, weeklies, journals and periodical conferences and seminars fostered the habit of questioning and discussion.

Yet old ways of thinking die hard, and they relapse frequently. Some of the new questions were hard to answer and demanded new methodologies and new combinations of knowledge which would take time to acquire. The aim of the Survey of Research in Economics was to present a critical account of the stimulating research done after independence in the important fields of Indian economics by Indian and foreign scholars to examine the gaps and to suggest sub-fields and priorities for further research. The survey presents a result of an extensive consultation and scrutiny process. The Survey of Research in Economics was published in seven volumes.

Economists tend to think of economic activities in terms of matching demand, and demand is determined by income distribution, which itself is the aim of planners to change, and tastes which are largely determined by advertisement and reflect the working of an unequal society.

Research priorities chalked out by the Survey are mentioned below:

(a) Illumination of the unorganized parts of different sectors;
(b) Identification of the obstacles to integration of the economy especially of unorganized parts, and devising of policy measures to remedy them;
(c) Conservation and economy in the use of water, energy, fuel, forests and scarce natural resources;.
(d) Behaviour of sectoral savings and their maximization and mobilization for plan purposes;
(e) Devising an income elastic tax system;
(f) Export promotion;
(g) Compulsory savings;

(h) Application of cost benefit analysis to public investment;
(i) Price changes and effects on factor supply;
(j) Signals of private sector and policy instruments for its control and regulation;
(k) Institutional and technological restructuring for the weaker sections;
(l) Regional and area planning;
(m) Problem of unemployment;
(n) Vertical mobility of labour;
(o) Resurveys of small areas;
(p) Study of economic effects of power structure;
(q) Problems of federalism; and
(r) Fundamental needs and choice among means of satisfying them.[31]

5.2 *Demography*

Interest in population as a field of research is still new, but it has attracted considerable volume of writings. To get research-oriented writings in this field has, therefore, involved a rather voluminous compilation of references which are presented in the form of classified and annotated bibliography. In the trend report, an attempt has been made to find out research content literature. This is followed by a general appraisal of the present state of research on population and related topics and then by an identification of research topics which seem to be more relevant in the context of development.

Assignment took a lot of time to appraise the volume of writings, including articles, papers, books, monographs, reports and even mimeographed papers. A generous help in the performance of this task was received from the Demography Research Centre of the Institute of Economic Growth.

The first comprehensive census covering most of British India was conducted during 1867-1872. Then in 1881 came the first complete census of population which was conducted on a uniform basis throughout India. Official reports giving a wealth of statistical information about the population have been available for the entire period covered by the census. This availability of massive data has not, however, helped the emergence of demography, the study of population, as a discipline. What we have for the period prior to

Second World War are occasional references to population problems in the writings of scholars on economic matters. After Second World War, population has formed a subject of more popular interest and of a serious study. The literature has grown tremendously and an infrastructure of some sort has been created for demographic research. It is difficult to say with certainty that demography is on the way to occupy its rightful place amongst social sciences. The present survey reviews the literature on population which has emanated from diverse sources and considers the yawning gaps in our knowledge about the multifaceted problem of population. It attempts further to suggest the line on which research may proceed in the interest of evolving demography as a discipline of knowledge on purposeful lines.

There are three main agencies in this field to collect demographic data:

1. *National Sample Survey Organization*

The National Sample Survey Organization was established at the instance of the late Prime Minister Jawaharlal Nehru and the initiative of late Prof. P.C. Mahalanobis in 1950. Its object may to obtain in a continuing manner comprehensive information on social, economic, demographic and agriculture characteristics through sample surveys on a country-wide basis.

2. *Research Programmes Committee of the Planning Commission*

The Committee sponsored series of city surveys. The original plan of city survey was to use it for the Second Five Year Plan, but due to delays these could not be used for that purpose.

3. *Fertility and Family Planning Surveys*

The surveys have acquired popularity because of the growing general concern with the problems of accelerating increase in the population over the last two decades. These social surveys focus attention on fertility and family planning and are obviously relevant as substantive contributions to demographic research.

Major work has been done in the area of family planning, urbanization, population size, reproductive performance, etc. The main concern of the growing demographic literature has been the variation in the size of India's population leading to consideration of reproductive performance. Another area of interest which seems to have attracted considerable attention is urbanization, next only to family planning. It accounts for 13 per cent of the aggregate.

The International Institute of Population studies, Bombay, originally called the Demographic Training and Research Centre was established under the joint auspices of the Government of India, the U.N. and the Tata Trust in 1956. Its contribution has been notable, but it remains the only institute catering to the training needs of Indian demography. The Indian Statistical Institute, Calcutta, offers a course in Demography in the form of an optional paper called "Population Studies and Vital Statistics".[32]

5.3 *Political Science*

A survey of research in political science is being published in five volumes by ICSSR.

Volume I covers: (1) Studies on the Indian National Movement, (2) Constitutional development, (3) Institutions of parliamentary democracy, (4) Political parties and pressure groups, (5) Leadership, (6) Judicial behaviour and process, (7) Judicial system in India, (8) Political performance and the policy process and (9) Political science and political system.

The remaining four volumes cover the following subjects of political science.

Volume II: (1) Processes of politics, (2) Federal politics, (3) State politics, (4) Urban politics, (5) Local politics, (6) Electoral politics, and (7) Comparative politics.

Volume III: (1) Caste and politics, (2) Politics of scheduled castes and scheduled tribes, (3) Religion and politics, (4) Students and politics, and (5) Violence and politics.

Volume IV: (1) Contribution of theory, (2) Political thought in Ancient India, (3) Political thought in Mediaeval India, (4) Political thought in modern India, (5) Indian writings on Western political thought, and (6) Marxian theory and analysis of India politics.

Volume V: (1) International relations, (2) Area studies, (3) Foreign policy studies and (4) Defence policy and analysis.

It also contains an overview of political science and the political system in India. The survey covers broadly the period up to 1970-71.

ICSSR proposes to bring out periodic reviews of research work done after the period covered by this survey.

Today there are 59 Political Science departments (second only to Economics). Another index of an excellent physical expansion is the number of Ph.D. theses submitted in the universities. While in the 40- year span (1911-50) covering the British colonial period only 148 Ph.D. theses in the social sciences were submitted in all the universities in India, in the next 20 year (1951-70), i.e. in the two decades after Independence, 2,576 theses were submitted (including 526 in political science and international relations).[33]

5.4 *Public Administration*

Survey of Research in Public Administration is published in two volumes. Public Administration as a discipline developed largely in the 20th century. Differing academic traditions in the various countries especially of the West, however, classified the discipline under Law, Political Science, Economics or even History.

In India, public administration is viewed both as a broader policy and implementative process. Its scope covers the manner in which policy issues in the country arise, formulation of public policy including the interaction between the legislatures, the bureaucracy, the legal systems, the institutional and technological systems designed for both policy formulation and implementation and, finally, the day-to-day management of public policy which determines its actual content.

Volume I of the Survey comprises the following chapters:

1. Study of Public Administration in India.
2. Politics and Administration.
3. Union-State Relations.
4. Research on Union and State Administration.
5. Headquarters Organization of Government.
6. District Administration.
7. Administration of Urban Areas.
8. Planning.
9. Budgeting and Financial Control.
10. Fiscal Administration.
11. Public Personnel Administration.

Volume II covered the period up to 1969 and dealt with eleven sub-areas including research methodology in public administration.

The Survey covers the period up to the end of 1969 and includes most of the research work on India done by Indian social scientists. The second survey of research covers the period of 1970-79. Where necessary, references have also been made to outstanding research work on India done by non-Indian scholars.[34]

5.5 *Management*

Management is a subject distilled in which out of many subjects. It is necessary to examine research in management in the following sections:

(a) Boundary of management study : the management function and its tasks;
(b) The nature of reach in management study : applied *vs* pure research and inter-dependence with other sciences; and
(c) The outlook and needs of research in management study.

The field of management is so diverse that it has no universally accepted focus. This is partly due to its complexity and expanse, and partly due to the variety of disciplines that converge upon it. Research in management may be more purposeful if the overall perspective of the field could integrate the differences and orientations into a pattern. If an overall perspective of management study does not have a pattern that integrates all the aspects, research would provide only knowledge about a part, rather than the whole of the subject under study.

It is, therefore, very essential to study management function and its tasks and discuss a framework for understanding the total subject. The field of research in management is fed by many streams, and a researcher has to use inputs from several disciplines. The special characteristic of research in management is the study of the confluence of multiple variables in the situation. Methodology is, however, essentially the same as in other fields of study. Thus management constitutes a distinct field of study by itself. A researcher has to follow necessarily the methodology of social science research. Just as the social scientist derives his hypothesis from available knowledge and proceeds to obtain data to his hypothesis, the researcher has to draw upon available knowledge and begin to examine the situation he is studying through data collected by him.

The main areas of research are general management and business history, organization and administration, personnel management and industrial relations, marketing, procurement and distribution, production operations, research and technology, finance, accounting and information control systems.[35]

5.6 *Sociology*

The idea of a massive programme of conducting survey in sociology was to identify the trend of development in various social disciplines in India.

The objectives of ICSSR surveys are the following:

1. They attempt to give a historical account of the trends of development in Indian sociology, social and cultural anthropology and social work. They serve as a background for the study of the survey reports included in these volumes.
2. Secondly, they try to summarize and highlight the main findings of each of the survey report and discusses their recommendations in terms of guidelines for determining priorities for research. The discussion also takes note of some areas of research, not covered in the present survey.
3. Thirdly, they attempt an assessment of the teaching facilities in terms of research areas covered by analysing the syllabi of different universities. A discussion of the availability of trained manpower is also relevant in this context. But as no adequate data on the subject is available the problem has only been briefly posed.[36]

M.S.A. Rao considers three phases of the development of research in social and cultural anthropology, sociology and social work. These are: (1) The phase of exploration, (2) The phase of subject as an academic discipline, and (3) The phase of diversification. It is interesting to know that the first two phases marked the development of the subject in the colonial period while the third phase had begun in the post-Independence era. It is, therefore, necessary to see these trends of development in the wider context of national problems, theoretical advancement and social needs — all of which have varied from time to time.

5.6.1 *Social and Cultural Anthropology*

Under social and cultural anthropology, tribal studies were the first to be initiated in India in the late report of the 18th century. Sir William Jones, in his inaugural address to the Asiatic Society of Bengal in 1774, defined the scope of anthropology as the entire field of studies concerned with man and nature. Such studies connected with social and cultural anthropology were published in journals and memoirs of the Asiatic Society. A few surveys of anthropological nature were published in the early part of the 19th century. But Anthropological research gained momentum during the last decade of the 19th century under Sir Herbert Risley, who himself was an anthropologist. He published *Tribes and Castes of Bengal* in four volumes. It is due to Risley's efforts that the Ethnographic Survey of India was established in 1901. The purpose of the Survey was to produce detailed ethnographic literature on Indian tribes and castes. Indian scholars particularly Anantha Krishna Iyer, S.C. Roy, Rai Bahadur Hiralal, B.A. Gupta, M.D. Nathubhoy, Lal Bihari Dey and a few others have contributed to the enrichment of literature on tribes and castes. S.C. Roy and Anantha Krishna Iyer could be considered pioneers of Indian ethnology. Iyer's work on the Cochin and Mysore tribes and castes and on the anthropology of Syrian Christians bears testimony to his scholarship. An important work on Indian anthropology is W.H.R. Rivers' *Todas* (1906). No less important is A.R. Radcliffe Brown's work on Andaman Islanders during 1906-8.

Anthropology developed as an academic discipline in Calcutta University at the initiative of Sir Ashutosh Mukherjee who was the then Vice-Chancellor. In 1920, S.C. Roy laid stress on field research with anthropological survey and the study of group in its entirety. He started the journal, *Man in India*, in 1921.

The diversification phase of social and cultural anthropology took place after the attainment of independence. It was a turning point in the development of social sciences in general. A significant trend was a shift in the emphasis from the study of tribal societies to the study of peasants and urban communities. Increasing facilities of the exchange of professors and students between India and USA resulted in a considerable influence of American anthropology on Indian anthropological studies.

The Ethnographic Survey of India established in 1901 was reincarnated in 1946 by the Government of India as the Anthropological Survey of India. In the 1950s Indian and foreign social anthropologists and sociologists took interest in the study of Indian societies. Particularly, their attention went towards the study of village communities.

5.6.2 *Sociology*

In 1914, a well-known town planner, human geographer and sociologist, Patrick Geddes, came to India. He was the man who influenced Radhakamal Mukherji. He was also the one who worked for the setting up of a department of sociology in the University of Bombay in 1915. And the first Ph.D. programme in sociology was started in this University in 1936. M.C. Pradhan was the first man to obtain his Ph.D. degree in 1938 for his research work on the *Untouchables in Bombay*. Another school of sociology was opened in Lucknow University. In the late 1930s and 1940s more universities introduced sociology as a discipline. Osmania University started teaching sociology as an optional subject in 1928. Poona University established the Department of Sociology and Anthropology at the Deccan College in the late 1930s.

Diversification in the field of sociology in the post-independence period was greater than in the field of anthropology. The trends of research in sociology and social anthropology favoured close association between them in the post-independence period. Another area of significance that emerged was political sociology. The subject includes elections, communications, communalism, backward class movements and the changing patterns of leadership at the village level. Another area of importance is industrial sociology. Research in the area was also promoted in the post-independence period. This subject covers worker, entrepreneurs, industrial, bureaucracy, industrial relations and trade unions. Sociological research in the post-independence period led to the growth of all-India professional associations.

5.6.3 *Social Work*

In India social work has a long tradition though its scientific orientation is recent. The origin of social work is associated with social reform. Reform activities in India took place in the early part of the 19th century. Persons like Raja Ram Mohan Roy, B.N. Malabar, Justice Rannade, Gopal Krishna Gokhale and Agarkar were the main architects who laid the foundation for a secular liberal and rational way of studying social problems. Brahmo Samaj, Prathna Samaj, Arya Samaj, Indian National Congress, Servants of Indian Society, Theosophical Society and Rama Krishna Mission were the organizations which contributed towards the reform of society.

Mahatma Gandhi also gave a lead to social reform and social activities during the early days of this century. The welfare of Harijans and tribal people, of women and children, socio-economic progress of the handicapped, rural welfare and leprosy relief were the areas in which Mahatma Gandhi took active interest in his life.

Sir Dorabji Tata Graduate School of Social Work was established in Bombay in 1936. It was a landmark in the development of social work education and research in India. The same school came to be known later as Tata Institute of Social Sciences. It started publishing the first journal on social work, *Indian Journal of Social Work*, in 1940. The second school of social work was established in Varanasi in 1947 by Kashi Vidyapeeth. Delhi School of Social Work was also established in the same year.

But social work education and research in India suffered in the absence of university recognition. However, Delhi University took the initiative and recognized it in 1948. This had its effect and during 1948–52, 15 schools of social work were started in different universities. In the 1950s research work of the Ph.D. standard in social work was undertaken. A few Departments of Sociology also encouraged students to undertake research on such social problems as crime, alcoholism, juvenile delinquency and prostitution.[37]

5.7 *Psychology*

Psychology as a science started in India with the establishment of a Department of Psychology in the Faculty of Science of Calcutta University in 1915. Research in psychology began thereafter. Review of psychological research in India has been done earlier by S.K. Mitra in 1955, B. Krishnan in 1961, D. Sinha in 1963 and S.D. Kapoor in 1965. These are valuable documents inasmuch as they have put on record the work done in the field. The ICSSR Advisory Committee on Psychology conducted a review of research in psychology in 1970-71. The Committee requested the psychologists to make a review of the research done in the area allocated to each individually.

These reviews show that the volume of work done in psychology is large, and that there has been a vigorous growth of psychological research in India, especially in the last 10 years. However, it is to be noted that the bulk of this research arose out of the process of the birth and development of scientific psychology in India.

Though the origin of psychology in India goes back to ancient times, the foundation of scientific psychology was laid only in the 20th century, as noted earlier, with the establishment of a psychological laboratory in Calcutta University in 1915. This was followed by Mysore where a Department of Psychology in the University of Mysore started functioning in 1924. The Indian Psychological Society was founded by G. Bose in 1922 and the Indian Psychological Association was formed in the year 1924, both having their headquarters in Calcutta. *Indian Journal of Psychology*, an official organ of the Indian Psychological Association, made its appearance in 1925. Soon after this, a psychological laboratory was opened in Lucknow, through an independent department of psychology did not exist. In 1946, Patna University started two full-fledged Departments of Experimental and Applied Psychology, although the work in applied psychology had started earlier at Calcutta.

Thus the period of a few decades before independence saw the beginning of scientific psychology, a scientific journal for the publication of research papers and a professional association to develop the image of the new science. In the post-independence period, 10 new university departments were added during the decade beginning with 1950. In the next decade, 17 more were added (UGC Report, 1968). At present, there are 33 university departments of psychology.

The rapid increase in research activity in psychology since 1950 can be seen both in the number of references in 10 reports and in the increase in the number of journals. The number of professional journals is another indication of the amount of research in the field. In 1950 there was one professional journal but now there are more than 12. A large number of trained psychologists are working outside the straight academic department in the universities. This is likely to influence psychological research in India. After 1950, there has also been a rapid progress in the number of publications on psychology as shown in the Table 2.5.

TABLE 2.5: Post-1950 publications in the years in different areas of psychology

Year	No. of publications
1951-55	325
1956-60	612
1961-65	865
1966 and after	1179
Total	2981

Source: A Survey of Research in Psychology, Bombay, Popular Prakashan, 1972, p. xxi.

Social psychology, clinical psychology and personality psychology were the major areas of psychological research. The rate of production is very high in social psychology because it is easier to produce papers. Experimental psychology remained neglected and the most neglected areas are physiological and comparative psychology. Contrary to the popular impression, neither much research has been done in the area of methodology, nor is there much published research.

Some of the basic requirements for research in psychology are as follows:

1. A good library of books and journals, particularly back volumes, is a prerequisite for research. ICSSR in collaboration with selected psychological departments can develop a research abstracting service.
2. Computational facilities are equally necessary. The Departments require small desk calculators, statistical tables and other aids.
3. Research activity is stimulated by social demand and appreciation. In research, social demand itself is an expression of appreciation. There should be demands for psychological research of different varieties from the government, semi-government agencies, industry and business, educational institutions and other organizations.
4. Budget is woefully poor for the development of research.[38]

ICSSR should set up interdisciplinary research teams including psychology for the study of salient social problems.

5.8 *Geography*

Indian geographers have by and large shown little interest in theoretical discussions on the nature of geography. The reasons are partly historical. When the controversy between the exponents of environmental determinism and possibilism was raging in the West, modern Indian geography had not been born. It did not yet get involved in the ideological turmoil through which modern geography acquired its philosophical foundations and its intellectual rigour.

Geography as a social science is concerned with the analysis of the spatial dimension of social phenomena and with the synthesis of natural as well as social variables within a regional frame. The future development of the discipline of geography as a social science should not be envisaged and planned in isolation from at least the immediate past. A major thrust to the development of geography at the professional level was given with the starting of the National Atlas Organization in the early 1950s. The decade of 1960-70 has been significant with reference to the contribution of Indian geographers, particularly in applied geographical studies.[39] ICSSR should give support for more geographical research of different regions of the country as regional studies. It should promote the following areas of geography on priority basis for geographical research. These are: Agricultural typology, Study of market centres, Techniques of area planning, Population and resources, Man and environment, Designing of industrial towns and centres, Geographical importance of the Indian Ocean region, Degree of the effectiveness of the "State Idea" in India, Electoral geography of India, Aspects of land reforms as related to landuse in hilly areas, Migration studies — rural and urban — and Plantations and refugee resettlements.[40]

6. Factors Responsible for Bibliographical Control of Social Sciences

Research in social sciences till the 1950s was mostly confined to universities, archives and a few research institutions like the Asiatic Society of Bengal (1784), Asiatic Society of Bombay (1804), National Archives of India (1891) and Bhandarkar Oriental Research Institute (1917). But in the post-independence period the research activity gains momentum on account of the following factors:

1. *Adoption of Planning as Chief Vehicle for the National Development*

Various government departments at national and state levels needed information and data for preparing their development plans. Therefore, various ministries, departments either undertook research projects by way of employing social scientists or got this work done through university departments and professional organizations.

2. *Setting up of Inter-disciplinary Research Institutes*

Social scientists of different disciplines got an opportunity to work together and share their experience for tackling problems of national and international importance in right perspectives.

3. *Role of Learned Societies*

Realizing the importance of research, they developed the infra-structure necessary for their members so as to promote their might in national development.

4. *Lead Taken by Commercial Organizations*

They set up research centres to keep their staff abreast with the latest techniques of management, marketing and technological advances.

5. *Expansion of Educational Facilities*

Many universities and institutions instituted research programmes leading to M.Phil., M.Litt, and Ph.D. degrees.

The cumulative effect of the above resulted in the setting up of many institutions in the country as shown in Table 2.6.

Table 2.6 makes it explicit that only 34 research institutes existed by 1950 whereas 139 such institutions came into existence during 1950-1980.[41]

In the field of economics, political science, public administration and sociology some research was done in Indian universities even prior to 1947, but research in social sciences attained to the full growth after 1947 only. Ultimately, a large volume of literature was produced which could not be properly utilized in the further growth process in the absence of its effective bibliographical control.

TABLE 2.6: Decade-wise growth of research institutes

Decades	Number of Institutions
Period up to 1900	8
1901-10	1
1911-20	1
1921-30	9
1931-40	2
1941-50	13
1951-60	38
1961-70	49
1971-80	54
1981-	5
Total	180

Source: B.M. Gupta et al, *Handbook of Libraries, Archives and Information Centres in India*, Delhi : Information Industry Publication, 1984, Vol. 1, p. 144.

Development of research in social sciences was affected by certain factors that were operative immediately after independence. Till 1947, there were only 17 universities and a few social science research institutions in existence. The grants given to them social science research organisations were quite meagre. This situation, improved considerably after Independence. Today, there are 150 universities (including deemed to be universities) and about 400 social science institutions. Though the development of social science research has always been slower compared to science and technology, it was considered necessary to accelerate it with a view to giving it a role in the economic planning of the country. Consequently, it received strong support from the government and ICSSR was born. This proved a turning point in the development of social science research in the country.

7. Socio-Economic Situation in Post-Independent India

Immediately after 1947, the Government of India found itself facing many social and economic problems. On the one hand, it was busy handling the havoc created by the partition. On the other, it had the country's completely shattered economy staring in its face. In the circumstances the National Government first thought of adopting planned economy through Five Year Plans. So the Planning Commission was set up in the year 1951. It was entrusted with the work of systematic economic planning with fixed targets. Although the targets were always short of expectation, they did wonderfully will to meet the priorities of the nation. For example, the First Five Year Plan (1952-55) gave importance to the improvement of national income; Second Five Year Plan to industrialization (1957-61); Third Five Year Plan to fertilizers, power generation, etc., (1962-66); Fourth Five Year Plan to complete those incomplete projects which yield immediate results (1969-74); Fifth Five Year Plan (1974-79) accorded top priority to projects capable of yielding results in the short run; Sixth Five Year Plan (1979-84) to rural development; Seventh Five Year Plan (1985-90) gave top priority to agriculture, employment generation and increase in productivity.

The need for planned development of the country was prompted to be more specific by the following factors: low standard of living, low span of life and high death rate, improper use of national resources, import of foodgrains, low progress in agriculture and industry, unemployment, higher value of import than of export, and growing population.

The Government of India was aware that economic development cannot be left to the whims and fancies of individuals. It realized that the distribution of resources should be regulated consciously by the organized agencies, and a favourable political and social atmosphere be created to ensure increase in investments. All this involved a lot of research work and consequently a large volume of literature was produced. Its proper utilization in the national development also necessitated proper bibliographical control.

8. Conclusion

Social sciences are now considered an important branch of knowledge pertaining to human activities and institutions. Social sciences are concerned with the disciplines that deal with human behaviour in its social and cultural aspects. It encompasses economics, political science, sociology, social and cultural anthropology, social psychology, social history, geography, public administration education, etc.

Social sciences are generally viewed relatively young in

comparison to natural sciences. They have gained recognition after a struggle of 200 years. There were two tendencies visible in the development of social sciences. The first was to drive towards unification for one single master social science, and the second was diversification of social sciences. But it is the second tendency that has won with the result that many disciplines and sub-disciplines have emerged today. In fact, social sciences are a major contemporary influence though their growth has been slow and tortuous.

Social sciences are as relevant to the rich nations as they are to the poor. Since independence, India has well-identified problems of its developing society wherein social scientists have acted as analysts. ICSSR and UGC have offered grants to universities and social science research institutions for promoting research. Development of social sciences can be assessed by the number of universities and colleges, university departments, research institutions, number of doctorates in social sciences and by the establishment of RPC, UGC, ICSSR themselves. The Association of Indian Universities has brought out a bibliography of doctoral dissertations of social sciences, which presents the development of social sciences. More than 1,000 doctoral theses in social sciences are submitted to the Indian universities every year.

Under the chairmanship of the late D.R. Gadgil, ICSSR conducted research surveys in the early 1970s in all the branches of social sciences to formulate the priorities and significant programmes in promoting social science research. Under this scheme the first survey of social sciences particularly in seven major fields was conducted. This and other surveys show a phenomenal rise in research literature. This necessitates its bibliographical control.

Information generated by social science research institutions, central, state and local government, international agencies, conference proceedings, conference papers, etc., have led to the growth of social science information which needs processing, documentation and presentation in the form of new information. This has also led to an "information explosion" for which a bibliographical control is necessary. In fact bibliographical control in the present day is considered a central theme of librarianship.

REFERENCES

1. R.N. Sharma, "India, Academic Libraries." In *Encyclopaedia of Library and*

Information Science. Edited by Allen Kent et al. (New York : Lekker), v. 39 Supplement 4, p. 203.

2. Charles A. Beard, *The Nature of Social Sciences* (New York : Charles Scribner, 1934), p. 230.
3. E.S.R.A. Seligman, "An Encyclopaedia of Social Sciences," (New York : Macmillan, 1934), p. 330.
4. Carl M. White, *Sources of Information in the Social Sciences : A Guide to the Literature,* 2nd edition. (Chicago : ALA, 1973), p. 1.
5. N.N. Gidwani, "Documentation on India." In *Comparative Librarianship.* Edited by N.N. Gidwani (Delhi : Vikas, 1973), p. 183.
6. S.C. Dube, "Role and Functions of Social Sciences." In *Research Methods in Social Sciences.* Edited by B.A.V. Sharma, D. Ravindra Prasad and P. Satyanarayana. (New Delhi : Sterling, 1985), p. 2.
7. S.C. Dube in B.A.V. Sharma, D. Ravindra Prasad and P. Satyanarayana eds., p. 5.
8. ICSSR Review Committee *Social Sciences in India : Retrospective and Prospective, a Report* (New Delhi : ICSSR, 1973), pp. 1-4.
9. S.C. Dube in B.A.V. Sharma, D. Ravindra Prasad and P. Satyanarayana, eds. p. 7.
10. B.A.V. Sharma in B.A.V. Sharma, D. Ravindra Prasad and P. Satyanarayana, eds., pp. 11-14.
11. Overviews and Recommendations. In *Report of Second Review Committee* (1978), p. 80.
12. *India 1985* (Delhi : Ministry of Information and Broadcasting, 1985), p. 100.
13. B.A.V. Sharma in B.A.V. Sharma, D. Ravindra Prasad and P. Satyanarayana, eds. p. 15.
14. M.L.P. Patterson in Collaboration with Wilham J. Alsparigh. *South Asian Civilization : A Bibliographic Synthesis.* (Chicago : The University of Chicago, 1981). Introduction.
15. S.P. Agrawal, *Social Science Information and Documentation : Search for Relevance in India.* (New Delhi : Concept, 1986) p.
16. ICSSR Annual Report, 1984-85.
17. R.P. Kumar, *Research Periodicals of Colonial India 1780-1947.* (Delhi : Academic Publications, 1985), pp. 1-7, (Published Ph.D. dissertation).
18. D.T. Lakadwala, Introduction, In *ICSSR Surveys of Research in Economics,* vol. p.1.
19. M.H. Gopal, "Criteria for Assessing Current Research in Social Sciences in Indian Universities." *Indian Economic Journal,* 32, 4 (April-June 1985), pp. 51-54.
20. M.S.A. Rao, *ICSSR Survey in Sociology and Social Anthropology.* (A Project Sponsored by the ICSSR). (Bombay : Popular Prakashan, 1974), p. xxix.
21. M.H. Gopal, pp. 45-54.
22. S.P. Agrawal, "Indian Social Science Periodicals," *Library Herald,* 22, 1 (April 1983), pp. 34-46.
23. Indra Deva, "Methodological Perspectives for the Study of Society in India". In *Contemporary India,* Ed. by Giri Raj Gupta. (Delhi : Vikas, 1976), p. 75-9.
24. Yogesh Atal, "Sociology in the Indian Campus". In *Contemporary India.* Ed. by Giri Raj Gupta. (Delhi : Vikas, 1976), p. 117.
25. P.C. Joshi, "Founders of the Lucknow School and Their Legacy Radhakamal

Mukherjee and D.P. Mukherjee—Some Reflections." *Economic and Political Weekly,* 21, 33 (August 16, 1986), p. 1457.

26. P.C. Joshi, pp. 1445-69.
27. M.S.A. Rao, p. xxv.
28. M.S.A. Rao, p.xxiv.
29. M.S.A. Rao, p. xxiv.
30. M.L.P. Patterson, p. xiv of Introduction.
31. D.T. Lakadwala, Introduction. In *ICSSR : A Survey of Research in Economics,* (Bombay : Allied, 1977), v.1, p. xix.
32. P.B. Desai, *A Survey of Research in Demography.* (A Project Sponsored by the ICSSR). (Bombay : Popular Prakashan, 1975), pp. 46-51.
33. ICSSR : *A Survey of Research in Political Science.* (New Delhi : Allied, 1979), pp. 210-211.
34. V.A. Pai Panindikar, "Study of Public Administration in India, a Survey." In *ICSSR's A Survey of Research in Public Administration.* (Bombay : Allied, 1973), p. 1
35. C.P. Rao, *A Survey of Research in Management,* 2 vols. (Delhi : Vikas, 1973) p. 1, 7.
36. M.S.A. Rao, Vol. 1, pp. xxi-xxii.
37. M.S.A. Rao, Vol. 1, pp. i-xvii.
38. S.K. Mitra, *Psychological Research in India.* ICSSR's Sponsored Project: (Bombay : Popular Prakashan, 1972), pp. xvii-xx.
    Second Survey of Research in Psychology covers the period 1971-76. This is a follow-up of the first which concerned the period up to 1969. This is in two parts. It was done under the chairmanship of Udai Pareek. (Bombay : Popular Prakashan, 1980).
39. Moonis Raza, *Geography as a Social Science.* ICSSR's Sponsored Project. (Bombay : Popular Prakashan, 1977), pp. xix-xx.
40. ICSSR Review Committee, *Social Sciences in India : Retrospective and Prospective, a Report* (1973), p. 128.
41. S.P. Agrawal and Manoharlal, "Social Science Research Libraries and Documentation Centres in India." In *Handbook of Libraries, Archives and Information Centres in India.* Edited by B.M. Gupta et al. (Delhi : Information Industry Publication, 1984), Vol. 1, pp. 144-46.

3

BIBLIOGRAPHICAL ACTIVITIES OF SOCIAL SCIENCE INSTITUTIONS A Survey

Introduction

This chapter is mainly a record of the survey carried out to get the views of the social science research libraries and higher education libraries about the state of bibliographical control of social science literature in India, and to elicit whether they feel any need for it or desire improvement in the existing state. Interestingly, majority of the respondents (96%) expressed need for it. Besides inquiry about the various bibliographical tools prepared locally or acquired readymade, it was also attempted to know the views about the functioning and perceptions of the National Social Science Documentation Centre (NASSDOC).

The survey findings indicate that social science institutions and higher education libraries are quite strong in the following subjects: commerce and trade, sociology, education, statistics, anthropology, geography, history, psychology, political science, etc. This list is in order of priority. Some of the newly emerging interdisciplinary areas are science and technology, agricultural economics and rural development, population studies, environmental studies, computer science, medical and health care and they all have social science relevance. These have developed and emerged because of the new challenges faced by society.

Indian social science research institutions and university libraries have of late become important centres of social science research. This is because of the growth of specialized collection. In fact, their collection is complementary to each other. The National Library, Calcutta, due to its peculiar character and location could not render much help to the social science research community. Hence, there is every likelihood of cooperation from such libraries as can meet the demands of scholars. This has resulted in strong links between university libraries and social science research libraries. Thus, there is also a need to have a system by which social science research could be systematized by getting good library cooperation from both.

Institutions, to whom the questionnaires were distributed are wellknown and recognized social science research institutions and university libraries of India. The following criteria were used to select institutions:

(a) Institutions which have a very significant collection in certain areas.
(b) Institutions which have been engaged in documentation activities for a long time.
(c) Institutions which have been referred to by foreign countries.
(d) Institutions where research facilities are available.
(e) Institutions which have been termed as depositories in different subjects.
(f) Institutions which are financed by ICSSR, and
(g) Libraries of national importance in the field of social sciences.

To collect the data about the bibliographical activities, a questionnaire was sent to 160 select social science institutions and universities in India. As customary in social scicnces, response was not encouraging. Only 61 questionnaires duly-filled-in were received back. (See Appendix-C). Up-to three reminders were sent to defaulters. The following institutions had sent replies expressing their inability to fill in the questionnaire. Some of the comments in brief are as under:

DRTC has suggested inclusion of library and information science in social science. Bombay University Library suggested a thorough revision of the questionnaire. Nehru Memorial Museum Library failed to receive the questionnaire, but provided information about their bibliographical activities. Heras Institute of Indian History and Culture regretted its inability to fill in the questionnaire because of the shortage of staff. The Institute for Social Science and Research, Vellore, could not reply as its librarian had left the institute. Madras Institute of Development Studies has provided little information about its documentation activities. The Director of NASSDOC has left it for others to fill in various queries pertaining to NASSDOC and its bibliographical activities. The Indian Institute of Public Opinion Pvt. Ltd., has also not filled in the questionnaire, but provided information of its publications, periodical surveys and polls about political opinion. The National Library authorities wrote, "the questionnaire is lengthy and will surely take some time to fill in with proper thinking". It took so much time that they could not fill it. The Indian Documentation Service, Gurgaon, had made a promise to send it but never kept it.

1. Objectives

The objectives of this survey were to assess:

(i) the present position of bibliographical control in India;
(ii) the collection and services of the social science institutions and university libraries in India;
(iii) the utility of bibliographical tools brought out by the social science research institutions and university libraries in India;
(iv) usefulness of the bibliographical activities of NASSDOC, and the extent to which it has been successful in controlling the social science information and bibliographical activities in the country; and
(v) to make a thorough analysis of the state of affairs of bibliographical control of social science literature in post-independent India to suggest a plan for its effective management.

TABLE 3.1: Social science institutions and universities*

Years	No. of Institutions	Percentage
Prior to 1947	11	18.6
1947-50	7	11.5
1951-60	15	24.6
1961-70	14	23.0
1971-80	13	21.3
1981-86	1	1.6
Total	61	100.0

* Data are based on the Survey which includes universities also.

After independence, there has been a rapid growth of universities as evident is from Table 3.2. The table indicates that in the decade 1961-70, as many as 42 new universities were set up which shows the tremendous growth of higher education in post-independence India.

TABLE 3.2: Establishment of universities

Years	No. of Universities/Deemed to be Universities
Prior to 1900	4
1901-10	2
1911-20	8
1921-30	8
1931-40	2
1941-50	12
1951-60	24
1961-70	42
1971-80	22
1981-85	15
Total	139

Source: Association of Indian Universities, *Universities Handbook: India*, Delhi, 1985.

Of the 61 respondents, only 11 (18%) institutions were established before 1947. However, social science institutions and universities have recorded a fast development from 1947 to 1980, but after 1980 the growth slightly slowed down and remained at that level.

2. Disciplines Covered by Social Science Institutions

Table 3.3 shows that most of the Indian social science institutions and universities reflect similar approach regarding the coverage of disciplines. Economics, sociology, anthropology, education, geography, political science, psychology, statistics, history, management, etc., are quite popular social science subjects. Library science, population studies, oriental studies, agricultural economics and rural development, science and technology, health care and family welfare, journalism, American studies, environmental science, banking and public finance, biographies, art and culture, social linguistics, computer science are comparatively new subjects and are developing fast. The subject of management developed during the last few decades has become an important branch of social science study.

TABLE 3.3: Social science subjects covered

Subject	No. of Institutions	Percentage
1. Economics	55	90.2
2. Sociology	52	85.2
3. Education	40.2	65.6
4. Psychology	38	62.3
5. Anthropology	37	60.6
6. Geography	37	60.6
7. Political Science	37	60.6
8. Statistics	37	60.6
9. History	36	59.0
10. Commerce & Trade	33	54.1
11. Public Administration	33	54.1
12. Social Work	26	42.7
13. Industrial Relations	25	41.0
14. Management	25	41.0
15. International Relations	24	39.3
16. Industrial Psychology	19	31.1
17. Law	19	31.1
18. Library & Information Science	7	11.5
19. Linguistics	6	9.8
20. Cooperation, Agricultural Economics & Rural Development	5	8.2
21. Population Studies	5	8.2
22. Indology & Oriental Studies	4	6.5
23. Medical, Health Care Family Welfare	4	6.5
24. Biography	3	4.9
25. Computer Science	3	4.9
26. Archaeology	2	3.3
27. Art & Culture	2	3.3
28. Banking & Public Finance	2	3.3
29. Environmental Science	2	3.3
30. Journalism	2	3.3
31. Science & Technology	2	3.3

Eugene Garfield's observation that the scientists of the Third World countries (particularly India) are engaged more in those areas of scientific research with which they are not immediately concerned, indicates that Indian scientists are busy with a highly technical research which a country like India can ill-afford. His observation may or may not be true in the field of social science, but two things are absolutely clear: (i) that Indian scientists are second to none, and (ii) that high technical research is not a monopoly of the developed countries alone.[1] New social science subjects are emerging because of the tremendous research activities going on in the traditional as well as the non-traditional subjects resulting in a flood of literature in various forms and formats. The U.N. and its agencies specially Unesco have contributed a lot to the growth of social science literature through its missions and units. After Second World War, a large amount of literature relating to poverty, illiteracy and hunger, etc., has been produced by their agencies. These are common problems faced by the Third World countries.

3. Collection

To support research activities in social sciences, availability of comprehensive and uptodate collection of books, periodicals, reports, etc., plays an important role. Leaving a few university libraries, many social sciences research institutions do not have comprehensive collection. Table 3.4 indicates that 25 (41%) libraries have a book collection ranging from 10,000 to 50,000 12(19.7%) libraries have a collection between 200,000 and 300,000 but these are the university libraries which include books on sciences and humanities, besides social sciences.

TABLE 3.4: Books

No. of Books	No. of Institutions	Percentage
Less than 10000	9	14.7
10000-20000	14	22.9
20001-50000	11	18.0
50001-100000	5	8.2
100001-200000	6	9.8
200001-300000	12	19.7
Above 300000	4	6.5
Total	61	100.0

3.1 *Bound Periodicals*

Nothing much is discernible from the figures shown in Table 3.5 because quite a few respondents have mixed up these figures with those of books. However, a majority, 47 (77%) of institutions maintain separate figures for bound volumes. It is clear from Table 3.5 that many institutions have a sizable bound volume collection –

7 (11.5%) institutions have above 20,000 bound volumes in their collection and these are mostly university libraries.

TABLE 3.5: Bound periodicals

No. of Bound Periodicals	No. of Institutions	Percentage
Less than 500	4	6.5
500-1000	8	13.1
1001-5000	10	16.4
5001-10000	8	13.1
10001-20000	11	18.0
Above 2000	7	11.5
Did not fill up the Column	13	21.3
Total	61	100.0

Prominent among social science research institutions whose library collection is beyond 100,000 books are the Asiatic Society and the ASRC. Among university libraries, Jawaharlal Nehru University Library, Rajasthan University Library and Karnataka University Library are the major university libraries and each one of them have a book collection of 200,000.

3.2 *Current Periodicals*

For special, academic and research libraries the most important research material are the current periodicals, and no research is possible without their use. A list of periodicals of any library is an indication of the strength or weakness of its collection (Table 3.6). The survey discloses that a few social science institutions and university libraries (21%) subscribe to between 200 and 500 journals, 14 (22.9%) institutions subscribe to between 501 and 1,000 journals, and 5 (8.5%) libraries are subscribing to between 1,000 and 1,500 periodicals. It is presumed that a good academic and social science research library may subscribe to about 300 journals in a faculty comprising a group of affiliated subject groups. Academic and research libraries subscribing to less than 300 journals are considered as below average. But it depends, more on the quality of journals than the mere numbers. Universities are multi-faculty institutions and should subscribe to not less than 500 journals subject to scrutiny of journals. Udaipur University Central Library, (established in 1961) still subscribes to only 300 journals, whereas university libraries of the 1970s subscribe to more journals. Jawaharlal Nehru University Library (established in 1971) subscribes to more than 2,000 journals. Bhai Gurudas Library, Guru Nanak Dev University (established in 1970), subscribes to 1,140 journals. Thus the growth of periodical collection is based on the library book budget, and the number of departments.

TABLE 3.6: Current periodicals

No. of Periodicals	No. of Institutions	Percentage
Less than 100	7	11.5
101-200	10	16.3
201-300	11	17.9
301-400	6	9.8
401-500	4	7.0
501-1000	14	23.0
1001-1500	5	8.0
1501-2000	2	3.3
Above 2000	2	3.3
Total	61	100.0

3.3 *Dissertations and Thesis*

Only eight institutions (13.1%) indicated that they maintain a separate collection of theses and dissertations (Table 3.7). Osmania University Library has over 3,000 theses and dissertations in its collection. This specialized collection is difficult to be maintained as theses are not published. It should not be difficult to acquire them because of the xeroxing facilities available in most of the research libraries. Yet social science research libraries are not strong in theses and dissertation collection. The National Institute of Mental Health and Neuro Sciences reports to have a good theses collection in its specialized field.

3.4 *Report*

Reports are the basic primary sources for social science research libraries and institutions of higher learning. Table 3.8 shows that a few research libraries maintain report collection, but this is to be further checked as a high majority of respondents did not fill the column. Thus only a few social science research libraries have report collection. Libraries of the National Institute of Small Industry Extension Training and the National Institute of Nutrition maintain more than 5,000 reports each in their collections. Reports are special material for many research libraries. Six (9.8%) institutions indicated that they have reports in their collection, but 55 (90.2%) respondents did not tick the column.

TABLE 3.7: Dissertations and theses

No. of Dissertations and Theses	No. of Institutions	Percentage
Less than 1000	3	4.9
1001-2000	2	3.3
2001-3000	2	3.3
3001-4000	1	1.6
Information not provided	53	86.9
Total	61	100.0

TABLE 3.8: Reports

No. of Reports	No. of Institutions	Percentage
Less than 1000	2	3.3
1001-2000	1	1.6
2001-3000	—	—
3001-4000	—	
4001-5000	1	1.6
Above 5000	2	3.3
Did not fill up the column	55	90.2
Total	61	100.0

3.5 *Microforms*

It is interesting that 24 (39.3%) institutions use microforms to maintain their research collection (Table 3.9). Bibliographical control of microforms is the foremost need in today's library world.

Despite rapidly increasing quantity of materials and their bibliographic complexity, the methods for controlling microforms of all levels – local, national and international – are inadequate. As production and distribution of microforms increase, the situation becomes more critical. In the United States the microform industry estimated that distribution and production would increase by 10 per cent annually. The current prediction is 20 per cent yearly. Moreover, a substantial part of the holdings in the United States is on microforms. Now the situation is that if there are 100 printed books, a library has 28 microforms, a ratio of less than 4.1. It is estimated and believed that microforms will not displace books, but they will become an influential part of library holdings.[2]

TABLE 3.9: Microforms

No. of Microforms	No. of Institutions	Percentage
Less than 5000	18	29.5
5001-10000	4	6.5
Above 10000	2	3.3
Did not fill up the column	37	60.6
Total	61	100.0

Indian libraries buy microforms to prove that they are not old-fashioned, and also to meet acute shortage of stacking space. It is true that they are not use in proportion to the heavy price paid for their acquisitions. This failure to utilize microform collections fully arises from the reluctance of readers to use them and unwillingness of librarians to process them adequately. Eighteen (29.5%) respondents indicated that they have less than 5000 microforms. Four (6.5%) libraries indicated that they have microform collection ranging from 5,000 to 10,000. The American Studies Research Centre and the Tata Energy Research Institute have over 20,000 microforms. But their use compared with books is not more. Some initiative, therefore, is necessary to persuade readers to consult them. The Indian Institute of Management, Bangalore, has over 10,000 microforms. India has one day to enter the stage where research and academic libraries will have to acquire microforms to save space, money and energy. The added advantage in storing microforms seems to be that their preservation is easy as these are not stolen or mutilated as the books often are.

3.6 *Other Documents*

Table 3.10 indicates that six (9.8%) institutions have reprints collection, three (4.9%) have educational films and manuscripts, two each (3.3%) institutions have paper clippings and maps and one each (1.6%) have reference collections, institutional publications, seminar papers, audio cassettes and syllabuses. The Anthropological Survey of India Library has a large collection of 4000 maps. JNU Library has 2,976 maps. The Asiatic Society of Bombay Library has over 10,000 coins and 2,357 manuscripts. The Bhandarkar Oriental Research Institute is a wonderful manuscript library with over 40,000 manuscripts. The Bharat Itihasa Samshodhak Mandal is another big library containing 15,00,000 original documents in Marathi, Persian and Kannada.

TABLE 3.10: Miscellaneous documents

Documents	No. of Institutions	Percentage
Reprints & Off-prints	6	9.8
Educational Films	3	4.9
Manuscripts	3	4.9
Paper Clippings	2	3.3
Maps	2	3.3
Audio Cassettes	1	1.6
Institutional Publications	1	1.6
Syllabuses	1	1.6
Coins	1	1.6
Reference Books	1	1.6
Seminar Papers	1	1.6
Did not fill up the column	39	63.9
Total	61	100.0

The H.C.M. Rajasthan State Institute of Public Administration had lost many of its important old valuable back volumes during the unprecedented flood in the year 1981. North Eastern Hill University and the Institute of Economic Growth possess a fine collection of *Census of India* from 1872 to 1951. The Institute of Economic Research, Population Research Centre and International Institute of Population Studies (IIPS) also have *Census of India* from the first

Census to 1951 on microfiche. Karnataka University Library has a remarkable collection of 12,000 U.N. documents, 15,000 government reports and 1985 theses and dissertations. The National Institute of Nutrition library maintains collection of 50,000 reprints in its own area of specialization. Osmania University Library is another wonderful collection of old 6,464 manuscripts, 7,217 U.N. documents and 3,000 pamphlets. Rajasthan University Library has 3,499 manuscripts, and Punjab University Library 1000 manuscripts.

4. Users

4.1 *Faculty Members*

Faculty members of any research and academic library are the main users besides research scholars and post-graduate students (Table 3.11). Only 36 (59%) respondents have ticked the column. Fourteen (22.9%) institutions receive more than 200 faculty members every years, whereas 14 (22.9%) institutions receive less than 50 faculty members.

TABLE 3.11: Teachers

No. of Faculty Members	No. of Institutions	Percentage
Less than 50	14	22.9
51-100	6	9.8
101-200	2	3.3
Above 200	14	22.9
Did not fill up the column	25	41.0
Total	61	100.0

4.2 *Research Scholars*

Table 3.12 shows that out of 61, 16 (26.2%) institutions receive less than 50 scholars. However, nine (14.7%) institutions receive more than 200 scholars a year. But most of the social science institutions have a limited number of research scholars as compared to university libraries. These scholars are engaged in doing Ph.D. or M.Phil degree. Few may be busy doing postdoctoral work or engaged in a book writing project.

TABLE 3.12: Scholars

No. of Research Scholars	No. of Institutions	Percentage
Less than 50	16	26.2
51-100	5	8.2
101-200	3	4.9
Above 200	9	14.9
Did not fill up the column	28	45.9
Total	61	100.0

4.3 *Post-Graduate Students*

Twelve (19.7%) institutions have reported that they receive more than 500 post-graduate students a year followed by Seven (11.5%) institutions which receive less than 50 students a year. Post-graduate students are future potential social scientists of the country (Table 3.13). But it is not clear why a large number (57.4%) of institutions did not fill up the column.

TABLE 3.13: Students

No. of Post Graduate Students	No. of Institutions	Percentage
Less than 50	7	11.5
51-100	3	4.9
101-200	2	3.3
200-300	1	1.6
301-400	1	1.6
401-500	—	—
Above 500	12	19.7
Did not fill up the column	35	57.4
Total	61	100.0

4.4 *Administrative Staff*

This category of users (Table 3.14) is not of committed scholars. Still they use libraries to upgrade their qualifications. Some scholars may in future venture into the realms of research. A good number of institutions (52.4%) did not indicate whether their administrative staff use the libraries. Twenty-two (36%) institutions indicated that their administrative staff use libraries where between less than 50 to 200 staff members make use of library facilities and only seven (11.5%) institutions receive above 200 administrative staff members to use the library resources. This is big number, and should be appreciated.

TABLE 3.14: Staff

No. of Staff	No. of Institutions	Percentage
Less than 50	10	16.4
51-100	4	6.5
101-200	8	13.1
Above 200	7	11.5
Did not fill up the column	32	52.4
Total	61	100.0

4.5 *Casual Readers*

Many readers are not members, but they visit libraries for some research need. Twenty-one (34.4%) institutions did not mention the number of casual readers they receive (Table 3.15). Asiatic Society Library receives 3,000 readers every month.

TABLE 3.15: Local outstation users

No. of Casual Readers	No. of Institutions	Percentage
Less than 50	3	4.9
51-100	3	4.9
101-200	3	4.9
Above 200	8	13.1
Only ticked but did not indicate the number	21	34.4
Did not fill up the column	23	37.7
Total	61	100.0

4.6 *Library Services*

Libraries have to lend their books and share its resources with other libraries through inter-library loan. Library services include reference service, reprographic service, bibliographic service, etc. Bibliographical services include indexing, abstracting, selective dissemination of information (SDI) current awareness service, documentation service, paper clipping service, consultation service and compilation of union lists and catalogues.

TABLE 3.16: Types of library services

Type of Service	No. of Institutions	Percentage
1. Reference/Readers Advisory Service	58	95.1
2. Inter-Library Loan Service	56	91.8
3. Lending Service	54	88.5
4. Reprographic Service	48	78.7
5. Bibliographical Service	46	75.4
6. Selective Dissemination of Information	7	11.5
7. Indexing & Abstracting	5	8.2
8. Any other Micrographic Service	4	7.0
9. Documentation Service	4	7.0
10. Current Awareness Services	4	7.0
11. Paper Clipping Service	3	4.9
12. Consultation Service	2	3.3
13. Medlars Offline Information Service	1	1.6
14. Film Show	1	1.6

The National Institute of Mental Health and Neuro Sciences offers Medlars Off-line Information Service to its users. Osmania University Library indicated film shows as their main service. Researchers want to find out what bibliographical services are available besides lending and inter-library loan service in the libraries. Fifty-eight (95.1%) respondents pointed out that they provide reference service to their users. This is a good response. Social science research libraries do not have a full-time reference librarian. Even an uptodate reference collection in libraries is also not available. Of course to keep uptodate reference collection is not an easy task. It is heartening to note that 48 (78.7%) institutions reported to have reprographic facilities. But still this response, though high, does not seem to be sufficient as reprographic service is a minimum service that any social science research library and university libraries should provide.

Forty-six (75.4%) social science research libraries and higher education libraries indicated that they provide bibliographical services to their users. Generally bibliographical work that they do is to compile a list of additions of the library. Only two (3.3%) institutions indicated that they provide consultation service. S.N.D.T. University Library is the only library which provides consultancy service to its users.

The bibliographical scenario as reported seems to be rosy, but the quality of bibliographical source is not good. Usually they produce work which is meant only for local consumption.

ICSSR North Western Regional Centre issues quarterly documentation lists. These are an index of articles appearing in the various journals received in the library. The Indian Institute of Education provides abstracting, translation, selective dissemination of information and current awareness service to its users. Jawaharlal Nehru University Library, NISIET and Institute of Economic Growth also provide SDI service to users.

Rajasthan University Library has set-up a micro-filming unit with facilities of preparing positive and negative films and making enlargements and slides. The Vaikunth Mehta National Institute of Co-operative Management provides current awareness service and documentation service. The H.C.M. State Institute of Public Administration, Centre for Policy Research and Centre for Research in Rural and Industrial Development provide Press clipping service. The National Institute of Health and Family Welfare provides micrographic service. The National Institute of Nutrition has brought out a guide to the library.

5. Need of Bibliographical Control

As Table 3.17 shows 59 (97.7%) respondents expressed the need for bibliographical control of social sciences which shows that the higher education libraries and social science research libraries have now realized the importance of bibliographical control and what remains to be done is to think of pathology.

TABLE 3.17: Need of bibliographical control

Response	No. of Institutions	Percentage
Yes	59	96.7
No	2	3.3
Total	61	100.0

5.1 *Reasons for Need of Bibliographical Control*

Only the Gokhale Institute of Public Affairs feels that there is not need of bibliographical control in social sciences for which it has offered no reasons. It is to be presumed that the meaning of bibliographical control is not clear to the library.

Table 3.18 shows that the respondents gave the following reasons for bibliographical control as: 55 (90.2%) indicated increased research activity, 45 (73.4%) indicated increased research output, 42 (68.5%) indicated more journals, 18 (29.5%) indicated interest of the Government, and 13 (21.3%) indicated availability of more grants as the basic reason, 15 (24.6%) indicated the interest of private organizations and commercial houses. The Administrative Staff College of India pointed out that the sponsored research is the main reason for bibliographical control. The Tata Energy Research Centre indicated that bibliographical control is necessary in the area of social aspects of energy. But the National Institute of Mental Health and Neuro Sciences feels that the need arose because of the growth in literature and lack of communication technology.

TABLE 3.18: Reasons for bibliographical control

Kinds of Activities	No. of Institutions	Percentage
1. Increased Research Activity	55	90.2
2. Increased Research Output	45	73.8
3. More Journals	42	68.5
4. Interest of the Government	18	29.5
5. Interest of Private Organizations/Commercial Houses	15	24.6
6. More Grants Available	13	21.23
7. Any other growth of Literature and Lack of Communication Technology	1	1.6
8. Sponsored Research	1	1.6

JNU Library has given the following priorities : increased research output, more journals, increased research activity, more grants available, interest of private organisations/commercial houses and interest of the government. Though all the above factors are important, priority also matters.

Local, state, national and international agencies are engaged in publishing information about the socio-economic aspects of human life which include health, security, environment, pollution control, poverty, etc. Ninety-six per cent respondents gave a firm commitment that concerts steps must be taken to improve the existing bibliographical situation, in other words effective steps ensuring that whatever is published is under bibliographical control. Social science institutions and higher education libraries will have to take up different bibliographical projects and share bibliographical tools. An order must be introduced and maintained to prevent any chaotic bibliographical situation. The quality of documentation work is poor, but it is hoped that the situation will improve with the advancement of information technology.

6. Attempt Made for Bibliographical Control

Thirty-nine (63.9%) respondents pointed out that they have made attempts at bibliographical control. This should be considered as a positive response, as majority of the institutions have been bringing out bibliographical tools for the last many years. Six (9.8%) respondents did not fill up the column showing that this category of non-committing respondents perhaps failed to understand the implications of the term. Sixteen (26.2%) respondents have never attempted bibliographical control. The following could be the reasons:

TABLE 3.19: Bibliographical control efforts

Response	No. of Institutions	Percentage
Yes	39	63.9
No	16	26.2
Did not tick the column	6	9.8
Total	61	100.0

1. Perhaps the existing bibliographical tools serve their purpose.
2. Their library collection is not strong and comprehensive.
3. They are not conscious of its real need.

7. Methods

Social science research libraries and institutions of higher learning use different methods in bringing out bibliographical works. Table 3.20 makes clear that the respondents are giving more importance to the compilation of subject bibliographies followed by indexes, abstracts and union catalogues than to surveys, production and surveys, etc. This is because the demand for subject bibliographies is more. Few institutions have attempted more than one method in achieving bibliographical control. Some have brought out periodical guides, retrospective bibliographies, selective dissemination of information and paper clippings. These activities are carried separately by institutions. Compilation of subject bibliographies seems to be the most important bibliographical activity of social science research libraries and institutes of higher learning. Much bibliographical work has to be done in this area because users find subject bibliographies extremely useful in their research. Indexing and abstracting activity falls in the next category of importance.

TABLE 3.20: Techniques and methods used for bibliographical control

Methods	No. of Institutions	Percentage
1. Compiling/Publishing Subject Bibliographies	24	39.3
2. Bringing out Indexing Journals	16	26.2
3. Bringing out Abstracting Journals	8	13.1
4. Compiling/Publishing Union Catalogue	7	11.5
5. M.Phil. and Ph.D. Survey in South Indian Universities	2	3.2
6. Book Production and Distribution	1	1.6
7. Periodical Guide	1	1.6
8. Retrospective Bibliography	1	1.6
9. Selective Dissemination of Information	1	1.6
10. Paper Clippings	1	1.6

8. Bibliographical Publications

Thirty-five (57.3%) respondents are found engaged in bibliographical activities. A few institutions are doing good work on social science research information and it is recognized by NASSDOC only. And recognition of bibliographical work means either getting financial help from NASSDOC or receiving subscription order from various libraries. Some bibliographical works are printed, but a large number of them are for local use and so are generally produced in mimeographed form. This includes accession list, a select list of articles or books, and ad-hoc bibliographies. Thirty-five (57.4%) respondents produce a total 61 bibliographical works on different subjects: social sciences as a whole, generalia, sociology, economics, American studies and technology. Bibliographical publications are produced one each in history, indology, management, political science, psychology and library and information science.

TABLE 3.21: Social science subjects

Subject	No. of Bibliographical Publications	Percentage
1. Social Sciences	21	34.4
2. Generalia	13	21.3
3. Sociology	8	13.1
4. Economics	6	9.8
5. American Studies	4	6.5
6. Technology	3	4.9
7. History	1	1.6
8. Indology	1	1.6
9. Library and Information Science	1	1.6
10. Management	1	1.6
11. Political Science	1	1.6
12. Psychology	1	1.6
Total	61	100.0

National bibliographical tools are: (1) *Index India* (Rajasthan University Library, Jaipur), (2) *Suchika* (Jawaharlal Nehru University Library, Delhi) and (3) *Indian National Bibliography* (Central Reference Library, Calcutta).

8.1 *Kinds of Bibliographical Publications*

Bibliographies, indexes and abstracts are the main bibliographical activities of institutions. Accession lists prepared are meant for local consumption, and though useful they have little value for other institutions unless libraries have an all-India membership, and also if their books circulate. Union catalogues brought out by NASSDOC is a healthy sign of library bibliographical control and a good network of availability of research materials is on the cards. The bibliographical scene shall change soon, and utility of union catalogues with the improvement in communication network and application of information technology particularly computers also shall improve.

TABLE 3.22: Kinds of secondary tools

Bibliographical Publications	No. of Institutions	Percentage
1. Bibliographies	19	31.1
2. Indexes	17	27.9
3. Abstracts	11	18.9
4. Documentation Lists	9	14.7
5. Accession Lists	3	4.9
6. Union Catalogues	2	3.3
Total	61	100.0

9. Source Documents

An institution while bringing out any bibliographical tool attempts to include such documents as are usually not indexed or abstracted in the existing bibliographical tools (Table 3.23). The purpose of any documentation activity is to provide the necessary information to its users as early as possible. Twenty-eight (45.9%) institutions use books, 27 (44.3%) periodicals and serials, 22 (36.1%) government publications, conference proceedings and papers, 20 (32.6%) theses and dissertations, 17 (27.9%) newspapers, 3 (4.9%) unpublished documents other than mentioned above and one (1.6%) each uses microforms and U.N. documents for bringing out bibliographical publications.

Osmania University Library uses U.N. documents for bringing out *Quarterly List of U.N. Documents and Reference Works Added to the Library*. This is less than half (46%) of the institutions which use books as raw material and mostly bring out accession lists of additions to the library. Hardly and professional acumen is required unless an accession list is an annotated one and books are of specialized nature. Still it is useful to know what new material has been added to a particular library. Twenty-seven (44.3%) institutions use periodicals to bring out indexes or a small cumulative index and abstracts. Indexes and abstracts are quite useful to social scientists or to specialists if a bibliographical work is brought out in the subject they want. Unfortunately institutions do not exchange their bibliographical publications, and this leads to a waste of energy and duplication. It would be quite unfortunate if it is suspended or discontinued by librarians and documentation officers. This may be either due to lack of use of a tool or no encouragement from users. Such reasons would not be surprising.

TABLE 3.23: Raw materials for compilation of secondary tools

Source Documents	No. of Institutions	Percentage
1. Books	28	45.9
2. Periodicals and Serials	27	44.3
3. Conference Proceedings	22	36.1
4. Government Publications	22	36.1
5. Theses and Dissertations	20	32.6
6. Newspapers	17	27.9
7. Pamphlets	13	21.3
8. Unpublished Documents	3	4.9
9. Microforms	1	1.6
10. U.N. Documents	1	1.6

9.1 *Suggestions for Improvement*

Assessing users'/subscribers' reaction is a must and a continuous process. This gives encouragement to those who bring out bibliographical tools. It is always necessary to know the reactions of subscribers/users. *Social Science Index* and other wilson bibliographical publications issue checklists to subscribers every year to find out which journal should be deleted and which to be included in future issues. For inclusion or exclusion of any journal, one has to give logical explanations. Indian social science bibliographical tools are *Index India, Guide to Indian Periodical Literature, Indian Press Index, documentation on Asia, Suchika*, etc. It is suggested that they should try to assess the usefulness of their tools through the checklist from users/subscribers to remain effective, but it is sad that 36 (59%) institutions do not issue checklists. Even otherwise this generally arrangement is found difficult by users because they do not find them convenient to consult, and therefore stop using them. Seventeen (27.9%) institutions do issue checklists to invite suggestions from users/subscribers regarding improvement in format contents and other features of a bibliographical tool (Table 3.24).

TABLE 3.24: Issuance of checklist to subscribers/users

Response	No. of Institutions	Percentage
Yes	17	27.7
No	36	59.1
Did not fill up the column	8	13.1
Total	61	100.0

9.1.1 *Intervals*

Five (8.2%) institutions indicated "occasionally", two (3.3%) "once in a year" and one (1.6%) each "once a month" and "irregularly". Though most of social science institutions and higher education libraries want to bring out bibliographical tools, they hardly ever attempt to know its usefulness. Few social science institutions and higher education libraries do invite suggestions from subscribers and users, but not on a regular basis. The issuing of a checklist at regular intervals should be given due attention so that the bibliographical tools remain useful in the years to come (Table 3.25).

TABLE 3.25: Frequency of issuance of checklist

Periodicity	No. of Institutions	Percentage
Occasionally	5	8.2
Once in a year	2	3.3
Once in a month	1	1.6
Irregularly	1	1.6
Did not fill up the column	52	85.2
Total	61	100.0

9.2 *Use of Computers*

Computer applications in libraries in India is a recent phenomenon.

Use of a computer is considered important and crucial in the changing circumstances. This is due to the technological impact. Our objective is to know whether social science research libraries and academic libraries use computers for bringing out bibliographical tools. Early 70's has been the period when the use of computers began. But social science institutions and higher education libraries have yet to use computers. It is pertinent to draw attention to the fact that two decades back there was hardly any library science department where a paper on computer applications in libraries was introduced. But now library science departments have introduced teaching of computer applications in libraries to train library science manpower with an access to computers. Computers are useful for preparing bibliographical tools. Table 3.26 indicates that only four (6.5%) institutions use computers. Fifty-one (83.6%) do not use computers (it means they do not have computers), two (3.3%) institutions point out that the computers are going to be installed soon. Four (6.5%) institutions did not fill up the column. A recent study shows that only 37 institutions including two university libraries use computers for different bibliographical purposes, but surprisingly not a single institution belongs to social sciences.[3]

TABLE 3.26: Use of computers for bibliographical purposes

Response	No. of Institutions	Percentage
Yes	4	6.5
No	51	83.6
Under proposal	2	3.3
Did not tick the column	4	6.5
Total	61	100.0

9.3 *Problems*

There are many problems in bringing out bibliographical tools like lack of staff, poor finance, lack of necessary equipment, poor response from users/subscribers, and lack of cooperation from staff/authorities (see Table 3.27). The major problem as indicated by 26 (42.7%) respondents is non-availability of competent technical staff who can shoulder the responsibility of bringing out bibliographical tools. Respondents have expressed their specific problems except the Administrative Staff College of India. The college does not have such problems. Some institutions have tick-marked more than one problem. Seven (11.5%) respondents have pointed out lack of cooperation from staff/authorities. Ten (16.4%) respon- dents indicated a poor response from users/subscribers is the main problem faced by the institutions.

TABLE 3.27: Problems faced by social science research libraries and higher education libraries

Kind of Problem	No. of Institutions	Percentage
Staff	26	42.7
Finance	18	29.6
Equipment	10	16.4
Poor response from Users/Subscribers	10	16.4
Cooperation from Staff/Authorities	7	11.5

9.4 *Financial Assistance*

A high majority 45 (73.8%) of respondents have stated that they do not receive any financial assistance from government or other agencies for bibliographical works (see Table 3.28). Only 10 (16.4%) respondents receive financial assistance from different sources for example: (1) North Eastern Hill University receives financial help from the ICSSR Regional Centre and the North Eastern Regional Council, (2) Bhai Gurudas Library of Guru Nanak Dev University received grant from the Government of India for preservation of manuscripts, (3) the ICSSR Southern Regional Centre receives a grant from the State Government, (4) National Institute of Rural Development gets full assistance from the Government.

Index India Project did receive financial support from ICSSR in its initial stages. ICSSR purchased few hundred copies of the Index and distributed them free to important research libraries all over the country.[4] ICSSR has been helping professional associations and institutions which are involved in bibliographical work since inception. Delhi Library Association brings out *Indian Press Index* for which it receives financial assistance regularly.

TABLE 3.28: Seeking of financial assistance

Response	No. of Institutions	Percentage
Yes	10	16.4
No	45	73.8
Did not tick the column	6	9.8
Total	61	100.0

9.5 *Familiarity of NASSDOC*

Fifty-four (88.5%) institutions (social science libraries and university libraries) are familiar with the services of NASSDOC. Surprisingly four (6.5%) institutions are not aware of the existence of NASSDOC. The rest did not fill up the column. The name of SSDC was changed to NASSDOC in 1986.

TABLE 3.29: Whether social science research libraries know about NASSDOC

Response	No. of Institutions	Percentage
Yes	54	88.5
No	4	6.5
Did not fill up the column	3	4.9
Total	61	100.0

9.5.1 *Use of NASSDOC's Services*

Twenty-six (42.6%) institutions have stated "seldom", 16 (26.2%) "frequently", and 12 (19.7%) "never" use the services of NASSDOC. Seven (11.5%) institutions did not tick the column. If the total response of "seldom" and "frequently" is taken together, a high majority of the institutions use NASSDOC services. Respondents who frequently use the services of NASSDOC were further probed. A few respondents, it was found, usually ask for various research studies, articles and subject bibliographies from NASSDOC. Institutions of higher learning and social science research libraries seek reference service, request union lists and catalogues, and subscribe to their secondary publications particularly *ICSSR Abstracts and Reviews*. They also seek reprographic and inter-library loan service from NASSDOC form time to time.

TABLE 3.30: Whether NASSDOC services are useful

Response	No. of Institutions	Percentage
Seldom	26	42.6
Frequently	16	26.2
Never	12	19.7
Did not fill up the column	7	11.5
Total	61	100.0

9.5.2 *Dissemination of Social Science Information*

It is essential to know the views of the respondents about the services rendered by NASSDOC — whether it disseminates to the desired or expected degree the social science information (see Table 3.31). Thirty (49.2%) institutions indicated that NASSDOC dissemination information about social science research and documentation activities. Nineteen (31.1%) institutions said NASSDOC does not disseminate the information and one (1.6%) respondent did not know anything about it. There is still ample scope for the dissemination of the information about NASSDOC and its social science research activities. Seven (18%) respondents did not tick the column, but the response shows that they do not want to express their views freely. It is just not enough to publish information about NASSDOC and its bibliographical activities in the different journals giving stereotype information. Something about the dissemination of information and activities should be done seriously. It is highly recommended that seminars/conferences, workshops and courses should be regularly arranged at ICSSR headquarters and regional centres to see that the social science researchers and librarians both know about its existence and its activities. The situation at present is not satisfactory. National-level planning is required so that regional centres spread over in different parts of the country to meet the desired goals. At present regional centres can be termed as purely reading rooms with minimum bibliographical activity.

TABLE 3.31: Respondents' views about the dissemination of information by NASSDOC

Response	No. of Institutions	Percentage
Yes	30	49.2
No	19	31.1
Do not know	1	1.6
Did not tick the column	11	18.0
Total	61	100.0

9.6 *Opinion About Bibliographical Control*

Fifty-one per cent respondents said that the bibliographical control situation in the country at present was not satisfactory and needed improvement. But 21 (34.4%) institutions felt that the bibliographical control was satisfactory, and 3 (4.9%) institutions were satisfied with the situation but added that it needs a lot of improvement. Six (9.8%) respondents did not tick the column. Table 3.32 makes it clear that though the situation of bibliographical control is improving, we have to go a long way to achieve it completely.

TABLE 3.32: Reactions of social science research libraries and university libraries about bibliographical control

Response	No. of Institutions	Percentage
Not satisfactory	31	51.0
Satisfactory	21	34.4
Satisfactory, but require improvement	3	4.9
Did not tick the column	6	9.8
Total	61	100.0

9.7 *Use of Bibliographical Services Produced by Other Institutions*

Thirty-two (52.4%) respondents seek the bibliographical help from other institutions; 21 (34.3%) stated that they do not; 8 (13.1%) did not tick the column (see Table 3.33). Cooperation among social science institutions for sharing the resources should be encouraged.

TABLE 3.33: Bibliographical help received from other institutions

Response	No. of Institutions	Percentage
Yes	32	52.4
No	21	34.4
Did not tick the column	8	13.1
Total	61	100.0

The institutions which mutually seek bibliographical publications from each other are the following:

A.N. Sinha Institute of Social Studies, Patna.
  Jawaharlal Nehru University Library, Delhi.
American Studies Research Centre (ASRC), Hyderabad.
  Central Institute of English and Foreign Languages (CIEFL).
  USIS Libraries in India.
Centre for Arid Zone Research Institute (CAZRI), Jodhpur.
  Agricultural Information System (AGRIS).
  Indian National Scientific and Documentation Centre.
Centre for Economic and Social Studies, Calcutta.
  NCAER Library, Delhi.
  National Institute of Rural Development (NIRD), Hyderabad.
  Commercial Services.
Centre of Research in Rural and Industrial Development, Chandigarh.
  ICSSR North Western Regional Centre, Chandigarh.
Council for Social Development, Hyderabad.
  NIRD, Hyderabad.
Giri Institute of Development Studies, Lucknow.
  NCAER Library, Delhi.
  Planning Commission Library, Delhi.
Indian Association of Special Libraries and Information Centres (IASLIC), Calcutta.
  National Library, Calcutta.
  Local Institutions.
ICSSR Southern Regional Centre, Hyderabad.
  Administrative Staff College of India (ASCI), Hyderabad.
  American Studies Research Centre, Hyderabad.
  National Academy of Agricultural Research & Management, Hyderabad.

National Social Science Documentation Centre, Delhi.
NIRD, Hyderabad.
NISIET, Hyderabad
Osmania University Library, Hyderabad.

Indian Institute of Education, Poona.
Gokhale Institute of Politics and Economics, Poona.
Literacy House, Lucknow.
Unesco Institute for Education, Hamburg (Germany).

Indian Institute of Management, Bangalore.
British Library, Bangalore.
Indian Institute of Mass Communication, Delhi.
Indian Space Research Organization (ISRO), Trivandrum.
United States Information Service (USIS), Madras.

Institute of Social and Economic Change, Bangalore.
National and International Institutions like the U.N. and its Agencies.

Institute of Economic Growth, Delhi.
Labour Bureau Library, Delhi.
NCAER Library, Delhi.
Reserve Bank of India Library, Bombay.

Institute of Economic Research, Population Research Centre, Dharwar.
Gokhale Institute of Politics and Economics, Poona.

Institute of Public Enterprise, Hyderabad.
Administrative Staff College of India, Hyderabad.
Indian Institute of Public Administration, Delhi.
National Social Science Documentation Centre (NASSDOC), Delhi.
Osmania University Library, Hyderabad.

International Institute of Population Sciences, Bombay.
Gokhale Institute of Politics and Economics, Poona.
Johns Hopkins University, USA.
Tata Institute of Social Sciences, Bombay.

Jawaharlal Nehru University Library, Delhi.
Indian Documentation Service, Gurgaon.
Rajasthan University Library, Jaipur.
University Libraries.

K.K. Handique Library, Gauhati.
North Eastern Regional Council, Shillong.

Management Development Institute, Gurgaon.

All India Management Association, New Delhi.

Indian Documentation Services, Gurgaon.

National Social Science Documentation Centre (NASSDOC), Delhi.

Marathwada University Library, Aurangabad.

Federation of Indian Chambers, New Delhi.

Jawaharlal Nehru University Library, Delhi.

Jayakar Library, Poona.

NASSDOC, Delhi.

Rajasthan University Library, Jaipur.

SNDT University Library, Bombay.

National Institute of Small Industry and Extension Training (NISIET), Hyderabad.

British Lending Library Division, U.K.

International Trade Centre.

United Nations Industrial Development Organization (UNIDO).

National Institute of Educational Planning and Administration (NIEPA), Delhi.

Library of Congress Book Procurement Centre, Delhi.

National Institute of Health and Family Welfare (NIHPW), New Delhi.

Libraries in the Field of Health, Population and Family Welfare.

National Medical Library, Delhi.

University Libraries.

Osmania University Library, Hyderabad.

INSDOC, Delhi.

NISIET, Hyderabad.

National Institute of Rural Development, Hyderabad.

Punjabi University Library, Patiala.

Neighbouring University Libraries.

Rajasthan University Library, Jaipur.

State Universities.

Ratan Tata Library at Delhi School of Economics, University of Delhi, Delhi.

JNU Library, Delhi.

Note: Italicisation line signifies that an institution is inter-exchanging bibliographical information from those institutions mentioned below it. This is an example of *inter-group* exchange.

The above list shows that normally university libraries or social science research libraries seek help from such organizations which have similar subject specialization. There is an urgent need to build up subject union catalogues and develop sectoral information system as part of national information system. This is possible if there is a will. L.S. Ramaiah's suggestion of establishing IULNET for Indian university libraries and social science institutions in the country[5] has paved the way for establishing INFLIBNET.[6]

9.8 *Images and Perceptions of NASSDOC*

Most of the respondents are satisfied with the performance of NASSDOC, but it needs a lot of improvement. Many have pointed out that the Centre is lagging behind so far as the quality of the services is concerned. To improve bibliographical services for social science researchers, the Centre shall have to undergo a complete overhauling. Present efforts and facilities are inadequate. The Centre should use computer facilities to provide efficient and expeditious services to social scientists.

Eleven (17.6%) respondents stated that the image of the NASSDOC is "very good". The comments of the remaining 58.8 per cent respondents are given below. The comments are general in nature, i.e. how do they view the image of the Centre.

A.N. Sinha Institute of Social Studies feels that ICSSR should draw a national policy for national information system of social sciences and should work out a plan for coordinating and integrating the activities of different social science organizations/institutes on bibliographical control.

Administrative Staff College of India realizes the importance of NASSDOC as a useful and necessary set-up in the age of information explosion.

American Studies Research Centre says that ICSSR is doing an excellent job in bibliographical control of social sciences, but there is scope for improvement. Grants awarded by it should be published. Its most publications are outdated.

Bhai Gurudas Library of Guru Nanak Dev University, appreciates the work of both the institutions — ICSSR and NASSDOC. They are doing pioneering work in social sciences. The compilation of union catalogue is commendable. The need is to keep it updated.

Centre for Studies in Social Sciences criticizes that ICSSR and NASSDOC are doing work currently from its Delhi office. Their regional centre should be organized in a better way to help the local researchers more efficiently.

Central Institute of English and Foreign Languages also comments that their documentation service is inadequate. They should bring out current contents of all Indian periodicals in social sciences, both in English and Indian languages, should be able to supply copies of the periodical articles to Indian Social Scientists. NASSDOC should publish retrospective subject bibliographies like the one they published on Indian education. They should try to build up a network of social science libraries in India, and should computerize their data bank and regional branches be connected to the central data bank with terminals.

Centre for Economic and Social Studies feels that a lot of scope for innovation and improvement is required.

Centre for Policy Research appreciates that NASSDOC is doing useful work in social science research.

Council for Social Development realizes that ICSSR has given good support to social scientists. There should be adequate emphasis on training also.

Giri Institute of Development Studies comments that they are doing at least work in a field which is more or less neglected. Cooperation from regional agencies is necessary in order to make NASSDOC more comprehensive and up-to-date.

IASLIC gives credit to NASSDOC for doing at least some work in the field.

ICSSR North West Regional Centre being a regional centre has to appreciate ICSSR for commendable job in promoting social science research in the country. The Council has done a remarkable job of setting priority areas of research in the social sciences.

ICSSR Southern Regional Centre remarks that it is a boon for social scientists and scholars who are engaged in social science subjects. Regional Centres should be provided with efficient staff and equipment like computer.

Institute of Development Studies realizes the importance of ICSSR and NASSDOC. It has very important status in the field of social science documentation services as well as bibliographical control.

Institute of Economic Research, Population Research Centre (Dharwar), says that ICSSR is working quite satisfactorily keeping in view the circumstances.

Institute of Public Enterprise praises that it is the only Centre which is having bibliographical control of social science literature in India.

Jawaharlal Nehru University Library feels that their bibliographical services are always behind schedule. They should to updated.

K.K. Handique Library of Gauhati University suggests that more improvement in future is desirable.

Management Development Institute (Gurgaon), comments that the Council since its inception has been doing commendable work through its documentation centre in providing documentation services in social sciences.

NCEAR suggests that the Council could play a major and active role in bringing about bibliographical control of social science literature in India through involvement of various institutions, coordination of their various bibliographical activities and most importantly acting quickly in this direction to help create bibliographic orderliness in the area.

National Institute of Small Industry and Extension Training, (NISIET) feels that because research in social science is in progress, documentation services are catching up.

National Institute of Mental Health and Neuro Sciences has no idea of ICSSR and NASSDOC as they do not have much correspondence with these organizations.

North Eastern Hill University Library criticizes that the service of NASSDOC is very slow. One article was requisitioned and a reply about its non-availability came after six months.

Osmania University Library appreciates that it is doing good work within the constraints.

Punjabi University Library comments it is striving to do the job.

Rajasthan University Library comments that ICSSR is doing a remarkable job in development of social science bibliographical control. There is a need for more cooperation at regional and national level.

Ratan Tata Library at Delhi School of Economics, University of Delhi, criticizes that the bibliographical activity is at low level and that too in isolation of potential users. Bibliographical output is unrelated to its usefulness. It also failed to elicit cooperation from many good useful social science centres.

SNDT University Library is not satisfied with the services of

ICSSR/NASSDOC.

Sukhadia University Library praises that both institutions are doing a good job in social sciences. It has developed its services, and hopes in the coming years it will do much more.

Vaikunth Mehta National Institute of Cooperative Management is quite satisfied with NASSDOC. It provides all bibliographical services for social science research and disseminates the required information. The institute further suggests that it should provide the bibliographical services in the disciplines other than social sciences.

10. Conclusion

The survey reveals that social science research and information in India is gaining ground as is evident from the increasing financial support received from different quarters, viz. ICSSR, Central Government and State Government funding agencies and UGC. Social science documentation activity has been developing through the efforts of many social science research institutions and university libraries since 1947. This is because of increased research output in the social sciences. With improved cooperation and coordination among such institutions the bibliographical control situation will improve further. These observations are based on the evidence of increasing grants, growing collection, and research output. Information technology used for information recording and dissemination would further speed up the bibliographical services. Library cooperation and resource-sharing among institutions engaged in research and teaching is becoming popular. Some institutions are getting cooperation even from the USA, the U.K. and West Germany. Such mutual linkages with other social science institutions and higher learning libraries shall help in improving the bibliographical control. Though mutual linkage is shown in the Map 3.1 no network of information system exists.

The survey further revealed that a high percentage of institutions of higher education and social science research have been realizing the need of bibliographical control for the last two decades because of: (1) increased research output, (2) increased research activities, and (3) more journals. Over 50 per cent of respondents have worked for bibliographical control in their own way. Only manually produced bibliographical tools are in vogue, and computer-based social science information services are yet to become the order of the day. To provide an expeditious bibliographical and information service to social science scholars, ICSSR should launch a "National Information system for Social Sciences" without any further delay.

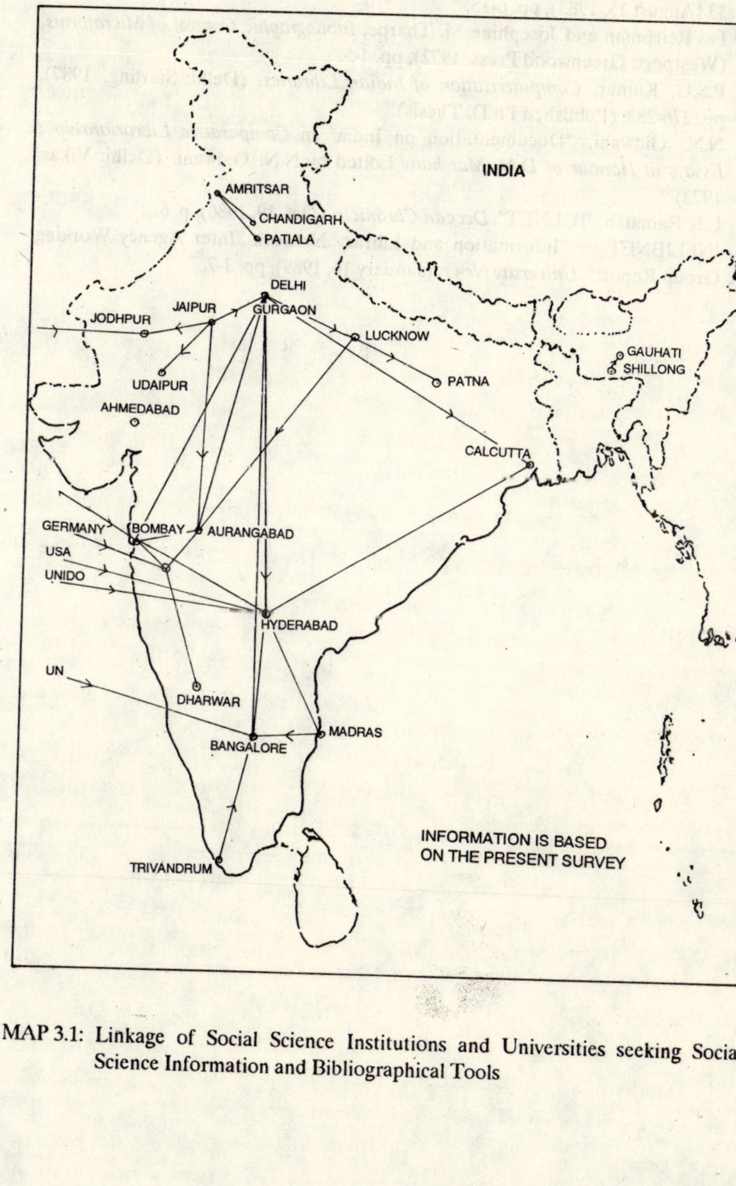

MAP 3.1: Linkage of Social Science Institutions and Universities seeking Social Science Information and Bibliographical Tools

REFERENCES

1. Eugene Garfield, "Mapping Science in the Third World". *Current Contents*, 5, 33 (August 15, 1983), pp. 6-15.
2. Fel Reichman and Josephine M. Tharpe, *Bibliographic Control of Microforms*, (Westport: Greenwood Press, 1972), pp. 4-5.
3. P.S.G. Kumar, *Computerization of Indian Libraries*. (Delhi: Sterling, 1987), pp. 276-283, (Published Ph.D. Thesis).
4. N.N. Gidwani, "Documentation on India" In *Comparative Librarianship : Essays in Honour of D.N. Marshall*. Edited by N.N. Gidwani. (Delhi: Vikas, 1973).
5. L.S. Ramaiah, "IULNET". *Deccan Chronicle*, (Oct. 19, 1986), p. 6.
6. INFLIBNET — "Information and Library Network. Inter Agency Working Group Report", *University News*, (January 16, 1989), pp. 3-7.

4

DOCUMENTATION ACTIVITIES IN SOCIAL SCIENCES

Introduction

The term "Documentation" was brought into use within the last 50 years or so, and it denotes the old idea "Bibliography". This verbal change has been made to indicate a shift in emphasis from macro-thought and macro-document to micro-thought and micro-document. It also refers to a shift from the past thought to the current nascent thought, and from service to the generalist to service to the specialist. Such specialists seek data, facts, knowledge, and modes of developing knowledge, within a severally restricted region of the universe of knowledge in which he is working and to which he is aiming to contributing a new thought.

Dr. S.R. Ranganathan, keeping in view his five laws of library science, defines documentation as:

> "promotion and practice of bringing into use of nascent micro-thought by specialists, and pinpointed, exhaustive and expeditious service of nascent thought to specialists. In spite of the continuous ever increasing cascade of nascent micro-thought on an ever-multiplying number of specialised subjects, communicated through several thousands of periodicals."[1]

ALA Glossary of Library and Information Science defines documentation in the following words:

> "Broadly, the systematic collection, organization, storage, retrieval and dissemination of specialized information, especially of a scientific or technical nature. More specifically, the acquisition, organization, storage, retrieval and

dissemination of documents."[2]

ASLIB defines documentation as:

"recording, organization and dissemination of specialized knowledge. Documentation does, in fact, embrace the whole gamut of operations from the discovery or creation of new knowledge through its publication, analysis, classification and 8arrangement to its arrival at the user; that is to say, report writing, publication, abstracting, classification, indexing, reassembly, presentation and dissemination."[3]

Documentation Division of the Special Library Association defined documentation in June, 1951, as:

"Documentation is the art comprised of (a) document reproduction, (b) document distribution, and (c) document utilization."[4]

The above definition is quite different from what is given by S.R. Ranganathan who gives more emphasis to documentation work and documentation service than to document reproduction, distribution and utilisation.

1. Documentation

S.R. Ranganathan, basically being a classificationist, always analyses concept into different facets. According to him documentation activity also has five facets like five laws of library science. These are: (1) Documentation work, (2) Documentation service, (3) Abstracting work, (4) Document reproduction service and (5) Translation service.[5]

1.1 *Documentation Work*

Documentation work consists of preparing documentation list by scanning the host micro-documents, picking out the macro and the micro-documents particularly the nascent micro-documentation work that should be brought to the notice of readers. It would be useful for them if a list is prepared in a most helpful manner.

Documentation work also includes preparing of Press clippings on a regular or ad-hoc basis. There are different kinds of documentation lists. It may be prepared on demand by a reader or a class of readers of be prepared in anticipation of demand. It may also cover a specific subject, or a specific region of knowledge covering a number of filiatory subjects, or the whole region of the universe of knowledge. A documentation list may includes the documents in a few specialized languages or it may cover all or many languages. It may confine itself to the documents produced within a country, or a region, or the world as a whole. It may be selective or exhaustive.

Documentation work may be done by a local library service, a national or state or an international agency. Normally a documentation list prepared on demand of a specific subject and usually selective in nature is done by a local library service. But lists of exhaustive nature and covering specified regions of knowledge are either done by national or international agencies.

1.2 *Documentation Service*

This is a term that denotes reference service in a restricted sense. It lays emphasis particularly on nascent micro-documents and on specialist readers. Documentation service is actually a long-range reference service of an intensive nature. This process includes:

1. Helping the inquire to formulate precisely his interest at the time.
2. Locating in the catalogue the entries for the documents covering inquirer's interest directly or indirectly.
3. Giving the documents to him if they are in the library.
4. Procuring the documents on inter-library loan, and
5. Giving a copy of the documents which he desires to own permanently.

Documentation service is an outcome of advancement of higher education and industries. Its need was earlier felt by technical and special libraries more than academic and social science research libraries. This activity gradually became a part and parcel of the duty of librarians and information scientists to provide documentation service to researchers, technocrats, industrial workers who otherwise find hardly any time to search and document important information relevant to their need. Gradually its need was felt in all branches of knowledge including social sciences. During, the last one decade, interestingly, the emphasis has shifted from "documentation" to "information". This is because of the impact of the changing attitude of researchers for pinpointed information and the use of machines to present information expeditiously and exhaustively.

1.3 *Translation Service*

According to S.R. Ranganathan, the pace of social science knowledge in Indian language is not so high as will justify the employment of a team of translators on a full time basis. Thus the economically way will be to get the translation done on piece work by a panel of permanent staff of translators. (However, Ranganathan warns that documentation does not mean that it includes translation). He suggests that a panel of translators in each language should be used rather than putting translation work on documentalists. It is not possible for a documentalist to know many languages, and mere knowing the language is not enough unless one has subject background. Otherwise one can imagine how monstrous the translation would become.[6]

2. Development of Social Science Documentation in India

Research in sciences has always swayed over social sciences and humanities, and, therefore, scientific documentation has stolen a march over other disciplins. This is because of the massive impact of science and technology on defence needs and public amenities have given it a natural priority in the budgetary allotment. Now social sciences are clamouring for an equal recognition and status, and a considerable work is being done in the university complexes and other national research organizations devoted to different disciplines of social sciences. Therefore, the need for documentation services in social sciences was felt.

Delay and neglect of documentation in the social sciences can be attributed to the following factors:

1. Demand for documentation is less in the social sciences.
2. Sufficient financial aid is not forthcoming.
3. Individual rather than cooperative research is the general rule.

4. Publications retain value for longer periods than in natural sciences.
5. Less emphasis on nascent thought in social sciences which is a prerequisite for documentation.
6. Absence of any standard vocabulary on the subject.
7. Absence of a scheme of depth classification.

Prior to the establishment of the National Social Science Documentation Centre (NASSDOC), social science documentation had been a local activity which depended entirely on the initiative of individual institutions to satisfy the needs of scholars attached to them. There has been hardly any documentation activity among research institutions. Consequently there has been a considerable duplication of effort. The distressing situation is that most research scholars are hardly aware of the facilities available to them though numerous documentation lists are brought out by several libraries. These lists are mostly mimeographed which are intended to provide current awareness service in a limited area of the social sciences and not of much significance to the social sciences and total body of research scholars, except in a few instances.

The Unesco Research Centre at Calcutta in early the 50s was a pioneer in bibliographical activities for the South Asian Region. It was bringing out an annual list of new books and articles appearing in periodicals published in India regularly. This was the beginning of documentation in social sciences in India and an effort towards bibliographical control of South Asian Publications. It was difficult to get literature in social sciences in English language in the absence of a national bibliography or any other current bibliographical tool. Another pioneering attempt was made by a commercial firm in Poona in 1955. The ambitious *Nifor Guide to Indian Periodicals, 1955-56* gives a listing of 2,127 titles classified by language, subject, geographic location and periodicity. But, today documentation has taken a new dimension due to the advent of computer technology. Now social sciences cannot be left out with the development of the new information technology.

3. Efforts Towards Setting up of a National Social Science Documentation Centre

During the last 30 years, the subject of social science documentation has been dealt in some detail in the professional circles. Several seminars and conferences have been held in the past which have helped to clarify the documentation needs in social sciences which finally led to the establishment of National Social Science Documentation Centre (NASSDOC) at New Delhi.

In 1959, the first library seminar on "Research in Social Sciences" was held under the auspices of the Indian School of International Studies and the Indian Council of World Affairs. The need of a national social science documentation centre was discussed in detail. The following projects for further pursuit emerged out of the discussion:

1. Survey of the holdings of periodical publications including those by the governments in the important libraries of the country so as to help the formulation of a policy for the coordination of acquisition and cooperation in service.
2. Preparation of a Union Catalogue of Learned periodicals in the social sciences in the important libraries in India.
3. Production and distribution of scientifically prepared trade catalogues of the publication of the Government of India.
4. Establishment of a 'National Social Science Documentation Centre' for the social sciences.
5. Promotion of research in the depth classification of the social sciences and their terminology.[7]

In 1960, a seminar on "International Relations and Regional Studies" was held at Bangalore under the auspices of the School of International Studies. A central library on international relations was recommended with a view to linking up with the work of the proposed "Indian National Social Science Documentation Centre" (INSSDOC). It proposed that the centre undertake responsibility to prepare a union catalogue of periodical holdings of Indian libraries and promote publication of documentation lists, inter-library loan services, translation of documents, micro-filming and reproduction facilities.

In 1962, a seminar on "Bibliographical Control" was held under the auspices of the Indian Library Association which was sponsored by the Ministry of Education of the Government of India. It recommended documentation work and services in different subject areas in the social sciences by 13 different agencies, setting up of a coordinating body for all documentation activities in the natural sciences, humanities and social sciences, a permanent Advisory Committee on Policy to implement the proposals, and functions of the coordinating body should be similar to those of INSDOC.[8]

In 1964, the third *Iaslic* seminar on "Session on Social Science Documentation in India" was held at Lucknow. It recommended that the functions of INSSDOC should be similar to those of INSDOC. It should request the Central Government to provide funds for the establishment of the centre for making a survey of the existing documentation services in social sciences in India, and request UGC to provide funds for compiling a union catalogue of periodical publications in social sciences.

In 1965, in the "Session of Social Science Documentation" of the Sixth *Iaslic* Conference at Trivandrum, recommended that a survey of the resources and documentation activities in the social sciences in India should be made. Thus, this *Iaslic* Conference reiterated the above recommendations of the past and stressed the need of surveys of social science institutions including universities.

In 1967, a survey of the activities in social science documentation in India was made by Girja Kumar. The data of this survey formed part of a working paper for the seminar on documentation in social sciences held at Delhi in 1967 under the auspices of the School of International Studies. Girja Kumar's paper on "Library Development in India: Retrospect and Prospect" was the main focus of the seminar. The most significant recommendation of the seminar was the establishment of a national documentation centre not only to undertake major projects, but also to coordinate documentation activities of other libraries in the countries.

The proposed functions of INSSDOC were (1) preparation of a union catalogue of periodical holdings in the social sciences in Indian libraries in a printed volume, and its maintenance on current basis on catalogue cards, (2) preparation of a comprehensive documentation list of periodical articles on social science disciplines once a month and to be cumulated in a printed volume of 1,000 pages in an annual volume, and (3) preparation of a comprehensive index to news a major newspaper of India.

In 1969, the last and final attempt was made. As an outcome of all the previous seminars and conferences, the Indian National Social Science Documentation Centre (INSSDOC) came into existence. The ICSSR established the long needed and cherished documentation branch of October 1, 1969 as National Social Science Documentation Centre (NASSDOC) at New Delhi which functioned with the collaboration of Jawaharlal Nehru University.

ICSSR asked Girja Kumar in 1969 to conduct a survey of 200 institutions consisting of research, university, government and other libraries. A detailed questionnaire was circulated to 187 libraries in December 1969. Of the 87 libraries which responded, 54 did not engage in any local documentation activity, and 43 admitted to having some kind of documentation activity to their credit. His survey findings furnished the following results:

> "Research libraries are doing maximum documentation work as compared to other types of libraries. However, Rajasthan University Library topped the list for preparing maximum number of cards followed by Delhi Library Association, Ministry of Industrial Development, Indian Council of World Affairs, K.K. Roy, Culcutta, Institute of Economic Growth, Karnataka University Library, Indian Institute of Management, Delhi School of Economics and National Institute of Economic Growth."[9]

3.1 *Difficulties in Social Science Documentation*

There are several problems to be tackled in documentation which are more acute in social science documentation due to the complexities implicit in the nature of the disciplines. Some of the major problems faced by the documentation are as follows:

(i) *Difficulty of Terminology*

Social science documentalists do not appear to have yet familiarized themselves with the elementary technical terms current in the field of documentation. It seems they are not very clear about the difference between the terms "Documentation Work" and "Documentation Services".

(ii) *Terminology in Social Sciences*

In the natural sciences the International Committee on Standard Terminology has been functioning for nearly a century. Practically every discipline in that group has a fairly stabilized technical terminology. So there is hardly any difficulty for the documentalist in understanding the true importance of any document to be included in a documentation list or to be brought into use in documentation service. On the contrary many subjects in the social sciences pose difficulties arising out of unstabilized terminology. But now that documentation enters into the field of social sciences, there is perhaps a chance for an agreed standard terminology in the social sciences to be taken and pursued with vigour.

(iii) *Main Subjects of Forming the Social Sciences*

Sociology is unquestionably accepted as a main subject of the field of social sciences. So is social work. But every subject rather entire universe of subjects has a sociological aspect. This tempts to bring in any of the subjects even from outside the field of social sciences. ICSSR has defined for the purpose of research, the subjects as constituting social sciences are: economic, commerce and demography, political science and government, administration and management, sociology, social and cultural anthropology, ethnography, social work and criminology, psychology and social psychology and human, political and economic geography. But the Council has excluded education and history from its purview of grants-giving scheme.

(iv) *Recognition of "Learned Paper" in Social Science Periodicals*

In the field of social sciences it is not at all easy to define a "learned paper" as it is in natural sciences. A consequence of the difficulty in recognizing a learned paper in social sciences leads naturally to the difficulty in deciding "learned periodical" for inclusion in the union catalogues of periodicals in social sciences.

(v) *Newspaper–like Publication*

A daily newspaper or weekly seldom has a learned paper on natural sciences. But in the field of social sciences, a newspaper often contains a record of such social phenomena as form the basis of research in social sciences. Therefore, while it is not practicable to include all newspapers and newspaper–like publications in the union catalogue, there should be a method of bringing the important papers in them to the notice of the research workers in the social sciences.

(vi) *Governmental and Institutional Serials*

Authentic material for research in social sciences is also found in serials—Government and institutional—such as administration reports and statistical tables. These should certainly be included in a union catalogue of periodical publications (i.e. periodicals and serials) in social sciences.

(vii) *Language Problem in Social Science Documentation*

India is a sub-continent with a variety of languages, customs, modes and usages. Currently the country is going through a language renaissance. Institutions of higher education are switching over from English to regional languages. This would mean that in any center for documentation, specially in the social sciences, it would be difficult to document publication in more than a dozen important Indian languages. But since the bulk of literature is in the English language, it would be desirable to have the documentation work in the English language for the present. For convenience, the entries for materials in Indian languages should be brought into the same sequence by transliteration, and the Roman script should therefore be adopted.[10, 11]

4. National Social Science Documentation Centre (NASSDOC) and its Documentation Activities

The Government of India established an autonomous body, ICSSR, in 1969, and then established in the Social Science Documentation Centre (SSDC) as its wing in 1970. Its objectives are to sponsor and promote research in social sciences and facilitate, its utilization which it does by awarding grants for research, and disseminate knowledge concerning social sciences. The name Social Science Documentation Centre was changed to National Social Science Documentation Centre (NASSDOC) in 1986.

NASSDOC has a unique position in the ICSSR set-up. The Centre performs the following activities:

(a) Building up a collection of reference material;
(b) Collecting (i) unpublished doctoral theses approved by Indian universities, and (ii) research reports of the projects undertaken by ICSSR and other social science research institutions assisted by ICSSR;
(c) Establishing duplicating, reprographic and micro-filming units;
(d) Striving for bibliographic control over social science materials;
(e) Providing select bibliographies on request; and
(f) Awarding study grants to scholars for working at libraries of their interest.

4. Research Collection

NASSDOC has a good collection of basic references in social sciences including bibliographies, indexes, abstracts, etc. It has a large collection of books on research methodology in social sciences, social indicators, and status of women. It also keeps the Council's priced/non-priced publications including those for which the Council has provided publication grants.

The collection of the Council is further augmented by several abstracts such as ICSSR Abstracts in Psychology, Sociology, Geography, Economics, Political Science, Public Administration, *Indian Dissertation Abstracts* and *Research Abstracts Quarterly*. Of special significance to researchers in social sciences is the library's collection of unpublished Ph.D theses and research project reports in social sciences.

The centre has a backfile collection of 90,000 social science periodicals. Current issues of most Indian periodicals are regularly received. Besides, important secondary and tertiary sources like *Social Science Citation Index, Social Sciences Index, Sociological Abstracts, Psychological Abstracts* and its own bibliographical publications are available for consultation.

Efforts are also made to obtain a copy of every unpublished doctoral thesis in social sciences accepted by Indian universities and also foreign unpublished theses on India. So far, 2,000 Ph.D. theses and 1,000 research projects have been collected. The following publications including journals are available on microfilm/microfiche: (i) *Anthropological Society of Bombay Journal,* (ii) *Annals of Indian Administration,* (iii) *Bombay Geographical Society Journals,*

(iv) *Economic Working Papers* (UK), (v) *Gujarat Research Society Journal,* (vi) *Indian Linguistics,* (vii) *Psychological Abstracts,* (viii) *Social Action,* (ix) Sharma, R.A., *A Bibliography of Moghul India, 1526-1707,* (x) Thurston, E. and Ramachari, K., *Castes and Tribes of Southern India,* (7 Vols), (xi) Ph.D. theses and research reports.

4.2 *Bibliographical Services*

NASSDOC provides the bibliographical services to users to ensure the optimum use of published and unpublished material and equipment. The services are inter-library loan, reprographic facilities, reference service, referral services and consultancy services. NASSDOC's "Bibliographies on Demand" is a useful service though the scholars have to pay for this service. The centre is engaged in exchange activities, and receives 1,900 periodicals. About 1,000 agencies are no exchange list. It also has an international collaboration, and acts as an Indian correspondent for international bibliographies on social sciences. It provides lists of Indian books on economics, political science and sociology to the International Committee for Social Science Documentation, Paris, for their respective volumes of bibliographies. It also provides data for *International Bulletin of Bibliography on Education.* Information about research institutions, social scientists, and information centres in India was also collected on behalf of Unesco for its data base during 1982. NASSDOC set-up the Inter-Library Resources Centre in collaboration with Jawaharlal Nehru University in 1975, where the local libraries were invited to deposit their non-current, infrequently used but important research serials.

4.2.1 *ICSSR Projects*

There are two kinds of programmes with NASSDOC:

(i) Projects undertaken by the Council directly or in collaboration with selected institutions, and
(ii) Projects assisted by the Council under its grant-in aid scheme.

Under the first category of programmes, ICSSR brings out the following publications.

4.2.1.1 *Union List of Social Science Periodicals (1971-)*

Four volumes of the union lists relating to periodicals currently available in Andhra Pradesh, Bombay, Delhi and Karnataka libraries were brought out in 1971– . The Delhi list was updated in 1978 and subsequently revised in 1982. It records availability of 5,174 periodical titles in 91 libraries in Delhi during 1982 without giving information about the availability of holdings of libraries.

4.2.1.2 *Union Catalogue of Social Science Serials (1970-76)*

Compilation of the union catalogue was the first major project undertaken on April 1, 1970, and formally completed on March 31, 1976. Thirty-two volumes giving the location of about 31,125 serials in 550 libraries in the 17 States and two Union Territories with a separate volume on National Library, Calcutta, have been published. The union catalogue by its very nature requires revision from time to time to provide information about the current status of periodicals/ serials in our libraries. In some cases, these may be weeded out by certain libraries. Libraries will have large holdings in the years to come than they have now. Unique holdings of some titles may also be discovered in the presently lesser known libraries. The revision of the union catalogue is not only necessary, but imperative if the time of social scientists is to be saved. It is, therefore, being considered to take up this work on a regular basis and make it a core activity and a continuing programme of NASSDOC. Maintenance of such catalogues at national level is a step towards bibliographical control of social science literature.

Union catalogues cover Andhra Pradesh, Assam, Bihar, Delhi, Gujarat, Jammu & Kashmir, Karnataka, Kerala, Madhya Pradesh, Maharashtra, Orissa, Punjab, Haryana, Himachal Pradesh, Rajasthan, Tamilnadu, Uttar Pradesh and West Bengal. These union catalogues proved extremely useful, but its coverage is for years 1971-76. It is hoped that NASSDOC would like to up-date the union catalogue as rightly remarked by its Director that such a catalogue by its nature requires revision from time to time to provide latest information about the current status of serials in libraries.[12]

4.2.1.3 *Union Catalogue of Newspapers in Delhi Libraries*

After the compilation of union catalogues of serials excluding newspapers, a preliminary edition of "Union Catalogue of Newspapers" reflecting holdings in Delhi libraries as on September 15, 1978, was brought out in mimeographed form, and was distributed to local libraries for reference. It was up-dated in 1983 and the information is intended to be maintained on cards. The latest catalogue covers 252 newspaper titles available in 36 libraries and newspaper offices.[13]

4.2.1.4 *Directory of Social Science Research Institutions and Directory of Professional Organisations in India*

NASSDOC has up-dated the two directories originally published in 1971, and the information is available on cards for reference. Such directories are part of the bibliographical activities of the centre and with a sure way to help social science scholars to get information.

4.2.1.5 *Mahatma Gandhi Bibliography*

The first volume in the series *Mohandas Karamchand Gandhi : A Bibliography* devoted to monographs in English was released on October 27, 1974. This was followed by volumes covering monographs in Sanskrit, Hindi, Bengali and Urdu. The remaining volumes are at various stages of compilation.

4.2.1.6 *Retrospective Cumulative Index of Indian Social Science Periodicals*

Along with the union catalogue project, NASSDOC planned to prepare a Retrospective Cumulative Index of Indian Social Science Periodicals right from their respective first volume. The Retrospective Index Project was started from April, 1976. NASSDOC has identified 240 periodicals for the project, and decided 1970 as the cut-off year. So far work relating to indexing of journals in education, psychology, anthropology and sociology has been completed. When the project is completed, it will mean bibliographical control of periodical literature published over the past 100 years, and it will be of potential utility to social scientists. This was one of the recommendations of the previously held seminars to have bibliographical control of retrospective social science literature.

The index is planned to be maintained initially on cards which can be consulted by scholars even while the work is in progress. It may be printed serially or computerized later on.

Initial experience of bringing out a volume of *Indian Education Index* under this series has been greatly appreciated, and is reflected in the demand for such work. This is, therefore, planned to be a long-term continuing service under which series of volumes are proposed to be brought out.

On compilation, the Retrospective Cumulative Index will have the following advantages:

(1) Index will provide reasonable bibliographic control of periodical literature published in this country during approximately the last 150 years.
(2) Union Catalogue volumes will provide location in the country of the needed volumes of any periodicals for quick and easy access.
(3) Inter-Library Resources Centre will try to provide access to these volumes or supply copies of required articles at reasonable cost.[14]

4.2.1.7 *Area Studies Bibliographies*

A project on Area Studies Bibliographies aimed at bringing together all social science material of research value pertaining to the different States and Union Territories started during the 1970s. Under this project, it was envisaged to bring out series of bibliographies covering material in social sciences available in any form and language exclusively related to the area concerned.

Under the supervision of a project director in each State, the compilation work is in progress in the following states:

1. Andhra Pradesh
2. Assam and other N.E. States of India
3. Bihar
4. Delhi
5. Goa, Daman & Diu
6. Gujarat
7. Haryana and Himachal
8. Jammu & Kashmir
9. Karnataka
10. Kerala
11. Madhya Pradesh
12. Maharashtra
13. Punjab
14. Rajasthan
15. Tamilnadu; and

Pradesh 16. Uttar Pradesh

About 2,500 titles in regional languages and about 2,000 titles in English have so far been received from various States and Union Territories.

4.2.1.8 *Language Bibliographies*

The project is wider in scope and seeks to cover research material in all disciplines of social sciences in India regional languages. The compilation work of bibliographies in Gujarati, Hindi and Kannada is in progress. The bibliographical data of about 3,600 publication is in hand.

4.2.1.9 *ICSSR-Assisted Projects*

A second category of the programmes (assisted by the ICSSR) with a grant-in-aid relates to the compilation of the following indexes and bibliographies:

(1) *Index of Articles on Agricultural Economics.*
(2) *Asian Social Science Bibliography*
(3) *Documentation on Asia*
(4) *A Directory of Behavioural Science Research in India*
(5) *Doctorates in Social Sciences*
(6) *Marathi Periodicals Index*
(7) *Kannada Periodicals Index*
(8) *Hindi Periodicals Index*
(9) *Children's Periodicals Index*

In addition to the above projects, ICSSR has also sanctioned grants-in-aid for the following subjects:

(1) Annotated Bibliography of Journals in Education, Psychology and Sociology.
(2) Bibliography on Foreign Research on Indian Political System.
(3) Bibliography of South Asian Linguistics.
(4) Children's Literature since Independence : A Bibliographical Study of its Social Impact.
(5) Encyclopaedia of Social Science in Marathi

(6) Indian Press Index
(7) Information Requirements and Suggestions for Developing Library and Information Services for Social Scientists in India.
(8) Preliminary Survey (Pilot Study) of Social Science Material in Hindi leading to encyclopaedia of Social Sciences.
(9) Socio-economic Implications of Puranic Legends : A Chronological Bibliographical Survey.
(10) Studies in Communal Behaviour with Special Reference to Hindu-Muslim Tension.

Besides ICSSR has provided a grant-in-aid of Rs. 11,70,000 to the Indian Council of World Affairs towards the maintenance of its Library during 1980-81.

ICSSR is quite liberal in helping them through grants-in-aid in purchasing published copies. *Indian Press Index* is one which gets the support both ways. But *Index India* which is one of the huge bibliographical works does not get any financial help. ICSSR should from time to time review its grants-in-aid policies to provide financial aid to compilation of indexes and bibliographies.

NASSDOC has been responsible for the following bibliographical tools since its establishment in 1969:

4.2.9.2 *ICSSR Research Abstract Quarterly (1971-)*

This has been appearing since October, 1971. Abstracts of reports of concerning research funded by the Council setting out the objectives, the methodology and major findings of the research are published in this journal.

4.2.9.3 *Indian Psychological Abstracts (1972-)*

It is a quarterly published regularly since January 1972. It publishes short abstracts of research work done in the discipline of Indian themes.

4.2.9.4 *Indian Dissertation Abstracts (1973-)*

This is a quarterly publication published since March, 1973. The journal publishes synopses of Ph.D. theses in social sciences submitted to the Indian universities. Each synopsis gives the name of the university awarding the degrees, the year and the name of the supervisor. The utility of this journal to the social science community and particularly to students is self-evident. It gives a state-of-research in social sciences and contribution to knowledge in different areas by students of various universities in India. This will help promotion of research, prevention of duplication of research, improvement in the quality of research, and dissemination of information on social science research among the universities. The coverage of dissertations in the journal extends to the disciplines normally recognized by the Council as falling within the scope of social sciences.[15]

4.2.9.5 *ICSSR Journal of Abstracts and Reviews (1972-)*

This is published in the following subject series:

(a) Sociology and Anthropology
(b) Economics
(c) Geography
(d) Political Science

These issues have been regularly appearing in print since January, 1972. The journal publishes abstracts of research as well as the reviews in the subject.

4.2.9.6 *Other ICSSR Publications/Series*

ICSSR has also brought out the following volumes of bibliographies:

Doctorates in Social Sciences		1857-1967
-do-	-do-	1968
-do-	-do-	1969
-do-	-do-	1970
-do-	-do-	1971

In another way ICSSR has promoted publication of good reference work by bulk purchase of the published copies of important secondary tools. In this category are included the following publications:

1. *Index India*

2. *Indian Behavioural Sciences Abstract*
3. *Indian Press Index*
4. *A Guide to Reference Material on India*
5. *Theses on the Indian Sub-Continent (1877-1971)*
6. *Indian Political Movement (1919-71)*
7. *Civil Disobedience and Indian Tradition*
8. *Hindi Sandarbh*
9. *Index to Calcutta Review (1844-1920)*

NASSDOC lists its future programme as follows:

(1) Establishing Micro-filming unit.
(2) Updating Union Catalogue of Social Science Serials/ Periodicals.
(3) A national information grid has also been on the planning board for sometime. The system is expected to link centres of excellence (in social sciences) of the country and make expeditious service to the seeker of information a sine qua non of coordinated cooperation among the constituents.[16, 17]

NASSDOC has made a lot of efforts to spread its activities.

4.3 *ICSSR Southern Regional Centre, Hyderabad*

The role of a regional centre is to act as the agent of ICSSR within the region; to act as the representative of the social scientists of the region and to bring their ideas and problems to ICSSR; to promote social science research and to serve as a link between social scientists of the region and the national and international community of social scientists. The ICSSR Southern Regional Centre has been responsible for the following bibliographical publications:

(i) *Current Contents in Social Sciences (1964-)*

This is a monthly mimeographed documentation list which has been regularly brought out since August, 1964. Approximately 100 copies are distributed to various social science libraries. It lists the contents of the articles received by the regional centre.

(ii) *Documentation in Social Sciences (1983-)*

This is a bi-monthly publication which provides information about articles from select journals. The latest issue was published on August 16, 1986.

(iii) *Social Science Information Bulletin (1983-)*

It is an annual publication brought out regularly since 1983. The latest is the 1986 issue available in the library. It provides information about the agencies and activities of social science research in South India.[18]

(iv) *Pradhan Vyasa Suchi (Telugu) (1978-)*

It is a half-yearly documentation list being brought out regularly since 1978. The latest issue available in the library is January-June, 1986.

(v) *Documentation Social Science (Urdu) (1978-)*

It is a half-yearly publication. This is being brought out since 1978. The latest issue available in the library is January-June, 1986.

(vi) Sharma, B.A.V. and P. Satyanarayana : *Ph.D Programme in Social Sciences in South Indian Universities*

The survey was presented to the 13th meeting of social scientists of Southern Universities at the Madras Institute of Development Studies on December 10-11, 1983. The Centre has brought out a useful survey of the functionary of Ph.D. programme in Southern Universities.[19]

(vii) *Union List of Current Social Science Periodicals : Hyderabad Libraries, 1987*

This is a union list of current periodicals available in 31 important libraries of the twin cities of Hyderabad. The union list provides social science researchers an information whether a particular library subscribes to the journal. But it fails to provide the holdings of the journals. The [illegible] includes some of the journals which are not scholarly. Since social science researchers read everything important to their research, it is not necessary that the list should contain only scholarly journals.

5. Other Social Science Documentation Agencies

Rajasthan University Library, Indian Council of World Affairs, National Library, Indian Documentation Service, Institute of Economic Growth, Ratan Tata Library at Delhi School of Economics, National Council of Applied Economic Research, Jawaharlal Nehru University Library, Karnataka University Library, Association of Indian Universities, and, of course, above all, NASSDOC are the major documentation centres. A variety of documentation activities are also performed, by many social research libraries and higher educational libraries.

The Institute of Economic Growth, Delhi, has been publishing *Asian Social Science Bibliography* since 1970. This is a continuation of *Southern Asian Social Science Bibliography* which was brought out by the UNESCO Research Centre on Social and Economic Development in Southern Asia. The 1966 and 1967 editions of the bibliography were prepared in 1970 and 1974 by the Institute of Economic growth at the suggestion of UNESCO. It is a regional social science bibliography covering references on Asian countries like Afghanistan, Burma, Cambodia, Sri Lanka, India, Indonesia, Iran, Korea, Laos, Malaysia, Nepal, Pakistan, the Philippines, Singapore, Taiwan, Thailand and Vietnam.

The fields covered are economics, sociology, social anthropology, social psychology, political science, social science and social data, education, communication and demography. The bibliography covers selective materials published in English not only within the country, but outside including books, articles from scholarly journals or reports, by government and other organizations. It covers 1,972 entries from 400 journals. The 1967 edition covers 2,285 entries from 400 journals. The entries are arranged classwise followed by author, subject and geographical indexes. Most entries have been provided with annotations. There is a considerable time lag between the appearance of the articles indexed and the release of the bibliography.

Another Noteworthy bibliographical publications is *Documentation on Asia.* It is a modification of *Documentation on Asian*

Affairs: Select Bibliography and Select Articles on Current Affairs. The annual was started in 1960 by the Indian Council of World Affairs. The 1960 edition was published in 1963 and the 1961 edition in 1966. ICSSR made a generous grant of Rs. 1,60,000 for bringing out the bibliographical service uptodate. (Details have been provided in the 4th Chapter).

One more bibliographical tool of national importance is *Index India.* It is brought out by Rajasthan University Library, Jaipur. This is a quarterly documentation list of India on material in English, combining in one sequence an Indian Newspaper Index, Index to Indian Periodicals, Index to Foreign Periodicals, Index to Composite Publications, Index to Bibliographical Profiles. It is cumulated annually. The index is selective in nature, but covers more than 1,000 periodicals. It attempts to cover literature on India in the field of social sciences and humanities excluding law reports and material on individual firms and banks. (Details have been provided in the 4th Chapter).

Guide to Indian Periodical Literature is a laudable commercial venture from the Indian Documentation Services. It is an alphabetical index covering author and subject in one alphabetic sequence. The current issue covers 440 Indian social science and humanities journals. It makes an attempt to be comprehensive though many important items are omitted. (Details have been provided in the 4th Chapter).

The Association of Indian Universities Library has developed a bibliography of doctoral dissertations as an effective tool in the dissemination of research information. Retrospective bibliographies covering the period 1857-1970 and 1970-75 were first to appear. Effective 1975, however, the bibliography was issued annually in two volumes. Volume I deals with natural and applied sciences while Volume II records doctoral degrees awarded in social sciences and humanities. In addition to the normal bibliographical details like the name of the research scholar, title of thesis, year of registration, and award of degree, the bibliography also gives the name and complete address of the supervising teacher. It also provides an availability note that seeks to inform whether a copy of the dissertation is available for consultation and use in the University library/ department or Registrar's office.[20]

The association has also brought out *Social Science : A Bibliography of Doctoral Dissertations Accepted by Indian Universities*

1857-1970. The bibliography is quite comprehensive and also shows the development of social sciences in the country since the beginning of the 20th century. It fills an important lacuna in social science research, and lists 2,810 theses in the following social science disciplines : sociology, political science, law, public administration, commerce, management, education library science, journalism and psychology.[21]

The A.N. Sinha Institute of Social Studies, Patna, publishes *Bihar in Print* every year. There is a time lag of at least three years.

ICSSR North Western Regional Centre, Chandigarh, brings out *Bibliography of Ph.D. and M.Phil. Theses in Social Sciences in Punjab University Library, Social Science Documentation List, Holdings of Social Science Journals in the Libraries of Chandigarh,* and *Bibliography of Punjabi Books (Social Sciences) in the Libraries of Chandigarh.*

K.K. Roy, Calcutta, has been bringing out *Bibliographia Asiatica : A Monthly Documentation List on Asia of Material in English* since 1968. This is a comprehensive index which includes scholarly works, research papers and documents, articles and editorials from leading newspapers, magazines, journals, economic and industrial reports, conference proceedings and commercial statistics by governments and international organizations listed under the names of all the Asian countries which are arranged alphabetically to facilitate quick reference.

It indexes more than 400 Indian journals of social sciences and humanities. Its format is also available in microform.[22]

6. Social Science Subjects

6.1 *Economics*

Economics has been a main plank of Indians social sciences since 1947. To develop the country's economy in a planned manner the Government of India gave importance to economics by setting up Planning Commission as an apex body of national planning. Prominent among the economics research institutes are the Institute of Economic Growth National Council of Applied Economic Research, Institute of Social and Economic Change, Indian Statistical Institutes at Calcutta, Delhi, Bangalore and Hyderabad, Gokhale Institute of Politics and Economics, Institute of Public Enterprise,

Institute of Applied Manpower Research and Delhi School of Economics at Delhi University. The following institutions have been engaged in documentation activities in the field of economics.

The field of labour is effectively covered by the Ministry of Labour through a bimonthly list on labour legislation. An Annual entitled *Labour Literature* is also issued from the same source. Supplementing this effort is the index of articles which appears as a regular feature in the *Indian Journal of Industrial Relations.* Bombay University Library issues a *Weekly Contents of Current Journals in Economics. Commercial Index* has been published from Calcutta since 1966 as a monthly documentation service. It fairly surveys the field and encompasses topics in economics, accountancy, company law, taxation and other matter relating to trade, industry, finance, etc.

Federation of Indian Chambers of Commerce and Industry, New Delhi brings out *Documentation Series* (selective journal articles). It has completed 19 volumes. It is an annotated index providing a comprehensive list of articles which appear in the newspapers, weeklies and fortnightlies of business and economics.

The Gokhale Institute of Politics and Economic, Poona, brings out *Fortnightly List of Articles on India.* This list which has been regularly appearing since 1967 is used for local consumption. The Institute's another organ is *Artha Vijnana* which has been appearing since 1959. It is a quarterly which is indexed in *Public Affairs Information Service* (PAIS) and *World Agricultural Economics and Rural Sociology Abstract,* which shows the reputation of the journal.

Index to Indian Economic Journals has been appearing on a monthly basis from Calcutta since 1966. This is brought out by the Information Research Academy. It scans 50 journals. The entries are arranged subjectwise, and supplemented by author and subject indexes. It is also available on microfilm.

The Indian Institute of Foreign Trade Library, Delhi, issues to fortnightly mimeographed services:

(a) *Documentation Lists*
(b) *The list of documents which are published and not for sale.*

The Ministry of Industrial Development issues : (i) *Documentation Service,* (ii) *Bibliography on Industry and Trade.* (The former is a monthly and the latter is an annual, but both are meant for official use only.) The Institute of Economic Growth, Delhi, brings out

Investment Planning and Project Evaluation. The Institute has been mainly responsible for bringing out *Asian Social Science Bibliography* on a yearly basis. The Institute of Public Enterprise, Hyderabad, brought out an *Annotated Bibliography on Public Enterprise in India* but was discontinued. The institute is development fast, but it is quite surprising that such a useful documentation list should have been discontinued.

The Institute of Applied Manpower Research, Delhi, brings out the following documentation lists:

(1) *Current Documentation* (1970-)
(2) *Manpower Documentation* (1970-)

The Manpower Documentation list has been regularly appearing since 1970, but was suspended from 1980 to 1986. It is published at the beginning of each quarter, provides information regarding books, reports and articles on manpower and related subjects received by the Institute during the preceding quarter. It is in three parts: *Part 1:* Annotated List of Manpower Titles and News Items on Manpower. *Part 2:* Index to Other Titles Processed by this centre. *Part 3:* Book Reviews digest featuring in condensed form, selected reviews of important publications acquired by the centre.

The Institute of Social and Economic Change, Bangalore brings out the following documentation lists for its local consumption.

(1) *Index to Current Articles on Social and Economic Change.* It is claimed that this is appearing regularly.
(2) *Agriculture and Rural Development Abstract:* It is brought out for local use and National Bank for Agriculture and Rural Development (NABARD) employees. The documentation list is financed by NABARD under an agreement against annual grant. Both the documentation lists are used for local consumption only. NABARD provides a grant of Rs. 1.1 lakhs per year towards periodical subscription.

The Ministry of Labour and Employment has been issuing, since 1957, a monthly documentation list known as *Bulletin of Current Awareness* (formerly called *Documentation Labour*) covering articles on labour and allied subjects. This is one of the earliest and systematic documentation services stated in the country. Monthly lists are cumulated every year and an annual volume is issued with index.

The National Council of Applied Economic Research, Delhi, brings out *Artha Suchi.* It is an index to Indian economic journals. The index was started in 1983 and has been regularly appearing quarterly since then.

It is a computerized index to government reports, journal articles, newspaper write-ups, working papers and discussion papers in the field of economics which are received in the field of economics in National Council of Applied Economic Research Library. *Artha Suchi* is processed on HP 3000 computer using MINISIS, a software package developed by the International Development Research Centre, Canada. It is available on-line, besides this printed version. The multiple access points like keywords help the users to broaden their searches and fast retrieval of information.

Artha Suchi covers literature on Indian economic and allied sectors published in over 100 journals and 10 newspapers received in NCAER Library. It is a valuable source of information and a useful tool for students, researchers and teachers.

The National Institute of Small Industry Extension Training, Hyderabad, brings out the following useful publications:

(1) *Sendoc Bulletin*. It is in three parts:

  (a) Industrial Technology
  (b) Economics and Development
  (c) Management and Behavioural Sciences

(2) *Appropriate Technology : Documentation Bulletin.*
(3) *Sendoc Current Accession List.*

The above documentation lists are uptodate and printed in time which serves the purpose of its clientele.

The Planning Commission library issues a weekly *Docplan* which indexes literature on economics and planning. The library also issues periodically special documentation lists on selected topics of interest under *Planning Bibliography Series.*

Ratan Tata Library at the Delhi School of Economics initially started with 4,000 volumes comprising the economics section of the Delhi University Library. The library has a fairly comprehensive collection which is extensive as well as intensive in the field of social sciences in general and economics in particular. The library brings out the following documentation list for local consumption:

(1) *Current Contents to the Periodicals Received in Ratan Tata Library:* This is brought out regularly on a fortnightly basis since 1971.
(2) *Book Review Index:* It is a monthly mimeographed publication.
(3) *Accession List:* It is issued monthly listing new books and regularly circulated among various departments. It covers all the subjects which fall within the scope of the Delhi School of Economics campus.
(4) *Documentation Lists:* It is a classified documentation list of articles and periodicals received in the library and is issued every fortnightly and distributed among the staff engaged in teaching and research.[23]

The Reserve Bank of India has been publishing the following monthly bulletin since 1947:

Reserve Bank of India Bulletin (1947-)

The text of the monthly bulletin appears both in English and Hindi. It is indexed in *Public Affairs Information Services.*

The Shri Ram Centre for Industrial Relations and Human Research, Delhi, brings out *Indian Journal of Industrial Relations* (1964-). This quarterly journal is indexed in *Guide to Indian Periodical Literature, Psychological Abstracts* and *Social Science Citation Index.*

The Tata Energy Institute, Bombay, publishes since 1976.

(1) *Energy Abstract Digest* (1976-)
(2) *Indian Energy Abstract* (1976-)

6.2 *Politics, Law and Public Administration*

Prominent among the political science institutions engaged in bibliographical activities are the Indian Council of World Affairs, Indian Institute of Public Administration, Institute of Indian Constitutional and Parliamentary Studies, A.N. Sinha Institute of

Social Studies and Nehru Memorial Museum Library.

The Indian Council of World Affairs also known as Sapru House is considered as a premier national institution of current affairs and documentation activities. Documentation work forms important part of the activities of the Sapru House Library, which is done on a regular basis after a separate unit was set-up in the library in 1966. Its documentation work is mainly related to the international relations and area studies.

The Council brings out the following three annual documentation lists regularly:

(1) *Select Articles on Current Affairs*
(2) *Documentation on Asia*
(3) *Indian and World Affairs : Select Bibliography*

The library brings out *Fortnightly List of Additions to the Library of Indian Council of World Affairs.* The arrangement of the list is helpful to the readers. It is arranged first countrywise and then subjectwise. *Weekly List of Articles* is also brought out every week. The library is also a depository of the U.N. and its specialized agencies' publications. In order to meet the special requirements of its clientele, the library prepared a *Special Index to India and U.N.* which is on cards and meets the requirements of users interested in the preparation of India in various organizations of the U.N.[24]

Press Clippings are a special class of research material, which are specially important in international relations and area studies. The library has been doing Press clipping work since 1960. At present there are over 80,000 clippings organized in 3,000 files available for consultation. Forty-two newspapers are being clipped regularly. The number of cuttings clipped per day average about 400 from newspapers covering various regions of the world. This shows the tremendous amount of documentation work being done by the library.[25]

The Indian Institute of Public Administration, Delhi, has been issuing a monthly *Abstract and Index of Articles* (1957-). About 150 periodicals are tapped for this service. It also brings out Documentation in *Public Administration.*[26]

The International Co-operative Alliance, Regional Office and Education Centre, Delhi, publishes *Documentation Bulletin for South East Asia* (1966-). The Bulletin contains the classified indexing list of articles on cooperation and allied subjects with special relevance to Asia selected from the periodicals received in the library of the International Cooperative Alliance Regional Office and Education Centre for South East Asia. This indicative indexing also contains the author's content of the articles wherever possible. The earlier issues of the documentation bulletin used to have a second part consisting of a classified list of books received by the bulletin.[27]

The Jawaharlal Nehru University Library has been bringing out the following documentation lists since 1971:

(1) *India and World Affairs : An Annual Bibliography* (1958-): So far period till 1959-82 has been covered. The documentation lists appears regularly in the journal, *International Studies,* which is the organ of the university.

(2) *Suchika : A Monthly Index to Periodical Literature in Social Sciences and Area Studies* (1980-): This is a useful tool for those actively engaged in research in international studies. The library brings out 250 copies regularly. The latest issue available in the library is of February, 1986. This is a meant for free distribution among its faculty members and also to other institutions.

(3) *JNU Dissertation Index* (1980): The Index is complied by Veena Taneja and A.R. Sethi. It was brought out in 1980. The publication date is not clear, but as it covers the period up to 1979, it is presumed that it must have been out in 1980. The Index includes Ph.D. theses and M.Phil. dissertations submitted to the various schools and centres of Jawaharlal Nehru University up to the end of 1979-80 academic year. The Index is divided into three parts:

Part 1 : Dissertations arranged by geographical areas.
Part 2 : Dissertations not susceptible to area approach have been classified by the subject in the second part.
Part 3 : Subject index to first two parts organized by POPSI, besides three other types of indexes.

It is a comprehensive index which is useful to social science scholars particularly doing M.Phil. and Ph.D. degree. The index is not particularly confined to political science but most dissertations deal with political science background. Each entry of the Index covers the full bibliographical information. It also provides a title of contents to show how a particularly dissertation has been designed.[28]

The Ministry of Home Affairs Library has been issuing a mimeographed classified list of articles on administration since 1967.

The Indian Law Institute issues an index every six months to its journal, *Indian Legal Periodicals* (1956-).

The Lok Sabha Secretariat also issues a very useful *Sessional Bibliography of Papers Laid on the Table and Statements Made by Ministers.* It is both authoritative and complete.[29] It also brings out the following documentation lists in the field of constitutional and parliamentary affairs :

(1) *Index to Lok Sabha Debates*
(2) *Privileges Digest*
(3) *Digest of Central Accounts and Constitutional Cases*
(4) *Abstracts and Index of Reports and Articles*

The above documentation lists are brought out to meet the ever-increasing needs of the Members of Parliament as well as political scientists and scholars on the subject.[30]

The Nehru Memorial Museum Library has been developed into one of the best well equipped and largest library on modern India. The library issues a documentation list known as *Selected Articles on Modern Indian History.* Another important checklist that they have broughtout is *List of Theses on Microfilms* (as on August 1, 1979). The Library procured microfilm copies of Ph.D. dissertations which have a bearing on modern Indian history. Up to 1979, there were 404 such theses available on microfilm for consultation in the Library. There is an author and title index listed in alphabetical order provided at the end of the list.[31]

The Delhi School of Social Work now known as Department of Social Work, University of Delhi, has been bringing out an excellent indexing tool called *Development and Welfare* (1958-). It is brought out regularly by the Department. It is selective indexing of articles, reports and other publications from a wide range of national and international sources. The focus of the journal is on the undeveloped and developing countries of Asia, Africa and Latin America about their social situation, developmental activities and welfare programmes. The position of the marginal, weaker section in the affluent world is also highlighted.

The index consist of two parts. The first part contains selective articles from over 1,100 journals in the areas of social history, education, health, human geography, law, psychology, sociology, social work, ecology, area studies, environmental studies, religion and philosophy. The second part consists of "Book Notes" section which provides information about the current publications on the developing world together with bibliographical details and annotations.[32]

The Gandhi Peace Foundation was established in New Delhi in 1964. The Foundation has undertaken a project of studying various tensions and conflicts in Indian society. As an aid to the study, the Foundation established a documentation centre in 1969 to take up the task of preparing bibliography continuously on selected areas for the benefit of scholars.[33]

6.3 *Sociology*

International Institute for Population Sciences, brings out *IIPS Library Acquisition List* (1958-). Though it is merely an accession list it is providing useful and, therefore, it has been kept up for so many years.

The National Institute of Community Development now known as National Institute of Rural Development (NIRD), Hyderabad, is responsible for the following useful bibliographical publications:

(1) *Cord Abstracts*
(2) *Cord Index*

S.N.D.T. University, Bombay, brings out (1) *Women's Studies: An Index to Indian Periodicals Literature* (1986-); (2) *Annotated Bibliography of Indian Periodicals for Children* (1979-). (This was brought out in English, Hindi, Gujarati and Marathi, but now it is discontinued.)

The university also brought out *Education of Woman in India since 1850-1967 : A Bibliography.* But this is now dated and not being kept uptodate. It brings out *Textile Information Resources in Select Libraries of Bombay.* For the first time it was brought out in 1981, but now it is discontinued.

6.4 *Education*

Important functions of the Association of Indian Universities (AIU) is to act as clearing house of information on higher education in the country. Towards this end the AIU Library is engaged in collecting building and developing instruments for the dissemination of research information. Over the years a valuable collection of books and documents on different aspects of higher education has been acquired. *University News* has been rendering a great service to those who care to be well informed about the development and research in higher education.[34] Earlier it was fortnightly but now it is weekly. Besides giving a news write-up about the Indian universities it also provide to important sections: (1) Research in Progress, (2) Theses of the Month: This helps the Indian academics to know the particulars of the doctoral dissertations submitted in Indian universities as well as research in progress. It helps to check duplication of research. Those scholars who are engaged in research find the *University News* an important and useful tool. The information is compiled on the basis of communication received from all universities in India.

Education is also well served by two quarterly services: (1) *Indian Education Abstracts* (1956-) issued by the Central Secretariat Library, (2) *Indian Educational Material* (1966-) issued by the Indian National Scientific Documentation Centre (INSDOC).[35]

The Indian Institute of Education, Poona, has undertaken a programme to bring out the "Writings on Indian Education", especially after 1947 to assist researchers and students of education in India under the general editorship of S.P. Agrawal. This is *Indian Education Index 1947-78*. The students of education and educational institutions will find this programme useful. This project could become possible because of the cooperation of ICSSR which allowed the Institute of use the index cards prepared for educational journals under its programme on *Retrospective Index to Social Science Periodicals* between 1947 and 1970. The last three decades have witnessed a phenomenal expansion of the Indian education system which has led to an equally phenomenal growth in educational literature, particularly the papers published in Indian educational journals. Attempts have also been made earlier to bring educational literature published in Indian journals under bibliographical control.

This Index is primarily a combined retrospective index to the contents of 26 Indian educational periodicals published in the English language. It gives access to more than 20,000 items published in these journals. It has two parts—a subject index and an author index. Full bibliographical details are provided in both the parts.

The Index covers all items including comments and replies, book review articles, obituaries, substantive reports of various committees, commissions, conferences and seminars. It covers the literature published between January 1947 — December 1978. A special feature of the Index is a list of the libraries where 26 journals with back volumes are available.[36] This is quite helpful because the social science scholars know where the document or information is available.

6.5 *Management*

The Administrative Staff College of India, Hyderabad, has been bringing out *Current Management Literature* (1971-). It is an abstracting tool regularly brought out by the College. The latest issue available is Volume 16 (1985-86). Though it is mimeographed its utility is international. It is listed in *Ulrich's International Periodicals Directory.* It should be appreciated, as only few social science research libraries engage in abstracting work.

The Indian Institute of Management, Bangalore, bring out: (1) *Recent Additions* — a monthly publication (discontinued due to the lack of professional staff); (2) *Current Press Clippings:* A fortnightly documentation list (discontinued due to lack of professional staff).

The Indian Institute of Public Administration also brings out a *Quarterly List of Abstracts and Index* of Articles which cover all aspects of public administration.

The Information Research Academy, Calcutta, brings out *Indian Management Abstracts.* This has been appearing regularly since 1972. It is edited by Partha Subir Guha.

The Vaikunth Mehta National Institute of Cooperative Management is responsible for bringing out the following documentation lists: (1) *Monthly List of Additions to the Library and Allied Subjects,* (2) *Monthly List of Articles on Co-operative and Allied Subjects.*

6.6 *Library Science*

The Indian Association of Special Libraries and Information Centres (IASLIC), Calcutta, is responsible for the production of *Indian*

Library Science Abstracts. It is a quarterly abstracting tool which has been appearing since 1967. So far 18 volumes have appeared. The abstracts cover articles including short communication published in library science periodicals issued in India. Proceedings of the conferences, and symposia held in India are also covered.

The Abstracts are classified according of *Colon Classification* (CC) and arranged under appropriate headings alphabetically by author index referring to the text by the serial number. The subject index is based on Preserved Context Indexing System (PRECIS). Initials of the abstractors are given at the end of each abstract.[37]

6.7 *Indology*

The Bhandarkar Oriental Research Institute has been publishing *Vedic Bibliography* (edited by R.N. Dandekar) since 1946. There was a gap of many years, but now it is being kept uptodate. Its first volume came out in 1946, second in 1961, third in 1973, and fourth in 1985. It is rated as the best bibliographical tool in the field of Indology.

Quarterly *Index Indo-Asiaticus* edited by Sibdas Chaudhari since 1968 reproduces the contents of important journals in Orientology both in English and other languages. This is brought out by the Centre for Asian Documentation. The journals chosen are important British, American, French, German, Hungarian, Indian, Pakistani, Thai, Japanese, and other publications. Articles are listed alphabetically by Author under the name of a journal. There is neither an author nor a subject index. The quality of the index is poor.[38]

6.8 *Psychology*

After Independence, psychology has been gaining importance as an independent research discipline. Many journals which have come up recently show that the growth of psychology is faster than other subjects. "Research Completed" and "Research in Progress" columns in the *University News* gives us the number of theses submitted and current research going on in Indian universities.

The contribution of ICSSR in bringing out *Indian Psychological Abstracts* is to be appreciated. The Council has been bringing out the *Abstract* since 1972. The Indian Psychological Association co-sponsor the *Abstract* along with the Council. It provides information about the advance book reviews, besides the abstracts of journal articles. It is well circulated throughout the country and outside India.

Guide to Indian Periodical Literature and *Index India* both cover *Indian Psychological Abstracts, Indian Journal of Psychology* and *Indian Journal of Applied Psychology.* Unfortunately journals like *Indian Academy of Applied Psychology Journal, Indian Journal of Behaviour, Indian Journal of Psychometry and Education, Indian Psychological Review* and *Indian Psychology* are not covered by both the indexes. *Indian Journal of Behaviour,* however is abstracted in *Indian Psychological Abstracts.* There is need to have a far and wide coverage of psychological journals by Indian indexing tools. It is surprising that the Indian psychological journals are represented well in foreign indexes like *Psychological Abstracts,* but not in Indian indexes and abstracts.

6.9 *Geography*

After Independence India developed its own geographical technology of producing geographical maps and atlases. It was found necessary to provide correct geographical facts to the Indian people. The then British Government was quite aware of its administrative responsibility to run the government efficiently. W.W. Hunter had brought out the first edition of *Imperial Gazetteer of India* in nine volumes in 1881.

The Government of India had also realized the need of revising gazetteers after Independence, and hence brought out the following:

Gazetteer of India: *Indian Union* 4 volumes (Delhi) Publication Division, (1965)

Volume 1 — *Country and People*
Volume 2 — *History and Culture*
Volume 3 — *Economic Structure and Activities*
Volume 4 — *Administration and Public Welfare*

New gazetteers are intended to educate not only the administrators, but the people in whose hands power ultimately rests. The gazetteers provide all the knowledge of the rich variety, and at the same time bring out the basic similarities underlying the outward differences. These gazetteers are important and significant bibliographical tools for geographers, as they provides various kinds of information pertaining to geographical details.

J.S. Sharma's *National Geographical Dictionary of India* is another commendable effort. But, in view of the minute geographical details of cities and towns, it cannot be compared with Chamber's *World Gazetteer and Geographical Dictionary.*[39]

Important work done in Indian geography is toposheets brought out by the Survey of India. This is the most authentic and painstaking geographical work done by the Britishers. Each and every part of the country has been surveyed and minute geographical details given. The toposheets are helpful in the development of regional planning.

Geography Teacher and *Geographical Observer* are indexed in *Index India* and *Guide to Indian Periodical Literature. Indian Geographical Studies Research Bulletin* and *Indian Geographical Journal* are indexed in *Index India,* but not in the *Guide.* Thus coverage of geographical journals in *Index India* is found better than in the *Guide.* However, overall coverage of geographical journals in both the Index and the *Guide* is poor.

6.9.1 *American Studies*

American Studies Research Centre (ASRC), Hyderabad, was set-up in 1964 as a bi-national institution to help Indian scholars to study American subject through its library. ASRC is basically a library having a comprehensive collection of American except science and technical subjects. It provides library facilities to those who are either engaged in full-time research on are teaching in Indian universities and colleges. Thus in order to have a full bibliographical control over current as well as retrospective literature of American studies. The ASRC has been bringing out various bibliographical tool since its inception. The following are the bibliographical publications:

1. *Acquisition List:* It is a mimeographed publication which comes out every quarter. This is a useful tool for users to know that is added to the collection. Being an all-India level library, ASRC acquisition list is quite in demand.

2. *American Studies Index to Selected Indian Periodicals:* It indexes the Indian journals subscribed by the library which publish articles on

American studies, and which are not indexed in any of the Indian indexing tools.

3. *American Studies Index to Selected Periodicals:* It indexes American studies journals which are not covered by the *Humanities Index* and *Social Sciences Index.*

4. *Indian Contributions to American Studies 1895-1977:* It is a complete checklist of books, articles, dissertations and papers in American studies by Indian authors.

5. *Indian Doctoral Engagement in American Studies:* It is a publication meant to acquaint scholars with the contents of dissertation at the M.Phil and Ph.D. levels and other scholarly monographs in American studies completed by Indian scholars.

6. *Indian Research in American Studies 1946-1977:* It is a list of dissertations accepted by Universities, and research in progress by Indian authors.

7. *Union List of Serials Available in ASRC and USIS Libraries in India 1986:* USIS post libraries in India had thought of bringing out a union catalogue which includes the periodical holdings of ASRC. This is useful if scholars want to know the location of a periodical along with a photocopy request. Union Catalogues are the important bibliographical tools which serve the purpose of bibliographical control of any subject. These data are also available on Wong Computer, therefore, subsequent revisions should be easy. The catalogue is in two parts-alphabetical and classified. The alphabetical list has been bound the classified list is being provided separately, so that individual parts may be reproduced as required. It is brought out by USIS, Delhi, in May. Introduction provides the information about the address of USIS port libraries and ASRC so that any scholar who wants to have information can contact any of the libraries.

ASRC has been regularly updating its checklists to provide latest information to scholars. The checklists are useful as they serve a dual purpose: they on a give a topic and, second, they indicate the availability of the material at the Centre.[40]

6.9.2 *African Studies*

Africa till the sixties was considered as a "dark continent", but slowly and gradually many old colonies broke away into small States and achieved independence. The Department of African Studies of the University of Delhi has been issuing a very comprehensive documentation list on Africa known as *Documentation List : Africa.* This is issued by the Delhi University Library since 1962. In October, 1966, it had to be suspended due to some unavoidable circumstances. However, its publication was resumed largely through the efforts of library professionals of the Delhi University Library. But there is a time lag of five years as it is evident from the 1967 Volume VI which was issued in 1972. The Documentation List collects articles on Africa published in various journals received in the Delhi University Library. The arrangement is under the specific subject in alphabetical sequence. The List contains the following parts:

(1) Periodicals Indexed
(2) List of Subject Headings used.
(3) Subject Part.
(4) Geographical Index.
(5) Author Index.

The list indexes 397 journals (received in the Delhi University Library) of all aspects of social sciences and humanities. This is any authoritative and standard bibliographical tool. Its only drawback is its time lag which should be reduced from five years to one.

7. Accession Lists, List of Periodicals and Local Union Lists

Social science research libraries and university libraries bring out accession lists, list of periodicals and union lists for local consumption and distribution purposes. Accession lists or list of additions proves useful to scholars who want to know about the books and periodicals being added to the library. With library co-operation, local libraries bring out a union list of periodicals with or without holdings. Institutions which bring out local documentation list (including accession lists) are as follows:

Osmania University Library brings out: (1) *Monthly List of New*

Additions to the Library: This is being brought since 1960. It is distributed free to all the departments of the University, and (2) *Quarterly List of U.N. Documents and Reference Works Added to the Library.*

The Library being a depository of U.N. Documents lists the U.N. reference general publications for the benefit of the scholars who are doing research on international organizations. The list is uptodate till 1985 and has been appearing regularly since 1983.

Karnataka University Library, Dharwar, has been doing extensive documentation work in the field of social sciences for the last many years. The credit for the initiation of such documentation lists goes to its former librarians. The library brings out:

1. *Catalogue of Periodicals:* The catalogue has been regularly appearing since 1954. For the time being it is under revision.
2. *Guide to Periodical Literature* the library brings out the guide since 1967, but now it is temporarily discontinued.
3. *Catalogue of Periodicals and Serlals of UNO:* This is being brought out since 1974, but now it is not being revised. The reason for discontinuation is not mentioned.
4. *Catalogue of Theses and Dissertations:* The catalogue has been appearing since 1960, and it is kept uptodate.
5. *Latest Additions:* The list of additions is being brought out since 1960.

The National Institute of Health and Family Welfare has been bringing out checklists and bibliographies from time to time. Since a list provided by its documentation centre is quite large it is not possible to list them. However, so far the Institute has brought out 33 publications in the form of bibliographies and checklists.

Gujarat University Library brought out the list of books on (a) education, (b) political science and (c) Gandhiana which were published regularly in 1974, 1975 and 1976 respectively. These have been discontinued.

The Indian Institute of Management besides regularly bringing out *Recent Additions and Current Press Clippings* is also responsible for preparing ad-hoc bibliographies and reading lists. The Institute maintains the following series:

(1) Bibliography Series
(2) New Digest Series
(3) Reading List Series
(4) Statistical Digest Series
(5) Pathfinder Series
(6) Reference Series

The National Institute of Nutrition receives reports, reprints, theses, slides, annual reports, current periodicals, advances, annual reviews and other serial monographs. The library is responsible for giving reference service, alert services and selective dissemination of information. Under the alert services the library provides (1) *Reprint Awareness List,* and (2) *Accession List.* Under the selective dissemination of information, the library brings out (1) *Annual List of Scientific Publications,* (2) *Subject Bibliographies,* (3) *Catalogue of Theses*, (4) *Nutrition in Health and Disease–Current Literature* – a bi-monthly list of articles scanned regularly from the primary periodicals and (5) *Catalogue of Periodicals Holdings.*

Bhai Gurdas Library of Guru Nanak Dev University brings out *Select Book List.* It is being up-dated for the last six years. The Gokhale Institute of Politics and Economics prepares *Fortnightly List of Articles on India.* Punjabi University Library brings out: *Periodica : Classified Index of Periodicals in Social Sciences and Humanities in the Library:* It is a mimeographed publication and has been appearing 'since' 1982. There is a time lag of three years.

Sukhadia University Library has been bringing out the following documentation lists for the last many years:

1. *Catalogue of Theses and Dissertations.*
2. *Acquisition List.*

Marathwada University Library brings out *Documentation List.* It is being published regularly since 1980.

The National Institute of Education Planning and Administration brings out the following documentation lists:

1. *Library New Arrival*
2. *List of the Documentation in Sub-National Levels*

North Eastern Hill University Library, brings out *Dissertation on*

North Eastern India — An Index to D.Litt., Ph.D., M.Phil., M.Ed. and M.Sc. Theses since 1982. It is in mimeographed form. It makes 300 copies for distribution purpose.

8. Current Trade Bibliographies

Trade bibliographies have been playing an important role in the book world in our country. Such bibliographies are national in scope, but usually record current books and the books which can be acquired through normal book trade channels. Prominent among trade bibliographies are *Books on India: Supplement to Index India* (1967-); *Indian Book Industry* (1969-), Delhi, Sterling (monthly); *Indian Books* (1974-75), New Delhi, Today and Tomorrow; *Indian Books* (1969-), Varanasi, Indian Bibliographic Centre; *Indian Publisher and Book Seller* (1951-), Bombay, Popular Book Depot; *Recent Indian Books* (1975-), Delhi, Federation of Publishers and Book Sellers; and *Publishing in India* (1979-) Delhi, D.K. Library Service.

Current trade bibliographies keep librarians and book lovers always well informed about what is being currently published in the country and which titles are in print. *Indian Books in Print* is a main source of information of books in print. Among the trade bibliographies *Indian Book Industry,* a monthly journal, is the best bibliographical publication which has successfully completed 19 years of its existence. It provides articles about the national book trade situation along with a subjectwise bibliography of current books. Publishers' advertisements are given in the journal about the new titles available with them.

8.1 *Periodical Guides*

Though India has completed 40 years of independence still we do not have a good periodical guide. Some effort has, however, been made to bring out a comprehensive guide to Indian periodicals during the last three decades. The first pioneering attempt was made in 1955 by a private commercial firm in India. *Nifor Guide to Indian Periodicals,* 1955-56, gives a listing of 2,127 titles classified by language, subject, geographic location and periodicity—all presented in Roman transliteration. The *Guide* provides a welcome introduction to the vast world of Indian periodicals. But in course of time the *Guide* has lost its usefulness because it was not being keep up-to-date. Not it is outdated. The same fate is of N.N. Gidwani's *Indian Periodicals : An Annotated Guide.* It came out in 1969, but no effort was made to keep it up-dated This guide is limited to English language titles. This group itself comprises 21 per cent of all periodicals published in India. This again was a pioneering effort, and it was thought that it would be revised, but in vain.[41]

In 1956, the Indian Government started to publishing the Annual Report of the Registrar of Newspapers (this title was changed to *Press in India* a few years ago). All commercial journals—from dailies to annuals—are supposed to be registered with the Government each year and furnish information on content, language and so forth. This annual list is an invaluable guide to the periodical publications of each Indian State, arranged by language and periodicity, and also presented in Roman transliteration. Since this is an annual, one can be reasonably sure that the statements of address and editorship are current. Though *Press in India* is indeed a huge and valuable compilation, it is not complete. Hence, as it is with *Indian National Bibliography,* the law of registry is apparently not enforced. Still it is real beginning towards bibliographical control of the periodicals published in India.

If Indian bibliographical tools have to serve the purpose, they have to be kept current with the monthly list of changes, additions and deletions, an essential qualification to make these lists a useful current bibliographical tool. It could be considered an achievement in the field of bibliographical control over Indian periodicals as these publications constitute the largest group of research literature.

8.2 *Directories of Libraries and Union Catalogues*

Importance of directories and union catalogues can not to be underestimated as these are the sure ways to achieve full bibliographical control in social science literature. One of the important links in achieving full bibliographical control is the location of material as discussed in the introduction. One may find a reference of a journal article or a book, but where is the journal article available in another aspect. ICSSR has paid attention to this and encouraged the academic institutions engaged in this kind of work. Important directories and union catalogues brought out by the professional organizations are the following:

(1) *Directory of Libraries and Who's Who in Library Profession in Delhi.* Edited by N.K. Goil, etc. Delhi, Delhi Library Association, 1964.
(2) *Directory of Libraries in Delhi.* Compiled by Surendra Kumar, New Delhi, Sterling, 1973.
(3) *Directory of Special and Research Libraries in India.* Compiled by IASLIC, Calcutta, IASLIC, 1962.
(4) *Indian Library Directory.* Compiled by S.R. Ranganathan and Others. 3rd edn. Delhi, Indian Library Association, 1951.
(5) *Indian Library Directory.* Edited by Joginder Singh and A.R. Sethi, 4th edn. Delhi, Indian Library Association, 1985.

S.R. Ranganathan had brought out a *Union Catalogue of Learned Periodicals Publications in South Asia* in 1953 which was published by the Indian Library Association. Another union catalogue of American serials known as *Union List of Learned American Serials in Indian Libraries* was brought out in 1966 by the Indian Council for Library Development. Both the catalogues served the research needs of social science scholars for many years. But union catalogues have to be revised from time to time.

ICSSR from its inception has been paying great attention the compilation of union catalogues. Union list and union catalogues of social science periodicals were immediately taken care of by the Council in the early seventies. But the problem with such tools is that there are to be up-dated from time to time in order to be useful to users.

8.3 *Government Publications*

Bibliographical control of government documents in South Asia has been a constant headache. This is because the government apparatus is huge and complex particularly in India. One has to struggle with the Central Government's proliferation of publications under a great number of ever changing bureaucratic ministries, departments, directorates and the like. One has also to deal with a similar variety of issuing agencies at the wing, state and territorial level of India. But this complexity is not unreasonable keeping in view the size of the land mass and population of India, and the diverse languages spoken. It is a formidable task for librarians to have control bibliographical government publications particularly of latter part of the 20th century of post-independent India.

Frank Campbell's monumental *Index Catalogue of Indian Official Publications in the Library, British Museum* was published in 1900 which covers the British period. Except this, till 1947 nothing was done towards government documents. *Indian National Bibliography* on government publications contributed for a limited period and only on a current basis. *Accession List : South Asia* is an extremely useful current bibliography. But there is no central and comprehensive listing that pulls together government publications at all levels.

Mohinder Singh's *Government Publications of India* surveys the nature and distribution of over 1,500 titles of Central Government documents and is of great help. The solution to this particular problem of bibliographical control is clearly of urgent, high priority. However, the bibliographical control of India government publications is another area which requires an in-depth study of an independent nature.

8.4 *Guide to Theses and Dissertations*

The Association of Indian Universities has for long been doing an excellent work by bringing out a number of bibliographies on the research completed in different disciplines. *University News* is an authoritative publication which helps Indian scholars to know the research work already done or being done in a particular field of research. ICSSR keeps track of social science dissertations submitted to the Indian universities. The Council in collaboration with the Association has been bringing out an important abstracting tool known as *Indian Dissertation Abstract* since 1973.

A bibliographical guide such as this would be a very useful tool because it is in theses and dissertations that all manner of new concepts are explored and new sources of information brought to light far in advance on publication. It is of great importance to scholars to keep abreast of work in their fields and to be able to obtain micro-film copies of the finished products.

Indian bibliographical control situation of social sciences is characterized by a variety of publications meant for the use of social science users. But one has to presuppose that the academic libraries and socials science research libraries are well developed, and users of such libraries know how to use the library in general and bibliographical sources in particular. But, unfortunately, this is not true. Indian social science scholars come with a very poor background of library knowledge, with a poor record of references and wrong concepts. This is because (1) the school library system in India is still non-existent, (2) college libraries are ill-equipped and (3) in university libraries user education programmes are still missing. Thus, in such a chaotic library situation to talk of ideal bibliographical control situation would be futile. To have an optimistic view, it is certain that the conditions shall change fast, and India will be able to take advantage of modern information technology in order to help social science scholars in pursuit of their research.

9. Conclusion

Social sciences remained a neglected sector in India till Independence. But after Independence the need for documentation services in social sciences was realized. This led to the establishment the Indian Council of Social Science Research in 1969 and its SSDC wing started a year later. Prior to this documentation activity used to be a local activity.

SSDC, now known as NASSDOC, has been doing a commendable job by providing documentation services to social science community through its publications and activities since inception. Documentation activities in social sciences reveal that the various institutions engaged should work in coordination so as to avoid duplication. This would also help in reducing time lag and making their bibliographical services uptodated and comprehensive. Unfortunately due to some problems peculiar to the Indian situation most of the documentation activities do not continue for long. As a result of documentation activities as Indian bibliographical tools also have a high mortality rate and incredibly high birth rate which is suicidal for the healthy growth of bibliographical control.

REFERENCES

1. S.R. Ranganathan, ed., *Documentation and its Facets,* (Bombay : Asia, 1963), p. 46.
2. Heartsill Young, ed., *The ALA Glossary of Library and Information Science.* (Chicago : American Library Association, 1983), p. 77.
3. Thomas Landau, ed., *Encyclopaedia of Librarianship.* 3rd rev. edn. (New

York : Hafner, 1967), p. 153.
4. Andrey N. Grosh, Documentation Division, SLA. In *Encyclopaedia of Library and Information Science.* Edited by Allen Kent and Harold Lancour. (New York Marcel Dekkar, 1972), vol. 7, p. 264.
5. S.R. Ranganathan, *Documentation : Genesis and Development.* (Delhi : Vikas, 1973), p. 48.
6. S.R. Ranganathan, *Documentation : Genesis and Development.* (Delhi : Vikas, 1973), p. 31-34.
7. S.R. Ranganathan, *Social Science Research and Libraries,* Papers and Summary Proceedings of the Library Seminar on Research in the Social Sciences, New Delhi, 2-4 January, 1959. (Bombay : Asia, 1960), p. 10.
8. S.R. Ranganathan, *Documentation : Genesis and Development.* (Delhi : Vikas, 1973), p. 221.
9. Anju Agrawal, *Information Requirements of the Social Science Research Scholars at Banaras Hindu University* (A Survey Project). Varanasi : Banaras Hindu University, 1976). (M. Lib.Sc. Dissertation), pp.81-82.
10. S.R. Ranganathan, *Documentation : Genesis and Development,* pp. 224-234.
11. Anju Agrawal, pp. 84-85.
12. S.P. Agrawal, "Social Science Documentation Centre." *Library Herald,* 21, 1-2 (April 1982 — September 1982), p. 50.
13. *NASSDOC Brochure.* (Date of Issue : March 3, 1986), p. 5 It is a mimeographed brochure issued by the Director of NASSDOC to disseminate the information about its activities.
14. *NASSDOC Brochure,* p. 6
15. S.P. Agrawal, p. 53.
16. S.P. Agrawal, Ibid.
17. *NASSDOC Brochure,* p. 8
18. *Social Science Information Bulletin,* 1 (January 1983).
19. B.A.V. Sharma and P. Satyanarayana, *Ph.D. Programme in Social Sciences in South Indian Universities.*
20. *University News,* (July 16, 1985), p. 18.
21. Association of Indian Universities, *Social Science : A Bibliography of Doctoral Dissertations Accepted by Indian Universities 1857-1970.*
22. K.K. Roy, *Bibliographia Asiatica : A Monthly,* 1, 1 (January 1960), Introduction.
23. Ved Bhushan and S.D. Vyas, "Social Science Information System," *Herald of Library Science,* 13, 2 (April 1974), pp. 117-118.
24. Ved Bhushan and S.D. Vyas, pp. 117-118.
25. Krishan Kumar, "Users" Survey of Sapru House Library", *Library Herald,* 12, 4 (January, 1972), pp. 246-248.
26. S.P. Agrawal, Manoharlal and Meena Walia. In *Building Library Collection and National Policy for Library and Information Services.* Edited by P.B. Mangla (Delhi : Indian Library Association, 1985), p. 131.
27. *Documentation Bulletin for South East Asia,* 1966.
28. *JNU Dissertation Index.* Compiled by Veena Taneja and A.R. Sethi. (Delhi : Jawaharlal Nehru University Library, 1980), Introduction.
29. Anju Agrawal, p.96.
30. Anju Agrawal, p.95.
31. Nehru Memorial Library. *List of Theses on Microfilms,* 1979.

32. E. Ram Reddy, *Social Science Information.* (Hyderabad : East West Affiliated Press, 1985), p. 49.
33. Anju Agrawal , p. 95.
34. *University News,* (July 15, 1978), p. 18.
35. Anju Agrawal, p. 94.
36. S.P. Agrawal, *Indian Education Index : 1947-1978.* (Delhi : Mansayan, 1980), Introduction.
37. *Indian Library Science Abstracts,* 18 (1984). Introduction.
38. M.L.P. Patterson. "Bibliographical Control for South Asia." *Library Quarterly,* 41, 2 (April, 1971), pp. 94-95.
39. S.D. Vyas, "Bibliographical Control of Social Sciences." *Indian Library Association Bulletin.* 15, 1-2 (January-June, 1979), p. 25-37.
40. S.D. Vyas, American Studies Research Centre Library, *Library Herald.* 20, 2-4 (July 1981 — March 1982), p. 139-150.
41. M.L.P. Patterson, p. 99.

5

MAJOR BIBLIOGRAPHICAL TOOLS A Study

Introduction

The major Indian bibliographical tools in social sciences are *Index India, Documentation on Asia, Indian National Bibliography, Indian Press Index, Guide to Indian Periodical Literature and Accession List : South Asia*. However, Agrawal does not consider *Guide to Indian Periodical Literature* a major Indian bibliographical tool, though it is a widely used bibliographical tool by Indian social scientists.[1]

Indian National Bibliography and *Accession List : South Asia* (both include India's current intellectual output) are the two current bibliographies which map the current book production. *Indian Press Index* is an important secondary tool brought out in mimeographed form by the Delhi Library Association. Another documentation tool of importance is *Suchika* which has lately been started in 1980, by the JNU Library. The Association of Indian Universities publishes *University News,* which includes references about journals, articles, etc. in education, dissertations submitted to universities and also the research in progress.

The present chapter is confined only to major current bibliographical tools, viz. *Index India, Guide to Indian Periodical Literature, Documentation on Asia, Indian National Bibliography, Accession List : South Asia* and *Indian Press Index.*

1. Bibliographical Problems

1.1 *International Scene*

It is unfortunate that social science research libraries could attract less attention of the library historians and bibliographers than the libraries in humanities and science and technology. An important reasons leading to little use of social science literature is the lack of adequate bibliographical services. Moreover, the existing bibliographical tools do not meet the specific as well as general needs of the social scientists.

Social science subjects are marked by an uneven development, poor efficiency and consequent low use of bibliographical services. For social scientists, primary sources are basically journals, monographs, survey reports, theses and dissertations. In order to find out the contents of journal articles and to save valuable time of social scientists it was thought to bring out secondary services exactly on the same lines as science and technology. In the social sciences, major secondary service are relatively few in number. CLOSS (Checklist of Social Science Serials) File identified only 160 current secondary titles. But when the scope of the secondary serials was widened to include primary journals, which carried secondary material, irregular and regular bibliographic bulletins and accession lists of libraries, the count reached, 1,000.

1.1.1 *Bath Study*

The University of Bath in England had the following programmes about social science information projects:

(1) INFROSS (Investigation into the Information Requirements of Social Sciences), and
(2) DISISS (Designs of Information System in the Social Sciences).

Work at Bath University has dealt with size, growth and characteristics of the social and monograph literature of the social sciences, and looked at the dynamics of literature by means of citation analysis and clustering of journal titles.

Bath Study emphasized on the use of bibliometric studies in order to know the trend and behaviour of social science journals and monographs. With the help of bibliometric studies, it could be found that in some areas of social sciences there is stability and in others there is change. Bath Study revealed that primary literature journals grow exponentially at about 3.5 per cent per annum, but there is no such firm trend in monograph literature. Moreover, there is no threat of document of information explosion (as it was feared in the 1960s) but one of austerity measures, financial stringency and diminishing returns on the use and production of documents in the present format from the users point of view. Document production may remain constant.[2]

Bath Study revealed that secondary bibliographical services in the social sciences developed late, both in comparison with services in science and technology and also in comparison with the development of primary journal literature in the social sciences. Between 1800 and 1910, world social science literature increased three and a half times, but the number of secondary services increased only from five to six. In fact secondary services increased after Second World War. In 1910 the ratio of secondary services to primary journal was 1:55, by 1940 it had decreased to 1:35, by 1970 it stood at 1:15, comparable to the 1:13 for science and technology.

The net effect of the growth of bibliographical control cannot be regarded as proportionate. Bath Study reports:

> "The tentative evidence available suggests that the main improvement in bibliographic control has been through new subjects rather than in the number of index of abstract entries listed per volume. The creation or proliferation of services may be an easier way of responding to the pressure for better control than attempting to expand and improve existing services."[3]

Development of information services in the social sciences does not reflect a planned and even growth up does it reflect any major variations and distinctions between disciplines and also between regions. Except psychology and sociology, indexing and abstracting services in other social science subjects have not kept pace with the increasing primary literature of their own fields. This difference in how effectively indexing and abstracting services have been able to control the growing literature of their own fields affects the number of services in each field. Thus the relatively small number of secondary serials in sociology and psychology may, in fact, reflect success in developing a few useful effective tools, obviating the development of a fragmented network of small services providing relatively limited coverage.

Dissatisfaction expressed by information workers with regard to the scope of the secondary services and their efficiency in controlling the bibliographical output in their respective fields is enhanced by the realization that social scientists make little use of these services. Findings of the INFROSS study at Bath University in 1971 noted that the use of even the international services in economics was very poor. *Journal of Economic Literature* was used by the only 18 per cent and *Index of Economic Articles* by 10 per cent of the economists surveyed.

The use of *Economic Abstracts* and *International Bibliography of Economics* was even more restricted, to five per cent and three per cent of respondents. The use of a similar tool in the other social sciences was comparatively low, e.g. *International Bibliography of Sociology* was used by only two per cent of the sociologists surveyed.

Low use of the bibliographical apparatus may in fact be a reflection on its efficiency in retrieving information. It has been suggested that the bibliographical services in the social sciences have been modelled along the lines of similar services in science and technology (which developed earlier) without taking into account the peculiarities of the subject. It is accepted that social sciences are characterized by a far greater variety of terminology and far less agreement on definitions than natural sciences. Thus bibliographical tools such as indexes which rely heavily on term for retrieving references are less effective.

Bibliographical tools attempt to identify the subject of documents and are frequently so organized as to facilitate retrieval references on one subject. However, the value-impregnated nature of social sciences makes it both impossible and pointless to separate the subject from its ideological framework. References to a document is made because of its conceptual perspective as much as its objective subject content. Social science researchers give great emphasis to conceptual frameworks and are consequently more interested in work which has been carried out by others of a similar persuasion than they are in knowing about work on the same topic, but looked at through a different framework. Unless bibliographical tools provide an indication of this framework, they are not found to be satisfactory.

Apart from the limited scope and efficiency of the indexing and abstracting services, the analytical evaluation of the literature which the natural sciences possess in the form of "Advances in . . . . ." and "Reviews of . . . ." have no parallel in social sciences. Bath Study also found that the ratio of reviews of literature to primary articles was 1:133 as compared to 1:45 in science and technology.

1.2 *Indian Scene*

In India, social science research institutions and universities are the important centres of social science research because of the rich and specialized collection in their libraries. In fact, their collection is complementary to each other. However, the National Library could not render much help to social science research due to its peculiar character and location. In India, more than anything else, development of university library's collections can be singled out as an important feature of the growth pattern of the library resources. But equally important are the libraries of specialized non-university and professional organizations and government departments. In modern times, such libraries have become major centres of social science research. Hence, there is much depends on the libraries of universities and social science research institutions. This has led to a strong cooperation between university libraries and social science research libraries. Still there is need to develop a system for strengthening the bonds of cooperation for the benefit of social scientists. Issues raised in this connection by Roberts appear to be correct, and was observation useful:

> "Today, higher education libraries have a particular importance for the social sciences and the social scientist. Universities and other advance institutions are major centres of social science research, and nearly every country has important collections in this sector . . ." "In the developing countries of the Third World, particularly in Africa and Latin America, the main social science collections have developed and are still developing within the higher education sector."[4]

According to Harsha Parekh, no estimate of the size, growth and characteristics of socials science literature in English and Indian languages has been made in India. True, comprehensive international studies have included Indian literature in their analysis but this has been acknowledgedly limited to select English language materials only. Studies of library use patterns by social scientists are scarce. While some studies of library use have been carried out, their limitations of scope and method restrict their value and utility to a considerable degree. Bibliographical services in the social sciences—abstracting journals, surveys of literature, union catalogues, etc.—which were practically non-existent 20 years ago have now been developed by the Indian Council of Social Science Research (ICSSR) and its documentation wing NASSDOC. But no feedback on their use and value is yet available. On this account one is made to take it for granted that their scope is limited, they suffer from time lag, poor arrangement and the quality of the information covered. Naturally, all these factors reduce their effectiveness. Therefore, a better understanding of the literature growth and use pattern in the social sciences in India would provide some guidance to authors, publishers, librarians, information service operators, and would also benefit the user of the information and communication system in the social sciences.[5]

In the words of B.S. Kesavan, "*Index India* and *guide to Indian Periodical Literature* are a very good start in social science documentation". M.L.P. Patterson comments, "to the extent that these two very important operations are meshed together, bibliographical control over Indian periodical literature, at least in English, will be greatly improved."[6] According to N.N. Gidwani, "bibliographies are solid highways to scholarly esteem and approval, without them it is difficult to carry on any research and serious study". Luther Evans, former Director General, UNESCO, has aptly said that without bibliographies the records of civilization would be an unchartered chaos of miscellaneous contributions to knowledge, unorganized and inapplicable to human needs. Gidwani strongly feels that for want of bibliographies the records of Indian culture have for so long remained a chaos causing serious handicaps for Indological studies. He confirms that it is a great event in the history of social science scholarship that ICSSR came into existence the year following the publication of Kesavan's overview.[7]

The Council had adopted a healthy policy of strengthening the existing services rather than launching duplicate ones itself. Its policy of formulating projects for institutions which possess the required potential to initiate and sustain a documentation service in specific fields is worth appreciating.

The number of periodical publication in social sciences in India is high, and the quality of a few is also equally high. Needless to say, these publications must be made available to serious scholars, and their contents made quickly and fully accessible through indexes. So far there has been a very serious lack of adequate indexing of Indian social science journals. And retrospective indexing still remains virtually blank. Some headway though has been made in "indexing current materials". According to M.L.P. Patterson, the situation in India is satisfactory in comparison to other South Asian nations, particularly Pakistan.[8]

2. Major Indian Bibliographical Tools

2.1 *Guide to Indian Periodical Literature* (Social Sciences and Humanities) (VI — 1964 — Gurgaon, Indian Documentation

Service).

Guide to Indian Periodical Literature was first brought out by Prabhu Book Service in 1964. It was a cumulative subject—author index to articles from about 140 selected Indian periodicals in social sciences and humanities. In the beginning, the few issues were compiled according to the *Dewey Decimal Classification system*. Later, after advice from C.R. Banerjee, former Deputy Librarian of the National Library, the arrangement was changed to dictionary order. Thus author and subject entries were arranged in one alphabetical order. The guide in the beginning appeared as monthly, up to January, 1967. Afterwards, it became quarterly with annual cumulation. In 1973 its title was changed to *Guide to Indian Periodical Literature.* It is edited by Sat Prakash Jain and indexes more than 440 Indian periodicals. All the issues of the *Guide* have followed the same pattern, focusing on the social sciences and the humanities and produced with more or less the same pattern and user aids.[9]

2.1.1 *Scope and Contents*

The Guide indexes articles and essays, including book reviews which appear in about 440 Indian journals devoted to social sciences and humanities. Each issue lists articles in periodicals published during the quarter, and issues are published two months after the quarter covered. Every number of the Guide follows the same format, providing subscription details, an introduction entitled How to use the (GIPL) *Guide to Indian Periodical Literature* list of abbreviations, sample entry, list of journal abbreviations, directory of journals, main index and list of publishers.

The introduction provides full information on the use of the guide, headings employed, arrangement of entries, level of bibliographical data and cross references. These data plus the list of abbreviations and sample entry provide users with all that is needed for an efficient use of the Index. The first list of journals is arranged by abbreviated titles used in the index and is followed by full tiles. The second list is arranged according to full titles and provides the editorial addresses, frequency and subscription price.

The main index is a combined subject and author listing of articles, which are arranged by author under each subject. The subject headings include geographic terms. When an article is too broad to be assigned a specific subject descriptor, it is entered under the appropriate geographical region, which includes Indian State. When an article on a specific region is concerned with a detailed topic, it is listed under the subject with a cross reference under the region. Subject headings are sub-divided where the amount of material and its quality so warrant. Furthermore, multiple subject entries are made when articles deal with more than one discrete topic. All subject and author headings are distinguished by bold capital letters.

Within each subject heading entries list article, author, abbreviated journal title, volume and issue number, date, pagination. Entries under author as the heading list title, journal abbreviation, volume and issue number, date, pagination. Occasionally in both types of entries the date and volume number appear in reverse order. Reviews are entered under author and provide information on book title, place of publication, publisher, pagination and price, if known, details of reviewing journal and indication that the entry is a review. Numerous cross references are provided for acronyms, alternative subject headings and joint authors throughout the index. It is assumed that the list of publishers at the end of each issue is devoted to firms whose works are reviewed, as journal publishers are covered in the list of journals. However, this is not clearly stated in the introduction.

2.1.2 *Analysis*

The guide compares favourably with similar indices produced in the developed countries. The quality of production, layout, preliminary matter, depth of indexing and ancillary features for the most part are all that one expects to find in a such a service. Each quarterly issue is published and distributed on schedule, usually reaching subscribers within six months. The content is similarly uptodate, with 80 per cent of the articles dated from the year of coverage. This is a particularly admirable record in view of the delays normal in journal publishing. It seems that the Indian Documentation Service has an excellent acquisition programme which is able to receive and process a number of journals quickly and efficiently. But this acquisition programme of the publisher is to the doubted because to subscribe for more than 400 journals for only indexing purpose does not appear to be economically feasible, despite the fact that Indian journals in social sciences and humanities are not so costly compared to journals in science and technology.

The range of periodicals scanned is most impressive and spans all fields in the social sciences and humanities. This breadth of coverage is matched by the detailed and carefully planned subject indexing, which is the best encountered in any Third World compilation of this kind. However, it would be useful if the introduction includes a note on the criteria for selecting journals to be scanned. If the emphasis is on scholarly, official and institutional titles, then how are these chosen? Are all contributions indexed or some articles are excluded? Finally, a detailed table of contents would make it more useful. John Mills points out that the *Guide* cannot be too highly recommended as a thorough and uptodate guide to Indian serials in the humanities and social sciences.[10]

During the course of a personal interview with the Editor, it was felt that the publication of this major bibliographical tool is not a financially profitable project. Because of the gradual fall in the number of subscribers, the Editor finds it difficult to continue its publication unless it secures a sufficient number of subscriptions. However, it would be sad indeed, if such an important bibliographical tool meets such a tragic end and for such reasons! University libraries and the libraries of social science institutions must come forward to help continue publication by way of extending subscription. It must be said that the quality of the *Guide* is extremely good and content accurate and the time lag between the period covered and publications is about four months.

2.2 *Index India* (V. 1-1967, Jaipur, Rajasthan University Library)

India gained a different status in the world of political, economic and social order after Independence. This resulted in increased research and multifaceted studies on India accelerating during the fifties. India and foreign scholars started taking keen interest in researches on Indian studies which was reflected in the increasing number of publications issued on various facets of India both in the country and abroad. Since most of the literature remained scattered throughout the pages of various journals, polytopical and composite books, transactions, proceedings and newspapers, it had become high impossible to keep track of the new information and knowledge about India. It is sad that most of the scholarly Indian journals did not even provide yearly cumulative index. This made the task of the researchers and scholars difficult. Scholars wasted their valuable time. Sometimes it used to take weeks to locate the relevant information on India. In the circumstance need for a reference tool which could furnish all such information about India was keenly felt. Foreign tools like *Reader's Guide to Periodicals Literature, Public Affairs Information Service, Social Sciences Index* did exist, but their coverage in terms of contents, scope and journals as regards to India was very selective and restrictive. Hence to meet this situation, the Rajasthan University Library, Jaipur, thought of issuing a single comprehensive Index on India.

The idea emerged out of a feasibility report which was received by the librarian of the Rajasthan University Library from the Harvard University, USA from comments and advice. This report prompted the authorities of the University of Rajasthan, and they felt that it would be desirable and in the fitness of things, if such a documentation service could be undertaken in India. This feeling was reinforced by a large number of requests for documentation aid received from research scholars and faculty members in the university. This move was further strengthened by professionally dedicated staff of the Rajasthan University Library who were fired with a spirit of dedication and enthusiasm and came forward to offer their services. Consequently an ambitious project known as *Index India* was launched in the year 1967.

2.2.1 *Growth*

Index India with time has grown into an important and valuable reference tool so far as its contents, number and variety of publications scanned are concerned. It began with 369 periodicals and now in its Volume 19 there are 1,357 periodicals out of which 750 are Indian and the rest foreign. The first volume of *Index India* was brought out in mimeographed form which contained 1,400 pages and had 35,363 entries. From Volume 2 onwards, the work of composite nature containing essays or articles on India by diverse hands was scanned and contributions were included.

2.2.2 *Aims and Scope*

This quarterly documentation service endeavours to index subjectwise all worthwhile articles, editorials, letters, comprehensive write-ups and notes published on any aspect of Indian in a select 1,300 journals and newspapers published in English language all over the world. It also indexes the contents of commemoration volumes, polytopical books, festschrifts and composite books containing contributions from diverse hands. The Index lists reviews of books on India and completed research (theses and dissertations) on India in India and abroad. Its coverage is oriented to such writings as surveys, reviews, analysis and such articles as interpret the Indian scene in its variegated facets. *Index India* combines in one sequence Index to Indian newspapers, Index to Indian periodicals, Index to foreign periodicals, Index to composite publications, Index to bibliographical profiles, Index to book reviews and Index to theses and dissertations. The number of entries as also the number of periodicals scanned in *Index India* since Volume 5 (1971) are shown in Table 5.1.

N.N. Gidwani, founder-editor of *Index India,* points out that:

> "India continues to be a focus of attention in all branches of knowledge, be it planning, economics, Indian philosophy, religion, and art and history, ... India is being studied and discussed. The Index helps to hold a mirror through which Indians see themselves through their own eyes and also as others see them. Its minute classification helps an avid researcher to reconstruct the subcontinent's political weather chart though the close scrutiny of what engaged the attention of the more articulate sections of the community and foreign observers from time to time."[11]

2.2.3 *Frequency and Time Lag*

Originally the Index was started as a quarterly and later attempts were made to make it a monthly. But on account of compelling reasons it was decided to continue it as a quarterly. As a matter of fact for the last few years it has been brought out as half-yearly. Further, to minimize the time lag it was being brought out as a cumulative annual for two years and then reverted back to quarterly as soon as the time lag was eliminated. It is true that the reduction in time lag will increase its usefulness. But it is difficult and a hazardous task to make it practically feasible because of the time-consuming process involved in its production, proof-reading and printing of such an elephantine service specially when the resource persons are limited. Time lag is also because of late receipt of literature specially the foreign periodicals and also for want of permanent staff earmarked for *Index India.*

TABLE 5.1: Yearly record of *Index India's* input

Volume	Year	Number of Journals (App.)	Total Number of Entries
5	1971	1078	47212
6	1972	1014	44267
7	1973	1176	34908
8	1974	1176	29484
9	1975	1178	32550
10	1976	1362	30370
11	1977	1175	34096
12	1978	1140	37206
13	1979	1303	33913
14	1980	1357	32757
15	1981	1056	36151
16	1982	1071	34298
17	1983	918	33143
18	1984	1098	32425
19	1985	1098	35341
20	1986	1200*	36000*
21	1987	1063	—

Source: 1. C.D. Sharma, A World Documentation List on Indian Affairs. In *30th All India Library Conference Souvenir,* Jaipur, 1985.
2. Actual counting of number of journals from the volumes of the *Index India.*
* Based on figures given by *Index India* Project.

2.2.4 *Finance*

Attempts were made to obtain financial assistance from the University Grants Commission (UGC) and the Government of India, but did not succeed. On the initial grant of Rs. 4500 made by the University of Rajasthan in the year 1968, the Index started rolling down and has built up a local found accumulated through its own earnings by subscription. Today it has its own printing plant in the basement of the library. Its financial base is insecure because of the non-realization of the cost of production of its individual volumes. Concerted efforts are on to increase its subscription so as to make it economically viable. At present there are less than 200 subscribers. ICSSR had extended financial help in its early phases by subscribing to a good number of copies for the university libraries and social science research institutions in the country.

Gidwani pointed out that *Index India* hardly gets any substantial support from its parent organization whereas *Indian Science Abstract* is fully supported by Council of Scientific and Industrial Research (CSIR) and is backed by the National Science Laboratory and other research organizations in India. It also receives generous cooperation from UNESCO, the National Science Foundation. However, in the case of *Index India* no such support has so far been forthcoming.

It was noted that the subscriptions of *Index India* had at one time gone up to 1,000, but slowly fell down to 200. Today, it has just 192 subscriptions. While doing cost benefit analysis, the net conclusion is that it is not a profitable venture. Total subscription amount can hardly meet the cost of production. Reasons for such a deplorable state of affairs may be;

(1) Its subscription rate has gone up to Rs. 600 (Indian) and Rs. 1200 (foreign) though keeping in view its size it appears quite reasonable.
(2) Many new competitive bibliographical services are available in the market like *Guide to Indian Periodical Literature, Indian Press Index,* etc.
(3) Social science research is yet to grow where it becomes necessary for social science researchers to consult bibliographical tools of this kind.
(4) It lacks effective advertising and marketing. Many institutions may not even be aware about its existence.

The financial situation of the Index for the above reasons is deplorable and needs immediate attention. *Sunday Standard* comments that the Index "is the cheapest reference service in the world". But surprisingly it fails to receive the necessary number of subscriptions. However, it is satisfying to note when the Editor reports that the future issues of the Index will seek advertisements to make the bibliographical tool a profitable venture from Volume 19 onwards. He has solicited the cooperation of academic institutions.[12] How far he will be successful is to be seen in the coming years.

That *Index India* has survived for such a long time despite heavy odds is a miracle. In 1979, UGC had sanctioned two posts, viz. Editor and Assistant Editor. Unfortunately both the positions still remain unfilled because of the indifferent attitude of the University Administration. The work is being carried out mainly by two staff members of the library deputed for this work and the rest of the work is done by the members of the library staff in not of duty hours. Payment is just nominal. In fact there is need to have more staff to work on the project as this is a stupendous work and requires serious attention towards the quality of the bibliography work.

Major international bibliographical tools follows alphabetical arrangement, but this Index has followed a classified arrangement. Subjectwise arrangement of the Index is difficult to produce, but it helps to avoid wasteful duplication of the same entries under different subject headings.

2.2.5 *Attempts Towards Improvement*

The Editor observes that the feedback from users about the usefulness of the Index are invited from time to time asking them as to how to improve the Index both in its contents and production. It was also discussed in one of the sessions of the "Seminar on Reference Sources on South Asia" held at the University of Rajasthan, Jaipur, in October, 1979. Taking note of these suggestions the Index India Management Committee set up a Review Committee consisting of Amrik Singh, Girja Kumar, S.C. Biswas and K. Navalani to re-evaluate the project and raise the standard of the Index further in terms of increased coverage as well as technical presentation of entries in *Index India.* The recommendations received from the Committee are in the process of implementation.[13]

Index India has been favourably reviewed both in India and foreign periodicals, and has gained a distinct prestige as a useful reference tool among the researchers and scholars interested to know the social, economic, or political or any such aspect of India. Credit for this goes to N.N. Gidwani, founder-editor and former Director of Rajasthan University Library, M.V. Mathur, former Vice-Chancellor of the University, and to Prof. Daya Krishna, first Chairman, Index India Management Committee, and C. D. Sharma, its Editor since 1982. All of them have played a significant role in making what *Index India* is today. Some of the reviews and comments from Indian journals are reproduced below:[14]

> "Apart from the comprehensive coverage there are several other welcome features of the publication. The classified arrangements of entries is such a relief. This helps to bring together the interrelated subjects in a logical sequence . . . . . a valuable tool of reference on current affairs."
>
> — *India Quarterly*

> "Here is . . . . a most useful reference volume which each library should be happy to possess . . . . . This certainly is the cheapest reference service in the world."
>
> — *Sunday Standard*

"Users of libraries will ever remain grateful to the Rajasthan University Library, Jaipur, for providing *Index India* . . . . at a nominal rate."

— *The Indian Pen*

2.2.6 *Comparison with Other Bibliographical Services*

If *Index India* is compared with INSDOC's *Indian Science Abstracts,* it is observed that both the services are produced by well-trained and experienced library staff. Both have institutional base. But it is highly pertinent to note that whereas INSDOC has provided full-time staff for producing *Indian Science Abstracts, Index India* is being produced by the voluntary effort of a few enthusiastic workers in out of duty hours. The Abstracts reports the work carried out by Indian scientists published in both Indian and foreign periodicals whereas *Index India* does not limit itself to the contributions made by Indian nationals only. It reports what is published on India. The Abstracts uses electronic hardware and the latest techniques for finalizing the entries and publishing them in journal form. Photographic method of reproduction saves drudgery of proof-reading while the Index is produced manually. Index India Project plans to bring out the Index on computer format.

While comparing the number of entries in *Index India* with other bibliographical services, the total number of entries is seven times more than that of *Indian Annual Bibliography of Asian Studies* with a lesser time lag. There are five times the number of entries in the *Guide to Indian Periodical Literature.* While comparing the number of entries in economics with that of *Index to Indian Economics* it is three times more. In the field of education, it reports 2,032 entries as against 798 in *INSDOC's India Educational Material* for the year 1969. Compared to *Documentation on Asia,* the Index's yearly coverage exceeds it by thirteen times and its chapter on India by fifty times.[15] But the Guha and Jayaswal study gives a different picture of *Index India.* They argue that the claim of the Index being comprehensive is doubtful. Except Communist countries, no other country will bring out such a voluminous bibliographical service without State support. In this respect the Index deserves encouragement by UGC and ICSSR to support its overall expenses of cost of production.

Gidwani feels satisfied that the needs of researchers are being met by *Index India.* He feels that what India needs today is retrospective documentation of those useful articles lying buried in the back files of innumerable journals and newspapers which may be effectively retrieved and put to productive use. There is a need to index those old journals which substantially published on India. Unnecessary duplication of documentation effort should be avoided. He suggests that it would be desirable to evolve a coordinated national policy and programme so that worthwhile efforts in local documentation can be given adequate support to enable them to be used at a national level.[16]

2.2.6.1 *Comparison of Index India and Guide to Indian Periodical Literature*

To compare *Index India* with *Guide to Indian Periodical Literature,* a sample checking of the list of periodicals of 1984 of the indexes was made. Both the *Guide* and the *Index* cover a large number of Indian journals of humanities and social sciences. While the *Guide* covers only Indian journals, the *Index* covers both Indian and foreign journals. The difference between both the tools is only in there policy. *Index India* provides information on India irrespective of whether the journals is published in India or a foreign country, but the journal article must deal with the India. The *Guide* on the other hand covers only Indian journals. While the *Guide* covers 440 Indian journals, *Index India* covers about 1,300 journals out of which 522 are Indian.

To find out the amount of duplication in both the bibliographical tools it was observed that 256 Indian journals were common. This is quite a big number, and we can ill-afford to have duplication of effort. *Index India's* percentage of duplication of journals accounts for 49 per cent (256 out of 522 Indian journals) as compared to 58.2 per cent (256 out of 440 journals) of *Guide to Indian Periodical Literature*. This is a serious waste. Some way should be found to avoid this duplication. Both the tools can serve the needs of Indian social scientists better if they go for specialization. Table 5.2 indicates the amount of duplication in the *Guide* and the *Index.*

It is suggested that the following steps should be taken to improve the utility of both *Index India* and *Guide to Indian Periodical Literature* (GIPL):

(1) GIPL can specialise in humanities journals and *Index India* should take care of social sciences. *Index India* should make

efforts to get almost all important journals of social sciences. If the Rajasthan University Library has a big subscription order, definitely the utility of *Index India* will increase. GIPL collects information of the journals from different libraries of Delhi rather than acquiring them.

TABLE 5.2: Duplication of Indian Journals in *Index India* and *Guide to Indian Periodical Literature*

Bibliographical Tool	No. of Journals Indexed	No. of Indian Journals	Common Journals in the Index and Guide	Percentage of duplication Journals
Index India	1000 (app)	522	256	49
Guide to Indian Periodical Literature	440	440	256	58.2

Source: Data based on the Checklist of Periodicals of *Index India* and *Guide to Indian Periodical Literature* of the year 1984.

(2) Secondly, journals to be included indexing should be selected on the basis of quality. Collecting information from any journal dealing with social sciences should not be a criteria. For example, institutional newsletters, house organs, daily newspapers, popular magazines, etc. can be left out. Of course such information is also necessary for social science research. It is suggested that for such publications a separate index can be brought out which will prove useful to social science scholars.

(3) Another possibility of avoiding duplication can be that *Index India* may cover only foreign journals which publish information about India, and the *Guide* can take care of Indian journals belonging to both humanities and social sciences. It could have been possible if both agencies are governed by ICSSR or UGC particularly in terms of finance. But this seems to be an ideal suggestion than practical one. The Guide is a commercial venture whereas the Index is institutional one.

2.2.7 *Suggestions for the Improvement*

Guha and Jayaswal study of *Index India* is an assessment of utility of the Index by information workers and information users. Important findings of this study are as follows:

(1) Entries do not represent the total number of unique items as most of the items are entered in other subjects because of multifocal nature.
(2) Entries of 1977 as compared to 1967 contains less number of entries, while the total number of journals have increased from 797 (1967) to 1,154 (1971). In 1977 only 34,096 entries were given in the Index as compared to 35,363 in 1967.
(3) *Index India* is selective and its claim of comprehensiveness is doubted. But it is a to be seen whether the Index claims that it is a most comprehensive tool.
(4) Subject headings used are not helpful to information seekers. For example, the term "pollution" is not used. For this, one has to see under "Sociology — Urban Sociology – Environmental Problems."
(5) A sample survey conducted in Jawaharlal Nehru University of Ph.D., M.Phil. scholars and Post-Graduate students indicated that the arrangement of the *Index* is difficult. The authors suggest that,
    (i) Alphabetical index should be given first and subject part later in order;
    (ii) More information be given about specific topics than general; and
    (iii) An orientation course should be conducted for the benefit of researchers to reap maximum benefit from the Index.[17]

There is another view given by Guha and Jayaswal that *Index India* lacks comprehensiveness. While comparing with *Indian and World Affairs : An Annual Bibliography,* they found that on "Foreign Relations of India," *Index India* lists only 814 items in the same period, i.e. 1975, while *India and World Affairs* lists 1,920 entries. Guha and Jayaswal have excluded newspapers and composite books because bibliography does not cover newspapers and composite books. They further found that some of the topic are not at all included in *Index India.* It is possible that the Rajasthan University Library may not be subscribing to some of the journals.

While comparing with *Guide to Indian Periodical Literature* in 1975 it covered 288 Indian periodicals whereas the *Index India* covered as many as 680 Indian periodicals in the same year. Today the *Guide* covers 440 journals whereas the *Index* covers more than 522 Indian journals.[18,19]

About the featuring of entries, *Index India* uses keyword out of context of index entries. This means it breaks chain-indexing. Guha and Jayaswal suggest, and it was also supported by information seekers, that *Index India* should follow the international pattern of standard abbreviations for periodicals. It brings a kind of mnemonic characteristic if they use the same abbreviations which have been used in international indexing tools. This seems to be a good suggestion which will certainly improve its utility as an index.

2.3 *Indian National Bibliography* (V.1-1959 — Calcutta Central Reference Library)

The first issue of *Indian National Bibliography* for 1958 began appearing at the end of 1963. This national bibliography was published quarterly and cumulated annually. Since 1964 issues have been appearing as monthly with annual cumulations. (However, between 1968 and 1970 no monthly issues were published. It is understood that annual volumes for these years await publication). Official and non-official material were listed in separate sections between 1958 and 1972 but in 1973 a single classified sequence was introduced. In 1970 a quinquennial cumulation for 1958-1962 was published, and two Sanskrit fascicules entitled *Rashtriya Grantha Suchi* and *Sanskrit Vibhag* have been issued for 1958-1962 and 1963-1967 publications. Information in *Indian National Bibliography* relies on compliance with the Delivery of Books (Public Libraries Act of 1954 and its Amendment Act No. 99 to 1956).

2.3.1 *Scope and Contents*

Indian legal deposit legislation stipulates that the Central Reference Library in Calcutta shall receive copies of all works published in the country. On the basis of this requirement, *Indian National Bibliography* includes books, pamphlets, official publications, first issues of periodicals or changed titles of existing serials. Newspapers and theses, maps, music and certain types of ephemera like trade catalogues, telephone directories etc. are excluded from coverage. The languages of works listed in *Indian National Bibliography* are Assamese, Bengali, English, Gujarati, Hindi, Kannada, Malayalam, Marathi, Oriya, Punjabi, Sanskrit, Tamil, Telugu and Urdu.

The annual cumulations are extremely late in appearing and

therefore it has little current bibliographical value. Current issues of *Indian National Bibliography* include a preface, list of abbreviations and language symbols, classified bibliography, author/title and subject indices. The preface provides some information on coverage and arrangement of *Indian National Bibliography,* but there is no table of contents. The main bibliography is organized by subject according to Dewey Decimal Classification with entries listed by their full Dewey numbers. For each of these numbers the subject heading is provided in bold type. Within the Dewey divisions entries are listed alphabetically by author when there is more than one item under a given number. The full cataloguing includes author (with dates when known), title, place of publication and publisher, date, pagination, details of illustrations, size, whether cloth or paper binding, price and series statement. Content footnotes are provided as necessary and language code is added at the bottom of entries together with the Colon Classification number. Names of authors and titles of work in Indian languages are transliterated into Roman script, and publications in all languages are arranged in a single sequence under each class.

Author/title index lists entries in a single alphabetical sequence and includes joint authors, editors compilers, translators and series titles. Author entries in the index contain brief bibliographical details (title, date, price and language). Reference is to the appropriate Dewey number in the main bibliography, but all other index entries in this sequence refer to author index citation rather than to the classified sequence. The subject index employs headings which are adopted from Dewey, again referring to the Dewey number in the main bibliography.

2.3.2 *Analysis*

The Indian publishing scene is characterized by vast volume, an extremely large number of publishers, works in many languages, overall poor quality in production and or generally low level of bibliographical control.[20] Most of the characteristics also apply to *Indian National Bibliography* (INB). On the one hand it is unrealistic to expect an indigenous national bibliography not to reflect the wider publishing situation, yet, on the other, such a compilation, as a country's publishing flagship, should show where and how potential improvements are possible. Unfortunately, *Indian National Bibliography* in its present form is unable to fulfil this ideal. In this context John Mills comments:

> "It is perhaps unfair to criticize the sub-standard physical qualities of a Third World national bibliography for it is a undeniable that compilers and publishers alike suffer from the constraints of inadequate financial support and staffing arrangement, outdated printing equipment and poor quality paper. South Asian publications, including *Indian National Bibliography,* seem particularly prone to these short comings, and one cannot expect vast improvements when the realities dictate otherwise."[21]

Indian National Bibliography could make certain small improvements which would greatly improve its appearance. In the main bibliography more adequate spacing between entries and either finer type or paper with a harder finish would do much to improve the poor legibility which hampers users. Furthermore, the assignment of running numbers to entries would simplify indices by obviating the need to use lengthy Dewey numbers.

Also in the indices it is not necessary to include full bibliographical details after author entire or to refer from titles back to author index entries. Much simpler would be straightforward Dewey or reference number after each index term, except when titles are needed to distinguish more than one entry under a given author.

However, INB still retains its value, but there are several criticisms requiring more definite attention by the compilers. Foremost among these is the increasingly dated publications of this bibliography. Earlier years issues were published and distributed within 12 months of compilation, but currently there is a three to four years time lag in the appearance of monthly number. Even worse, annual cumulations now seem to be eight years behind schedule. This poor record also extends to the content of individual issues. In the December, 1977, number for example, only 40 per cent of the entries carry 1977 imprint. Such figures indicate that INB has little value as a current bibliographical record, and without uptodate annual cumulations in particular very few potential users will want to spend time with this compilation even for retrospective purposes. Moreover, this current bibliographical record does not represent cent per cent India's total output of book production. It hardly claims to cover 60 per cent of published documents.

A second critical area lies in the subject, which in general is an extremely useful feature for those who require a more detailed topical approach than that permitted by the classified sequence. Unfortunately, several features in this index detract from its usefulness. First, cross references are non-existent. Thus one who searches under "theology" will not find any information, but there are likely to be entries under "Roman Catholic theology". Second, terms in descriptive clusters are not always permuted, which means that one cannot search under secondary keywords with any degree of confidence. For example , "Exercises: Personal hygiene" does not also appear under "Personal hygiene exercises". Both of these failures must be remedied if the subject index is to have a substantial reference value.

Finally, the lack of both a table of contents and a list of publishers must be remedied in future issues. The former can be easily compiled, and it would be an immensely valuable feature, especially when it includes an outline of the main Dewey classes. The latter which ought to indicate addresses as well as names, is more complex to provide, but it is an essential feature in view of India's massive publishing industry.

J.S. Mills exposes the limitations of INB in seeking to become a more effective record of Indian published literature. However, a serious effort must be made to meet this challenge, for, in its present state, INB is altogether too inadequate for most user requirements.

2.4 *Documentation on Asia*

(V.1 - 1960 — New Delhi : Published for Indian Council of World Affairs, 1963) edited by Girja Kumar and V. Machve. (Vol. 4 was published in 1974, publisher varies). As the title indicates, it is a subject bibliography of articles and documents on Asia.

The necessity of bibliographical control of social science literature in this region was felt for long. Therefore, in the 60s, the authorities of the Indian Council of World Affairs decided to bring out a bibliographical service for social science researchers. Girja Kumar, the then librarian on ICWA, stated the need and usefulness of bibliographical control as under:

> "Systematic presentation of references to recorded knowledge and their location in the shortest possible time becomes imperative for promoting research. The same objective is achieved through the bibliographical control of current and past knowledge. If a scholar were to be presented, so to say, on a

platter all the references to a specific subject of his or her interest, it would cut short considerably the period for any research work."[22]

The starting of this bibliography was possible because the coverage of *Bibliography of Asian Studies* which is published annually in the *Journal of Asian Studies,* listing books and articles in major Western languages on the social sciences and humanities, was poor.

Girja Kumar, the then Editor had felt that an ideal bibliography of current literature on Asia should include books, articles and documents published in all major languages of the world as well as in most languages of the area. But, unfortunately, it could not be made possible because of the diversities of languages.

2.4.1 *Scope and Contents*

The bibliography covers, in full or summary, speeches, statements, resolutions, white papers, agreements and reports from official and non-official sources. Documents are taken from varied sources including government, political parties and public organizations. Documents included in the tool are very significant as these are a primary source material for primary research. Besides a variety of sources such as official gazetteers, parliamentary debates committee and commission reports, press releases, embassy bulletins, publications of international organizations, political party publication, newspapers, periodicals and press agency bulletins, books and pamphlets have been tapped for selection. The Editors preferred the most authentic sources for selection of documents, but in their absence secondary sources have been utilized.

2.4.2 *Problems*

Availability of material on different countries of Asia has been the main problem and, therefore, various political parties, research institutions, organizations and government departments of all countries of Asia were contacted for ensuring an uninterrupted flow of source material. Except China, India and Indonesia most countries were not able to send their publications.

Another problem faced by the compilers of this indexing tool was diversity of languages, and abrupt changeover from Western language to area language as a means of intellectual communication. This handicapped any attempt at thorough documentation of many areas in Asia.

Preface of the first volume (1960) indicates that contributions appearing in weekly periodical publications were not considered for inclusion for the reasons stated by its then Editor, Girja Kumar:

> "It is difficult to see how many respectable research contributions in the field of regional studies could be made without taking into consideration the partisan views or objective interpretations as reflected in the weekly Press. Publications like *New Statesman* and *Economist* interpret hot news in its bare essentials. They look at the events from a special angle which illuminates several hidden meanings in the political and economic development. This kind of information is specially useful in evaluating the historical events."[23]

The Editor felt that any political party organ like *New Age, Janata* and *Mankind* representing sectional interest is a new genre of literature and is basic for any study of national politics. Since such literature is now generally accepted as a legitimate field of interest to research, it is included in *Documentation on Asia*.

2.4.3 *Classification*

Arrangement of entries is based upon an ad-hoc classification, which is largely guided by the schedules of Ranganathan's Colon Classification. The Editor writes in the Preface that employment of an ad-hoc classification is temporary. The present experiment has reinforced the belief in the efficacy of a faceted scheme of classification with detailed schedules. Other advantages of classified arrangement is that it has helped to avoid duplication of entries.

2.4.4 *Rendering of Names*

There are a lot of difficulties in the rendering of Asian names. Thus there is a need for standardization of names. Systematic studies at national and international level will make the task easier for cataloguers. However, problems regarding rendering of several Asian names remain unresolved, because of lack of proper guidance in the existing codes.

Geographical and subject schedule follow introduction. The arrangement of geographical schedule is easy which is based on the Colon Classification order. For example, 4 is given to South Asia and 5 to West Asia whereas subject schedules entries are fitted in each geographical division. This arrangement is based on the Colon Classification order with some amendments.

So far its use as a helpful bibliographical service is concerned, it depends upon researchers' approach to find out his research needs. Though helpful, many times researchers do not consult bibliographical tools. Partly blame may also be put on libraries where such useful bibliographical services are not brought to the notice of scholars and teachers of the subjects.

Citations from periodicals publications are arranged in the following order: Name of the periodical (in italics), volume number (in bracket), date of publication, pages. For example : *New Statesman* 59 (1517) : Ap. 9: 512-14. The year is omitted if it is current.

The language of a document, apart from English, is indicated against each source in the Bibliography. The tool also includes separate sections for bibliography of periodical publications, books and reports. There are two parts of index—subject index and author index. This kind of arrangement is helpful as users may find it easy to consult the tool.

2.5 *Accessions List : South Asia* (V.1-1962 — New Delhi : American Libraries Book Procurement Centre)

The Centre was set up under Public Law (PL) 480 Programme on Overseas Acquisition by American Libraries. Under this programme the Library of Congress acquires publications from a number of developing countries of the world for selected libraries in the United States. The list covers selected publications from India, and there are similar lists for Pakistan and Indonesia. But now these are merged under its new title *Accessions List : South Asia.* The list is arranged by language of publication with each language section separately alphabetized by author, within each language section commercial and government monographs are listed in a single alphabet. Monographs in series and annual publications are also included with the monographs. Government publications are indicted by an asterisk preceding the code number.

The list is issued by the American Libraries Book Procurement Centre, New Delhi. The first issue of *Accession List* came out in July, 1962, under the title *Accessions List India.* It is a monthly record of the publications acquired by the U.S. Library of Congress American Libraries Book Procurement Centre, New Delhi. The Public Law (PL) 480 Programme made it possible for the Library of Congress to acquire Indian documents. This programme is also made possible by financial support from the American research libraries receiving the publications, the cooperation of the Government of India, help of the Indian book trade and efforts of the citizens of India working on the staff of the Centre.

They have identified the following U.S. libraries where a good number of copies of a particular work are sent:

Library of Congress
University of California Library, Berkeley
University of Chicago Library
Cornell University Library
Duke University Library
University of Hawaii Library
University of Minnesota Library
University of Texas Library
University of Washington Library
University of Wisconsin Library
Yale University Library

All the libraries participating in the programme have agreed to lend these publications under the terms of the American Library Association's Inter-Library Loan Code.

Each book is assigned a code number which indicates the country of origin, the language in which the book is written and the serial number within the language group. Starting with the January, 1963, issue, newspapers and periodicals were listed twice each year, in January and July. A cumulative author index is issued annually in the December number. A sample entry is given below.

I-E — 581
Roy, KSHITIS. Rabindranath Tagore, a life story, tr. from the Bengali by Lila Ray. (Delhi, Publication Division, 1961) 92 p. (Biography)

The list is selective in nature and does not include all publications. For example, it excludes certain textbooks and Indian editions of current Western works. It includes Central and State Government publications on a selective basis. It is highly reliable for currency, accuracy and completeness of bibliographical details.

An annual cumulative volume list of serials is also brought out on an annual basis. The list of serials is extremely helpful. The *Accession*

List : South Asia is highly useful. In certain ways, it is more useful than the *Indian National Bibliography* because it is published promptly and is relatively comprehensive. Its bibliographical details are uptodate and serve as a better substitute in the absence of *Indian National Bibliography.*

2.6 *Indian Press Index* (V.1 — 1968 — Delhi : Delhi Library Association). Edited by C.P. Vashisth.

2.6.1 *Scope*

The Delhi Library Association started the *Indian Press Index* as a monthly indexing journal with effect from April, 1968. This index indexes all the signed or unsigned articles, special write-ups, editorials and important statements and letters published in 17 daily English newspapers of India. The Association also brings out a separate quarterly supplement to the Index covering the book reviews published in all these newspapers. The project is a contribution of no small measure in the field of documentation of newspapers in India. It should be useful to librarians, journalists, scholars, educationists, public administrators, business executives and other specialists who use newspaper media for reference and research work. *Indian Press Index* still possesses some value of merit, despite coverage being limited to 17 English language newspapers.

2.6.2 *Coverage*

The following English newspapers are indexed in the *Index.*

Amrit Bazar Patrika, Assam Tribune, Business Herald, Deccan Herald, Economic Times, Financial Express, Hindu, Hindustan Times, Indian Express, Indian Nation, Madhya Pradesh Chronicle, National Herald, Northern Indian Patrika, Patriot, Statesman (Delhi ed.), *Times of India* (Delhi ed.) and *Tribune.*

The Index is in three parts:

(1) Subject Part
(2) Geographical Index
(3) Author Index

2.6.3 *Arrangement*

Arrangement of entries in the Index is under the specific subject in alphabetical sequence. As the entries have been grouped under different specific subject heading in current usage, the users may use the subject part of the Index itself to find out the reference.

2.6.4 *Indian Book Review Supplement*

A *Quarterly Book Review Supplement* of the books reviewed in these newspapers is also compiled. The subject and author index are given in the end of each issue of the Supplement to entry number where the detail of the publications are to be found. This has been appearing since 1968 on a quarterly basis.

A useful guide about the availability of the back files of newspapers in Delhi libraries is also provided. This is helpful as otherwise a user would be grouping in the dark. Another useful service is that xerox copies of articles indexed in the Index are available — the Association has made the arrangement. This helps in achieving full bibliographical control of newspapers being published in India. But this service should be publicized through their journal *Library Herald.*

2.6.5 *The Problems*

There is a time lag of three years which should be reduced to one, if the tool has to serve its real purpose. Another problem is that of adequate resource persons to compile it on a full-time basis. At present, it is being done by professionals on a part-time basis. Further the Association is publishing the Index in mimeographed form. This should be immediately dispensed with as its paper is of poor quality, and equally poor is mimeographing. It is suggested that in order to let it have a long life for use in libraries, good quality paper should be used. Hence its copies should be printed. It is hoped that its utility will increase with its better appearance and simple arrangement.

Giving opinion about the state of affairs of the bibliographical control in the South Asia region, M.L.P. Patterson feels that it is far better, particularly in India. He says:

> "It is fair to say that a great deal has been accomplished in the past fifteen years to establish control over South Asian periodical literature, but we must recognize that there is a long way yet to go. In particular, we may say that coverage of India is far better than that of Pakistan, Ceylon and Nepal; and within coverage of India itself, that of English language materials is far

and away more satisfactory than that of non-English."[24]

3. Common Problems in the Social Science Bibliographical Tools

The position of major Indian bibliographical tools cannot be considered as satisfactory. Their proper development has been hampered by the following common problems for the last many years.

3.1 *Finance*

Social science research gained momentum with the establishment of ICSSR. Besides its multifarious activities, ICSSR has supported bibliographical ventures by way of procuring multiple copies of such publications as well as providing financial assistance to such bodies as venture to bring out bibliographical tools. But it is not possible to continue or extend such help for ever. Institutions bringing out such bibliographical tools have to have financial self-sufficiency. Funding agencies like UGC, Planning Commission, etc. which provide financial help for such bibliographical ventures also have their limitations. The present study reveals that majority of the bibliographical ventures have suffered on this account.

3.2 *Manpower*

Most of the bibliographical tools brought out in India do not have full-time professional staff to work for them as is evident from the working of *Index India* and *Indian Press Index*. These are run by part-time professionals. Documentation work is a full-time job and it should be done carefully and vigorously in order to produce faultless, efficient and authentic tools which would increase their utility. It has been observed that there is a dearth of specialist indexers and cataloguers with a sound knowledge of various social science subjects in social science research libraries and higher education libraries. Library science schools should pay due attention to their training programmes to cover this important aspect of library service. Competent reference librarians will be able to impart effective user education to scholars for making efficient use of bibliographical tools and other resources.

3.3 *Information Technology*

Most of the Indian bibliographical tools in the field of social sciences are still produced manually. Right from the selection of material to the production of bibliographical tools, hardly any modern means or technology is used. In the field of social sciences use of computers in India still appears to be far off. As the situation prevails to bring out efficient and authentic bibliographical tools use of modern means of information collection and technology will be found an asset, particularly use of computers. With the advent of micro-computers many bibliographical services could be produced on a small scale. Establishment of data banks in social sciences and availability of their information online will greatly help in achieving bibliographical control. Agencies responsible for bringing out *Index India* and *Guide to Indian Periodical Literature* should undertake feasibility study in this regard.

3.4 *Duplication*

It may not be possible to completely eliminate duplication, but it could be minimized to a large extent. It is there because of the lack of coordination and cooperation in sharing of resources at the national level. Such problems are often discussed in seminars and conferences, but no concerted effort is made to avoid it. Duplication is a wasteful effort and must be vigorously fought. It would be desirable to evolve a coordinated national policy and programme to give adequate support to local documentation activities which can be used at national level, and the right agency is ICSSR which is playing an important role.

3.5 *Lack of Abstracting and Citation Machinery*

During the last two decades, it could have been possible to effect bibliographical control of journal articles by bringing out comprehensive indexes, but even abstracting of articles of Indian journals is still not done effectively. (ICSSR is engaged in abstracting of social science dissertations and journal articles on a selective basis). A large number of journal articles are still not abstracted indicating how woefully our abstracting machinery is. Except psychology, sociology and to some extent library science, in other subjects abstracts are not made of journal articles. It is an avoidable obstruction. . . . in the bibliographical control of social sciences.

Another area which has emerged during the last one decade is the use of citation techniques. It is to be noted that Eugene Garfield's *Social Science Citation Index* hardly covers Indian journals, and there is no separate social science citation index for Indian journals.

Hence, an effort should be made in this direction by ICSSR. Social science scholars have to run from pillar to post for citations in the absence of such bibliographical tools. Therefore, it would not be a day too soon if an *Indian Social Science Citation Index* is launched to help social science research.

3.6 *Grey Literature*

Grey literature is generally not available for acquisition through normal publishing channels. It utility remains unused in the piles of vertical files. Conference proceedings, papers, monographic literature, typescripts, reprints, xerox copies, preprints, statistical data, etc. are the documents which are not indexed in any of the bibliographical tools. Such useful information also needs proper dissemination for their use. NASSDOC can think of bringing out such a useful tool for the benefit of social science scholars who otherwise do not know the existence of grey literature.

3.7 *Time Lag*

Time lag reduces the reference utility of a bibliographical tool. Many Indian bibliographical publications suffer on account of this problem. In the case of *Indian National Bibliography* and *Indian Press Index,* it is intolerable. To some extent *Index India* also suffers from this problem. This may be on account of late receipt of journals as well as inadequate and part time professional staff. But it is a serious problem, and deserves due attention for annual publications one year and for quarterlies three months may be taken as permissible time lag.

3.8 *Bibliographical Control of Retrospective Literature*

Bibliographical Control of retrospective literature is also linked with current bibliographical control. Girja Kumar and N.N. Gidwani pleaded for retrospective documentation. They felt that current literature of social science produced in the country was under bibliographical control, whereas retrospective literature was yet to be covered. ICSSR has made on effort to cover retrospective literature. Still some areas remain. These should be taken up as new projects by ICSSR.

3.9 *Lack of Appreciation or Awareness*

Publishers of *Index India* and *Guide to Indian Periodical Literature* say that these are not profitable ventures, because both the bibliographical services how failed to get adequate number of subscribers. *Index India's* present subscription order is around 200 copies and of *Guide to Indian Periodical Literature* 500. There are a number of libraries attached to universities, colleges, social science research institutions, government departments and some leading public libraries were these tools would be found useful. Subscription under of these bibliographical tools is not commensurate with the member of such libraries. This could be so due to financial constraints, but the real reason appears to be lack of appreciation or awareness about the utility, of the bibliographical tools not only on the part of the scholars and researchers, but also on the part of the management of the libraries and institutions concerned.

4. Conclusion

Emergence of secondary sources in social sciences was late. Development of information and bibliographical services in social sciences does not reflect planned and even growth. There is low use of bibliographical tools because of lack of awareness of the tools. Secondly these tools have not been user-oriented as is revealed by the Bath Study and the present survey (Chapter V).

Social science institutions and universities are the important centres of social science research, but scholars have to depend more on the resources of university libraries. Such libraries have taken a lead in producing bibliographical tools to serve the requirements of social science scholars. This activity got further impetus with the emergence of ICSSR/NASSDOC which produce union catalogues, indexes and subject bibliographies, etc.

The major bibliographical tools have common problems like finance, manpower, technology, publication, time lag and lack of awareness. Some of the problems are directly related to social sciences — lack of abstracting and citation machinery, grey literature, bibliographical control of retrospective literature, etc. The declining number of subscription orders for *Index India, Guide to Indian Periodical Literature* and other tools is surprising as on the one hand social science literature is growing and on the other, there is low use of such tools. It shows that the bibliographical tools are not user-oriented. Therefore, if it is desired that social science scholars use these tools their format and get-up will have to be changed to suit their requirements.

REFERENCES

1. S.P. Agrawal and Manoharlal, "Social Science Research Libraries and Documentation Centres in India". In *Handbook of Libraries, Archives and Information Centres,* B.M. Gupta et al. (New Delhi : Information Industry Publication, 1984-85), p. 153.
2. Stephen Andrew Roberts, "Social Science Libraries and Collection". In *Encyclopaedia of Library and Information Science.* V. 28, Edited by Allen Kent, Harold Lancour and Jay E. Daily. (New York : Marcel Dekker, 1980), pp. 62-64.
3. Bath University, *Size, Growth and Composition of Social Science Literature.* (Bath, University of Bath, 1975) (DISSIS Research Reports, Series A, No. 2).
4. Stephen Andrew Roberts, p. 61.
5. Harsha Parekh, "Social Science Literature. Size, Use Patterns and Bibliographical Services." *Economic and Political Weekly,* 17, 35 (August 28, 1982), pp. 1423-25.
6. M.L.P. Patterson, "Bibliographical Control for South Asia." *Library Quarterly*, 4, 2 (April 1971), p. 96.
7. N.N. Gidwani, "Documentation on India." In *Comparative Librarianship : Essays in Honour of Prof. D.N. Marshall.* Edited by N.N. Gidwani. (Delhi : Vikas, 1973), p. 181.
8. M.L.P. Patterson, "Bibliographical Controls for South Asia." *Library Quarterly* 4, 2 (April, 1971), p.95.
9. Vijay Kumar Jain (ed.) *Guide to Indian Periodical Literature* (Social Science and Humanities). (Gurgaon : Prabhu Books Service, 1968). Preface.
10. In John Mills' book which is under print (the references have been taken from the proofs of his book. The book is yet to be published) pp. 133-144.
11. N.N. Gidwani, "Documentation of India." In *Comparative Librarianship : Essays in Honour of Prof. D.N. Marshall.* Edited by N.N. Gidwani (Delhi : Vikas, 1973), p. 193.
12. *Index India,* V. 18 (1985), Preface, C.D. Sharma (Editor; *Index India*) writes in preface about the new policy which will be effective from V. 19 onwards.
13. C.D. Sharma, A World Documentation List on Indian Affairs. In *30th All India Library Conference Souvenir,* (January 28-31, 1985), p. 60.
14. *Index India Brochure* (this brochure gives information about subscription rates and reviews about the Index).
15. N.N. Gidwani, *Comparative Librarianship,* p. 192.
16. N.N. Gidwani, p. 195.
17. B. Guha, A.K. Guha and P.K. Jayaswal, "A Decade of Index India" *Herald of Library Science,* 22, 3-4 (July — October, 1983), pp. 174-185.
18. *Index India* (1984).
19. *Guide to Indian Periodical Literature* (1984).
20. Harsha Parekh, p. 1424.
21. In John Mills book which is under print (The reference has been taken from the proofs of his books. (The book is yet to be published) pp. 138-144.
22. *Documentation of Asia,* V. 1 (1960). Edited by Girja Kumar and V. Machve (Delhi: Allied Publishers, 1963). Girja Kumar writes an introduction about the use of the Index in its preface.
23. *Documentation on Asia.* V.1 (1960). Edited by Girja Kumar and V. Machve (Delhi : Allied Publishers, 1963). Girja Kumar writes an introduction about the use of the Index in its preface.
24. M.L.P. Patterson, p.98.

6

INFORMATION NEEDS AND EXPECTATIONS OF SOCIAL SCIENCE SCHOLARS AND RESEARCHERS
A Survey

Introduction

Bibliographical control is now a central theme of library and information science. To know the situation of the bibliographical control in India, it is necessary to survey, on a national level, the information needs and expectations of social science scholars. For this 500 questionnaires were distributed all over the country among selected social science libraries and institutions of higher learning. To assess the information needs and expectations of social science scholars and researchers, an attempt is made to find out the use of Indian bibliographical sources, viz. *Accession List : South Asia, Artha Suchi, Documentation on Asia, Guide to Indian Periodical Literature, Index India, Indian National Bibliography* and *Suchika*. The attempt is also made to know the actual purpose for which they use bibliographical sources. An effort is made to find out the arrangement of bibliographical sources and how far the bibliographical sources are uptodate, and meet their information and bibliographical requirements.

An endeavour was made to seek users' suggestions for the improvement of existing bibliographical sources. To know from social science scholars which they considered the best bibliographical sources and best libraries in India, two separate questions were also designed. It was also found necessary to know the reading habits (number of hours devoted in the libraries) of social science scholars.

Comments and suggestions were invited.

1. Methodology

Questionnaires were distributed to social science research libraries and university libraries by registered mail (self-addressed postage paid envelopes). But as usual the response was not encouraging because of the indifference to social survey research by respondents. Out of 500 questionnaires distributed, 148 were received back. Thus the response rate comes to 30 per cent. This too could be achieved by sending several reminders and making personal contacts. The questionnaires were distributed in August, 1987, and those received up to January, 1988 have been included in this study.

2. Sampling

To survey each and every institution to find out the information needs of social science scholars and researchers in terms of money, accuracy, time and lack of research staff to study the entire population of social science scholars in the country is difficult. Questionnaires were sent to selected social science institutions and institutions of higher learning which have been covered in Chapter 3, and in addition to that some more selective institutions were also included based on geographical considerations. The idea was to get the national response of the institutions irrespective of their reputation. Most of the social science research libraries were largely concentrated in Delhi, Bombay, Calcutta, Bangalore, Hyderabad, Madras, Jaipur, Lucknow and Trivandrum. Delhi being the national capital is a big centre of social science research libraries. Selection of institutions was based on geographical sampling because efforts were made to cover the selected institutions of all the regions, i.e. South, East, North, West, Central and even North-East. Reasonable representative response could be received from all over the country except from the deep South.

Minimum 10 and maximum 50 questionnaires were sent to different institutions depending on their calibre and reputation. Table 6.1 indicates the response.

TABLE 6.1: Response to the Questionnaire received from social science institutions and universities

Institution/University	No. of Questionnaires sent	Response received
North Zone		
Banaras Hindu University, Varanasi	25	10
Delhi University, Delhi	25	1
Department of Social Work, University of Delhi, Delhi	25	11
ICSSR North-Western Regional Centre, Chandigarh	25	8
Jawaharlal Nehru University, Delhi	50	37
Rajasthan University, Jaipur	50	6
Sukhadia University, Udaipur	20	3
East Zone		
A.N. Sinha Institute of Social Studies, Patna	25	16
Centre for Studies in Social Sciences, Calcutta	10	8
Gauhati University, Gauhati	25	5
West Zone		
Gokhale Institute of Politics and Economics, Poona	25	1
S.N.D.T. Women University, Bombay	20	7
Sardar Patel Institute of Economics & Social Research, Ahmedabad	10	4
South Zone		
American Studies Research Centre, Hyderabad	25	12
Andhra University, Waltair	25	9
ICSSR Southern Regional Centre, Hyderabad	25	10
Institutions which failed to return duly filled in Questionnaires		
South Zone		
Centre for Development Studies, Trivandrum	20	0
Institute of Social and Economic Change, Bangalore	20	0
Madras Institute of Development Studies	10	0
North Zone		
Lucknow University, Lucknow	10	0
West Zone		
Nagpur University, Nagpur	20	0
East Zone		
North-Eastern Hill University, Shillong	20	0
Total	500	148

3. Purpose

The purpose was to collect information on the following:

(1) Total information requirements of the social science users.
(2) Research problems of social science scholars in the use of bibliographical sources.
(3) Best bibliographical sources.
(4) Best libraries.
(5) Major areas of research in social sciences.
(6) Other bibliographical sources which are not mentioned in question 6.3 (see Appendix A).

Some of the findings are really startling. The National Library of Calcutta is found to be less used by social science scholars as compared to other research libraries. Due to the emergence of a number of research libraries, social science scholars' needs are now met quite effectively without the help of the National Library. A galaxy of social science subject fields is given in Table 6.5. This enormity of subject fields has created difficulties for the librarians to meet the demands of researchers effectively.

Rise of educational and special libraries in social sciences is of historical significance in India particularly after Independence. Development of university libraries can be considered as an important feature of the growth pattern of library resources. However, equally important are the libraries of specialized agencies of professional institutions, and of government departments. Higher education libraries have a particular importance for the social sciences and the social scientists. The universities and other advanced institutions are the major centres of social science research.

Jawaharlal Nehru University Library (JNU) and Ratan Tata Library at Delhi School of Economics (RTL), Institute of Economic Growth, Indian Council of World Affairs, Nehru Memorial Museum Library, NASSDOC, ANS Institute of Social Studies, and Indian Institute of Public Administration, are major national social science research libraries in both contemporary and historical terms, although the primary purpose of JNU and RTL is to support university teaching and research. Some university libraries which have many departmental and seminar libraries in social sciences have a fine collection on social sciences particularly to meet the university requirements.

It is presumed that social science collections are still developing within the higher education sector. The history of social science libraries and its collection is largely recent and contemporary. Collections are still, for the most part, in the process of development. Acquisition of materials in numerical terms has been substantial. However, fullest use of the social science collection is yet to be made.

Like the emergence of social science libraries themselves, the history of the bibliographical exploitation of social science collections is also recent. In India, major secondary bibliographical undertakings are relatively few in number, particularly where the secondary literature of abstracting and indexing tools is considered separately.

Although *Indian National Bibliography* covers material of relevance to the social sciences, it has not developed to meet, and it has not been designed to meet the particular needs of social scientists in the way it is arranged, classified and indexed. *Guide to Indian Periodical Literature* and *Index India* are the two major indexing tools in the field especially for the journal literature. However, *Suchika* (brought out by Jawaharlal Nehru University Library) is also considered as a good checklist of its collection on international relations.

Social sciences have grown rapidly since Second World War, characterized by rapid educational expansion in this field in the 60s and 70s. Many social science libraries and collections have not, and could not have developed to anything like full potential in more ways than just acquisition alone. Social science libraries will undoubtedly develop to a greater degree in the next few decades in spite of financial constraints. In India, a new social science is being forged owing much to European and American models.[1]

4. Age Group

The study revealed that more than 50 per cent of the social science scholars were below the age of 30 years, 38.5 per cent fell in the age group of 30–40. Only 8 per cent were in the age group of over 40. Most (above 90%) were below 40 years of age. Table 6.2 gives the number of scholars falling under different age groups.

5. Qualifications

Table 6.3 shows that 72 (48.6%) are M.A., 48 (32.4%) M.Phil. and 28 (18.9%) Ph.D. degree holders. In the early 70s, UGC recommended that teachers must have either an M.Phil. degree or a Ph.D. Many universities in the country have now introduced M.Phil. courses in social sciences. And the establishment of ICSSR in Delhi and its regional centres in different parts of country has given a boost to research in these sciences.

TABLE 6.2: Age group of social science scholars

Age Group	No. of Scholars	Percentage
Below 30	78	52.0
30 – 40	57	38.5
41 – 50	12	8.1
51 – 60	0	0.0
61 – 70	1	0.6
Total	148	100.0

TABLE 6.3: Qualifications of social science scholars

Qualifications	No. of Scholars	Percentage
M.A.	72	48.6
M.Phil.	48	32.4
Ph.D.	28	18.9
Total	148	100.0

6. Designations

Table 6.4 gives the designations of social science scholars. It shows that more than 77 (52%) scholars are engaged in full-time research. Teachers form a big group of scholars who keep themselves engaged in serious research as 29 per cent of them are lecturers, 6 per cent readers and 0.6 per cent professors. Another category is of research associates. They are senior research scholars, whose job is to do their own research, and simultaneously guide junior scholars. This group constitutes 4 per cent of scholars. A small group of librarians (2%), social workers (0.6%), NSS Coordinators (0.6%) and assistant teachers of the school (0.6%) are also engaged in research. The biggest group is of full-time/part-time research scholars who constituted 52 per cent the total respondents.

TABLE 6.4: Designations of social science scholars

Group of Social Science Scholars	No. of Scholars	Percentage
Lecturers	43	29.0
Readers	9	6.0
Professors	1	0.6
Research Scholars	77	52.0
Deputy Directors	2	1.3
Librarians/Teachers	4	2.7
Assistant Coordinator	1	0.6
Social Worker	1	0.6
Research Associates (Fellow)	6	4.0
Did not fill up the column	2	1.3
Total	148	100.0

7. Fields of Research Interest of Social Science Scholars

Research interest of social science scholars projects an interesting panoramic view. A variety of social science topics are available to Indian scholars to do either research or to have a strong interest in the subject. This subject classification has a high degree of overlap, but what is interesting is to know that many social science scholars are interested in inter-disciplinary subjects. The subjects have been arranged alphabetically, in order of priority. It is economics and its sub-classes, political science and its sub-classes, sociology and its sub-classes, history and its sub-classes, geography, law, anthropology, commerce, psychology, education and their sub-classes. These are basic traditional social science disciplines where research is going at a faster speed than in subjects which have developed due to the immediate need, and partly due to distillation process. These are journalism, library and information science, management, area studies, etc. A number of scholars have also shown their interest in the subject of humanities besides retaining their main research interest in the social science. Scholars have indicated interest in more than one subject and few of them have shown interest in social sciences as a whole. Some social science scholars were also found interested in miscellaneous subjects which are: agriculture, defence studies, mathematics, research methodology and knowledge in general.

Table 6.5 reveals that Indian scholars are now more concerned with local, state and national social issues than international. Another interesting approach seen in the social science research is the development of inter-disciplinary subjects like medical anthropology, agricultural economics, political economy, health economics, agricultural geography, social geography, social psychology, political sociology and military sociology.

TABLE 6.5: Subject interest of social science scholars

Main Fields of Interest	Number of Scholars	Percentage
Anthropology		
Anthropology	10	6.7
Ethnicity, Ethnography and Medical Anthropology	1 each	0.6 each
Commerce		
Accountancy, Banking, Commerce and Marketing	1 each	0.6 each
Economics		
Economics	25	17.6
International Economics	4	2.7
Agricultural Economics, Development Economics, Indian Economics, Public Finance and Statistics	3 each	2.0 each
Economic Growth, Micro-economics, Monetary Economics, Political Economy and Regional Cooperation (SAARC) and Regional Development	2 each	1.3 each
European Economic Community, Health Economics, Industrial Development, Industry, Land Reforms, Micro-economics, Marxism Theory, Policy Analysis, Politics of Labour, Soviet Political Economy, State Finance, Welfare Economy, Union State Financial Relations, Transportation, Development & Taxation and Development Finance	1 each	0.6 each
Geography		
Geography	8	5.4
Agricultural Geography, Industrial Geography	2 each	1.3 each
Environmental Geography, Evolution of Geographical Thought, Social Geography and Study of Wasteland Utilization	1 each	0.6 each
History		
History	18	12.2
American History	4	2.7

(*Contd.*)

TABLE 6.5 (*Contd.*)

Main Fields of Interest	Number of Scholars	Percentage
Cultural History, Mediaeval History and Modern Indian History	2 each	1.3 each
Archaeology, Intellectual History, Economic History and History of the Far East	1 each	0.6 each
Law		
Law	4	2.7
International Law	3	2.0
Law of the Air and Space	2	1.3
Environmental Law, Labour Laws and Law of Sea (Maritime Law)	1 each	0.6 each
Political Science		
Political Science	21	14.2
International Politics (including international relations)	15	10.1
Indian Government and Politics, Political Theory, Public Administration, South Asian Politics and Foreign Policy	3 each	2.0 each
Agrarian Politics	2	1.3
China Politics, Comparative Politics, Contemporary Political Process, Economic Influence of Politics, Election, Gandhian Thought, Govt. and Politics, International Organizations, Politics of India and Pakistan, Political System in India, Politics of Nuclear Weapon, Politics of Third World Societies, Role of Superpower in South Asia, Sino-Indian Relations, Soviet Policy, State Progress in India, U.N. and Peace Studies and World Crisis	1 each	0.6 each
Psychology		
Psychology	12	8.1
Social Psychology	5	3.4
Mental Health	3	2.0
Clinical Psychology and Organizational Psychology	2 each	1.3 each
Industrial Psychology and Psychometric Methods	1 each	0.6 each
Sociology		
Sociology	23	15.5
Social Work	9	6.0
Demography, Rural Sociology and Women	6 each	4.0 each
Political Sociology, Rural Land Use and Planning, Development and Community Development, Health and Welfare	3 each	2.0 each

(*Contd.*)

TABLE 6.5 (*Contd.*)

Main Fields of Interest	Number of Scholars	Percentage
Caste, Class and Politics, Family and Child Welfare, Social Defence and Correctional Services, Social Policy and Tribal Development	2 each	1.3 each
Changing Patterns of Social Structure, Communalism, Community Study, Folk Culture, Gerontology (Aging), Health, Indian Caste System, Indian Society, Industrial Sociology, Military Sociology, Mural Social Structures, Nature of Soviet Study, Social and Political Process, Social Aspects of SC/ST, Landless Labour of India, Social Ecology, Social Inequality, Social Medicine, Social Movement, Social Problems, Social System in India, Theories of Soviet Dynamics, Voluntary Action, Urban Sociology and Youth Work	1 each	0.6 each
Journalism		
International Communication, Mass Media and Culture Communication	2 each	1.3 each
	1	0.6
Education		
Education	8	5.4
Teaching	1	0.6
Library and Information Science		
Library Science	6	4.0
Documentation and Bibliography in Regional Language	1	0.6
Science and Technology		
Sciences	5	3.4
Computers, History of Science and Technology	2 each	1.3 each
Management		
Management	6	4.0
Social Statistics and Stochastic Process (Operation Research)	1 each	0.6 each
Social Sciences		
Social Sciences (All)	4	2.7
Islamic Social Science	1	0.6
Area Studies		
West Asia	3	2.0
Africa and South Asia	1 each	0.6 each

(*Contd.*)

TABLE 6.5 (*Contd.*)

Main Fields of Interest	Number of Scholars	Percentage
Humanities		
General Literature (including English)	14	9.45
Philosophy	8	5.4
Art, Hindi, Humanities (All), Languages, Social Linguistics, Music	1 each	0.6 each
Miscellaneous		
Agriculture, Defence Studies and Mathematics	3 each	2.0 each
Research Methodology	2	1.3
General Knowledge	1	0.6

Indian social science scholars are largely interested in the subjects of immediate concern and the social problems our country is facing today. Thus a high percentage of research is being done in social sciences which are of immediate concern to the Indian people.[2] On the other hand, Indian scientists have engaged themselves in research in such areas which are of no immediate concern of our country. It does not mean that India should lag behind in the international field in top scientific research.

Social science research is becoming mature partly due to the opening of new social science institutions and partly due to more universities. In the early 70s many inter-disciplinary area departments were opened in different universities to encourage young scholars to take up such research problems as are different from traditional subjects. To illustrate a few, Jawaharlal Nehru University has many area studies departments. They are: West Asian Studies, American Studies and Russian Studies programme. Rajasthan University has South Asia Study Centre. UGC has approved the following (see Table 6.6) area study centres in different universities.[3,4]

Area studies has promoted a rapid development of library resources within the area. A meaningful research in area studies is getting support from the universities given in Table 6.6 for which UGC has provided liberal finds to make even field trips to the subject countries.

TABLE 6.6: Area study centres approved by UGC

University	Name of Area Study Centres
University of Delhi, Delhi	African Studies Centre
Osmania University, Hyderabad	Centre for area Studies Regional Planning and Urban Development in the Indian Ocean Countries
University of Srinagar, Srinagar Jammu & Kashmir	Centre for Central Asian Studies
North Bengal University, Raja Ram Mohanpur Distt., Darjeeling	Centre for Himalayan Studies
Calcutta University, Calcutta	Centre for South and South East Asian Studies
Madras University, Madras	Centre for South and South East Asian Studies
Bombay University, Bombay	Centre for Soviet Studies
Sri Venkateswara University, Tripura	Centre for Studies of Indo-China
Gokhale Institute of Politics and Economics, Poona	Centre for the Study for East European Socialist Economics
Banaras Hindu University, Varanasi	Centre for Studies of Nepal
Aligarh Muslim University, Aligarh	Centre for West Asia Studies
Bombay University, Bombay	Centre for East African Studies
University of Delhi, Delhi	Chinese and Japanese Studies Centre
Jawaharlal Nehru University, Delhi	Gulf Studies Centre, Soviet and East European Studies Centre and American Studies Centre
University of Rajasthan, Jaipur	South Asia Study Centre

8. Bibliographical Control of Information Explosion

The first question designed is whether there is any need of bibliographical control. A majority of scholars 76 (51.3%) are of the opinion that there is a need for it, but 47(32%) do not feel the necessity. The question posed is perhaps a bit technical as is evident that many scholars are not aware of the meaning of "bibliographical control". In Table 6.7, 15 (10.1%) scholars have indicated that they "do not know about bibliographical control, (9.6%) did not tick either "Yes" or "No" column indicate that they did not understand the question. One scholars has openly admitted that he is not clear about the question. Majority (51.3%) of them ticked "Yes" indicating that social science scholars are aware of the need for a strong bibliographical control.

TABLE 6.7: Necessity of bibliographical control

Category	No. of Scholars	Percentage
Yes	76	51.3
No	47	32.0
Do not Know	15	10.1
Question is not clear	1	0.6
Did not tick	9	6.0
Total	148	100.0

8.1 *Use of Bibliographical Sources*

In Table 6.8 113 (76.3%) scholars use subject bibliographies followed by 95(64.2%) abstracting journals and 69(46.6%) indexing journals. Local documentation list is used by 50 (33.8%) scholars. Documentation lists received from outside organization are used by 48 (32.4%) scholars and the union catalogue of serials and journals by 39 (26.3%) scholars. Subject bibliographies is considered as a major secondary source useful to social science scholars. Surprisingly social science scholars prefer abstracts to indexes. Unfortunately, union catalogues of serials and journals could not make much impact on social science scholars. There are two reasons:

1. ICSSR union catalogues are of poor quality. The problem with these is that of uptodateness. A large number of scholars have remarked that such catalogues are not kept uptodate.
2. Scholars do not know the utility of such tools.

TABLE 6.8: Use of type of bibliographical sources

Bibliographical Sources	No. of Scholars	Percentage
Subject Bibliographies	113	76.3
Abstracting Journals	95	64.2
Indexing Journals	69	46.6
Local Documentation List Received from Outside Organization	48	32.4
Union Catalogue of Serials and Journals	39	26.3

TABLE 6.9: Frequency of use of bibliographical sources in a year

No. of times used in a year	Subject Biblio-graphies	Abstracts	Indexes	Local Documen-tation List	Documentation List (outside)	Union Catalogues	Total
10 and above	38	28	19	10	8	10	113
9	--	--	--	--	--	--	---
8	--	--	2	1	1	--	4
7	2	--	2	2	--	--	6
6	5	7	2	3	3	1	21
5	4	7	3	2	2	3	21
4	5	4	2	3	3	5	22
3	3	8	5	7	5	4	32
2	8	8	5	2	8	3	34
1	5	5	6	8	6	8	38
Total	70	67	46	38	36	34	291

There are two trends which are absolutely clear from Table 6:9 (i) Social science scholars use secondary sources heavily, (ii) Use of subject bibliographies, followed by abstracting and indexing tools is the routine/method adopted by most scholars. The figures 10 and above depict the same behaviour observed in the total number of times used in a year.

8.2 *Use of Available Bibliographical Services*

Over 50 per cent respondents use secondary tools "regularly" and "most often" where 27 per cent and 19 per cent scholars use "usually" and "occasionally". One respondents said that he had not used any of the secondary tools (see Table 6.10). Perhaps, he is a fresh scholar who does not know the use of such tools. It is surprising that the use of bibliographical sources at post-graduate level is little. But the overall use of secondary sources in social science research is quite heavy.

TABLE 6.10: Use of bibliographical services

Degree of Frequency	Number of Scholars	Percentage
Regularly	40	27.0
Most often	37	25.0
Usually	40	27.0
Occasionally	28	19.0
Not at all	1	0.6
Did not fill up the column	2	1.3
Total	148	100.0

8.3 *Popularity of Use of Indian Bibliographical Sources*

An enumerative list of popularly known bibliographical tools was mentioned to elicit information (see Table 6.11). However, this list is not a comprehensive list. So the answers given by the social science scholars are not surprising. *Guide to Indian Periodical Literature* is the most used index in India than *Index India, Indian National Bibliography, Accession List : South Asia, Documentation on Asia and Suchika.*

TABLE 6.11: Use of Indian bibliographical sources

Bibliographical Source	Number of Scholars	Percentage
Guide to Indian Periodical Literature	58	39.2
Index India	49	33.1
Indian National Bibliography	48	32.4
Accession List : South Asia	35	23.6
Documentation on Asia	35	23.6
Suchika	30	20.2
Artha Suchi	14	9.4
ICSSR Abstracts and Reviews	1	0.6
AIU & UGC Publications	1	0.6

The order of merit list in the use of Indian bibliographical sources is startling. While there is no dispute about *Guide to Indian Periodical Literature* getting first bibliographical preference, *Suchika* getting second preference and pushing *Index India* and *Indian National Bibliography* to third spot within the first priority sector is quite surprising. When it comes to second preference, *Index India* tops the list pushing *Guide to Indian Periodical Literature* to the third spot. This means if these tools are available in a particular library, the predictable behaviour of social science scholars in using bibliographical tools will be the same as evidence in Table 6.12.

8.4 Use of Other Bibliographical Sources

Table 6.13 describes the list of other bibliographical sources used by social science scholars. This list also provides a panoramic view of foreign and Indian bibliographical sources. Few scholars have responded to this question and, therefore, it is difficult to know the use of bibliographical sources other than mentioned in Table 6.11. The indicated tools are ICSSR documentation bulletins, library science indexing tools—like *Library and Information Science Abstracts, Development and Welfare, Dissertation Abstract International, Sociological Abstracts* and *ICSSR journals*. *ICSSR Surveys of Research* are the tools on which social science scholars depend heavily. A large number of sources have been indicated by one scholar each. In indicating actual bibliographical tools, a few of them have named general bibliographical sources from where they find information of the references. These are archival records, bibliographies given at the end of a book, footnotes, book reviews, dissertations, and indexes of the various journals.

TABLE 6.12: • Order of merit of Indian bibliographical tools

Order of Merit	Guide to Indian Periodical Literature	Index India	Indian National Bibliography	Documentation on Asia	Accession List South Asia	Suchika	Artha Suchi	ICSSR Abstracts and Reviews	Total
	Number of persons who indicated their order of priority								
1	2	3	4	5	6	7	8	9	10
1	27	12	12	5	8	14	4	2	84
2	12	18	14	10	5	2	3	—	64
3	6	14	8	8	7	5	4	—	52
4	3	22	3	4	4	5	—	—	41
5	2	—	1	2	4	1	1	—	11
6	1	—	1	—	1	1	3	—	7
7	—	1	—	2	1	1	1	—	6
8	—	—	—	—	—	—	—	—	—
Total	51	47	39	31	30	29	16	2	265

TABLE 6.13: Use of other bibliographical sources

Bibliographical Sources	Number of Scholars	Percentage
Special		
Library and Information Science Abstracts, ICSSR Documentation Bulletin and Library Literature	3 each	2.0 each
Development and Welfare, Dissertation Abstracts International, ICSSR Journals, ICSSR Surveys of Research, Sociological Abstracts and Tata Institute of Social Science Bibliography	2 each	1.3 each
ABC Political Science., A Bibliography of Contents; Political Science and Govt., Banking Statistics, Bibliography of Women at Work, Bibliography of Asian Studies, Bibliography on Women Studies, Bibliography (Prepared by Women's Research wing of SNDT University, Bombay) Books in Print, Central Institute of English and Foreign Languages (CIEFL) Documentation List, Congressional Index, Current Contents, Current Literature on Science of Sciences, Digest of News and Views, Documentation Fortnightly, Encyclopaedia of Educational Research Abstracts, Explanatory Notes on Current Statistics, Hindu, Historical Abstracts, IIPA Documentation List, Index Islamicus, Index to U.S. Government Periodicals, Indian Abstract, Indian Educational Review, Indian Library Science Abstracts, International Political Science Abstracts, International Psychology Abstract, Muslim World Book Review (U.K.), New York Times, Public Affairs Informations Service, Reader's Guide to Periodical Literature, Report on Currency and Finance, Research Abstracts, Reserve Bank of India Bulletin, Selective Bibliography of National Security Council, Social Science Citation Index, Social Work Research and Abstracts (National Association of Social Work), U.N. Bibliographical Information and University News.	1 each	0.6 each
General		
Archival Records, Bibliography Mentioned in Back page of Books, Bibliographies or References given in Footnotes, Bibliographies given at the end of Relevant Books, Book Reviews, Dissertations, Existing Research Works, Indexes of Various Journals, Research Articles and Books on Specific Subjects	1 each	0.6 each

8.5 *Purpose of Using Bibliographical Sources*

A high percentage of scholars (86%) have indicated the purpose of using bibliographical sources as "doing research", followed by "writing papers" (52%), "writing dissertations and theses" (39.2%). Few scholars (11%) use bibliographical sources for "presenting papers in the seminars/conference/workshop", followed by writing books (20%) and guiding research" (7%). Only 3 per cent respondents use bibliographical services to write articles in newspapers (Table 6.14). It is explicitly clear that a high percentage of scholars use them for their research purpose. It shows that in teaching one does not use many bibliographical tools. Only when one engages in research, he has to consult them and then only the importance of secondary tools is realized. Therefore, at college and school levels a teacher a post-graduate students hardly uses bibliographical sources.

TABLE 6.14: Purpose of using bibliographical sources

Purpose	Number of Scholars	Percentage
Doing Research	127	86
Writing Papers	77	52
Dissertations and Theses	58	39.2
For Teaching	41	38.0
Writing Books	29	20.0
Presenting Paper in Seminar/ Conference/Workshop	16	11.0
Writing Reports	16	11.0
Guiding Research	10	7.0
Any Other Purpose (for knowledge and for newspapers)	4	3.0

5.6 *Arrangement of Bibliographical Sources*

It is an important to know the reactions of researchers about the arrangement of bibliographical tools. In most bibliographical tools the arrangement is not helpful. Thus the usefulness of any tool is doubtful. To have an effective bibliographical control, it is necessary that the bibliographical tools are designed and arranged from the users' point of view. Over 37 per cent scholars have agreed that the arrangement of most of the bibliographical tools is helpful but can be improved further as indicated by 57.4 per cent scholars. They want a new innovation in information storage and retrieval systems, and are less satisfied with the present ordering of bibliographical sources. Two (1.3%) respondents say that they are unhappy with the arrangement of bibliographical tools. Five (3.4%) scholars have indicated that they cannot say anything about the arrangement of bibliographical tools (see Table 6.15).

TABLE 6.15: Arrangement of bibliographical sources

Level of Arrangement	Number of Scholars	Percentage
Helpful	56	37.0
Helpful, but can be improved	85	57.4
Not helpful	2	1.3
Cannot say	5	3.4
Total	148	100.0

8.7 *Meeting Information Needs*

Information needs of 62.8 per cent scholars are met in a "limited" way, whereas 31 per cent scholars are satisfied with the comprehensive coverage of the bibliographical tools (see Table 6.16). Six per cent respondents could not say whether bibliographical tools meet their information needs. Our information 'sources' and bibliographical tools are not properly designed and arranged to cater to the needs of social scientists. It is high time effort is made to improve the arrangement of bibliographical tools. The time is not far when computers and other information retrieval machines will rescue social science research libraries to make bibliographical sources more user oriented. Social science scholars say that Indian bibliographical tools do not lend much help to them. Nine (6%) scholars cannot say whether bibliographical sources meet their information needs.

TABLE 6.16: Whether bibliographical sources meet information needs of social science scholars

Meeting Information Needs	Number of Scholars	Percentage
Comprehensive	46	31.0
Limited	93	62.8
Cannot say	9	6.0
Total	148	100.0

8.8 *Uptodateness of Bibliographical Sources*

To know their reaction about the uptodateness of bibliographical sources, it was difficult for the scholars to answer the relevant questions. Because nineteen (12.8%) scholars wrote cannot say. Therefore, the answers given by them are indifferent 43.2 per cent indicating "yes" and 41.9 per cent indicating "no" little offers to judge the uptodateness of bibliographical sources. If the reply of respondents is added to the "no" category they form a majority showing that bibliographical tools have to be maintained upto date.

TABLE 6.17: Uptodateness of bibliographical sources

Category	Number of Scholars	Percentage
Yes	64	43.2
No	62	41.9
Cannot say	19	12.8
Partially	1	0.6
Did not fill up the column	2	1.3
Total	148	100.0

8.9 *Suggestions for Improvement*

The following suggestions which are of similar nature have been put together in order of preference. The number of scholars and percentage is mentioned in brackets.

(1) Bibliographical tools must be latest and upto date 16(10.8%).
(2) Services of the librarians could be extended in tracing the sources early in order to avoid waste of time in tracing them by researchers—15 (10%)
(3) Computerize the bibliographical sources—6 (3.8%)
(4) Subject bibliographies should be increased—2 (1.3%)
(5) Bibliographical sources should have a more comprehensive coverage University bibliographical sources should be interchanged to enrich the sources—2 (1.3%)
(6) A bibliography on any subject should not have much technology. It should be simple which may be easy to follow by layman also.
(7) Uptodate sources are to be provided of whatever biblio-

graphical tools there are. They must reach the users do not know about their location, even if libraries have them.

(8) University libraries should be managed, and not casually looked after in the case of bibliographical sources.

(9) The modern systems should be followed and innovations are needed to save the readers time.

(10) Bibliographies of American source materials on Soviet and East European Studies would be extensively useful for the development of area study programmes in India.

(11) Bibliographical tools should have more flexible subject titles, incorporating the latest development in the field of study.

(12) Bibliographical sources should be like those of a particular country : political history, economic history, intellectual history, social history.

(13) Irrelevant references should be removed from bibliographical publications.

(14) Bibliographical information should be centralized.

(15) Subjectwise and authorwise lists of the research work being pursued in different universities in India should be prepared.

(16) A lot of research is being carried out on Indian problems by many foreign universities, particularly American. Their bibliographies should be prepared.

(17) Libraries have failed to provide the information they have with them, besides improving bibliographical tools.

(18) Bibliography can be improved using interconnected computerized system of information. If you have that, and each researcher is given information, you can publish periodically the complete index of availabilities.

(19) A broad framework of a library's bibliographical sources should be given to scholars.

(20) More precise information regarding the various sources should be prominently disseminated to research scholars in published form. More foreign bibliographies should also be incorporated properly indicating the best of convenient means of obtaining them.

(21) Some young scholars should be sent to the USA and the Soviet Union especially to collect all existing bibliographical sources. Also European countries and U.N. Information Centre should be requested for all bibliographical sources for all subjects.

(22) Bibliographical information services have not been made

comprehensive and upto date. On classified and specialized topics, no bibliographical information services are available. An attempt should be made to find out the solution to this problem also.

(23) Many readers suffer from information gap about the bibliographical sources. Often there is no proper dissemination about the current bibliographical sources they possess. There is need for:

(1) more coverage of articles
(2) proper display
(3) upto date information
(4) Subject-cum-author index for the improvement of the bibliographical index.

(24) Coverage (areawise) of bibliographical sources should be widened.

(25) Foreign abstracting/indexing journals are not comprehensive. They do not include all published information in the subject area. The subject coverage of these journals has to be improved. Further, it will be helpful if they include a note relating to the availability of source documents.

(26) In India it is very difficult to gather information or even to exactly know what is being published where. Anthropological journals of our country have no specialization. Hence bibliographical sources have to be improved.

(27) More exhaustive documentation is needed in the field of political philosophy and philosophy.

(28) (a) Detailed abstracts will be more desirable.
(b) Need of specific bibliography dealing with very specific subjects (for example) instead of one bibliography like *Artha Suchi* which includes everything in economics, specific bibliographies dealing with specific topics should be desired.

(29) Current awareness bulletin of research in economics is needed.

(30) There should be many copies of bibliographical sources which should be displayed and arranged according to the subjects and area.

(31) Every library must have some basic geographical works or tools as reference sources, e.g. gazetteers, guide books, hand-books, almanacs, bibliographies of bibliographies. These would be useful in research work.

(32) Documentation centre should be established in the library and cards for each of the issues prepared by social scientists should be maintained.

(33) Information regarding the technique, design and methods is needed for further improvement.

(34) While making the index of different subjects, author and titlewise, it will be more convenient for a user if the index is made bifurcating different fields within a subject (such as taxation, public borrowing, deficit financing, planning, growth, etc., in economics) so that it is convenient for a researchers to go through the needed materials.

(35) Author Index is more helpful.

(36) Theme specification should be included in bibliographical tools.

(37) It would be a welcome enterprise, if some way is found out to indicate the main thrust and focus of books along with bibliographical sources.

It is an important to consider the suggestions given by the respondents seriously. The above first five suggestions are significant. Bibliographical tools should be uptodate. Librarians should extend help in using bibliographical information and making of subject bibliographies, computerizing bibliographical sources and making bibliographical services comprehensive. All these are very significant suggestions made by social science scholars. These need immediate attention. While making plans these suggestions should be incorporated and known social science scholars are invited whenever any important decision is taken in this regard by the decision-making bodies. This will help both ways. Social science scholars will have their complaints attended to and those who are publishing bibliographical tools will get an idea of consumers' needs and expectations. This partnership is essential if bibliographical works are to be produced. There is an urgent need to have cooperation of social science academic community which should from time to time let the library know what are their bibliographical interests and library needs. This would also help in planning the bibliographical resources, library facilities and effective services befitting the need and requirements of the social science community.

9. Best Bibliographical Tools

The best bibliographical tool in order of priority is *Guide to Indian Periodical Literature* followed by *ICSSR Surveys of Research, Development and Welfare, Dissertation Abstracts International, Index India, International Political Science Abstracts* and *Library Literature* (Table 6.18). These are the most favoured bibliographical tools. Surprisingly the majority of the scholars failed to indicate the best bibliographical tool in their own fields. Social science scholars are desperately in need of a bibliographical tool which can meet most of their research requirements. They consult well-known bibliographical tools like *Index India* and *Guide to Indian Periodical Literature,* but their failure to indicate the best bibliographical tool is astonishing. It seems they are unable to decide which is the best tool. It is argued that silence indicates lack of knowledge about the best bibliographical tool in the social sciences.

TABLE 6.18: Best bibliographical tools

Bibliographical Tools	Number of Scholars	Percentage
Guide to Indian Periodical Literature, ICSSR Surveys of Research Development and Welfare, Dissertation Abstract International, Index India, International Political Science Abstract, Library and Information Science Abstracts, Library Literature and Sociological Abstracts.	3 each	2 each
Accession List : South Asia, African Bibliographical Review (London Publication), American Psychological Abstract, Annual Journal or Bulletin Published by Indian Law Institute, Artha Suchi, Bibliography of Asian Studies, Books in Print, CIEFL Documentation List, Congressional Index and Abstracts, Encyclopaedia Brittanica, Encyclopaedia of Educational Research Abstracts (Baroda University), Indian Dissertation Abstract, International Encyclopaedia of Social Sciences, Index Islamicus, Library and Information Science Abstract, Public Affairs Information Service, Reader's Guide to Periodical Literature, Reserve Bank of India Bulletin, Shanker Sen Gupta : Bibliography of Folklore, Survey of Economic Literature, Times of India Directory, U.N. Bibliographies, Vedic Bibliography, Women in India : Bibliography (Sage Publication)	1 each	0.6 each

9.1 *Best Libraries*

Importance of research libraries having significant collection in special fields can never be underestimated. It is ironical that India is still far behind in managing libraries of higher education and social science research. There is a little fear of subjectivity when the respondents mention their own library as the best library. This creates a situation where it is difficult to judge the best library. Secondly social science scholars receive UGC and ICSSR scholarships, and they consult well-known higher education and social science research libraries. It is because of this reason they consider JNU library as the best library (see Table 6.19).

TABLE 6.19: Best libraries

Libraries	Number of Scholars	Percentage
Jawaharlal Nehru University Library, Delhi	29	19.6
Indian Council of World Affairs, Delhi	21	14.5
ANS Institute of Social Studies, Patna, Delhi University Library including Ratan Tata Library of Delhi School of Economics, Delhi, Nehru Memorial Museum and Library, Delhi	16 each	10.8 each
American Studies Research Centre, Hyderabad	13	8.8
Indian Council of Social Science Research Library (NASSDOC), Delhi	11	7.4
Department of Social Work Library, University of Delhi, Delhi	10	6.8
National Library, Calcutta	9	6
Indian Institute of Public Administration, Delhi, Institute of Defence and Strategic Analysis, Delhi, Osmania University Library, Hyderabad	8 each	5.4 each
Banaras Hindu University, USIS (Delhi)	7 each	4.7 each
British Library, Delhi, Gokhale Institute of Economics and Politics, Poona, ICSSR Southern Regional Centre, Hyderabad, Punjab University Library, Chandigarh, V.S. Krishna Memorial Library, Waltair	5 each	3.3 each
Central Secretariat Library, Delhi	4	2.7
Bombay University Library, Bombay, Indian Institute of Management, Ahmedabad, Rajasthan University Library, Jaipur, SNDT University Library, Bombay	3 each	2.0 each
Administrative Staff College of India, Hyderabad, Central Institute of English and Foreign Languages Library, Hyderabad, Centre for Studies in Social Science, Calcutta, Indian Institute of Foreign Trade,		

(*Contd.*)

TABLE 6.19 (*Contd.*)

Libraries	Number of Scholars	Percentage
Library, Delhi, Institute of Economic Growth, Delhi, Max Mueller Bhawan, Delhi, Planning Commission, Delhi Sardar Patel Institute of Economic & Social Research, Ahmedabad	2 each	1.3 each
All India Women's Conference Library, Archaeological Survey of India, Arms Control Association, Association of Indian Universities, Bureau of Public Research and Development, Centre for Defence Information, Connemera Library, Madras, District Central Library, Waltair, Forest Research Institute, Dehradun, Gautami Granthalaya Rajahmundry, Gujarat Institute of Area Planning, Ahmedabad, Indian Council of Medical Research, ICSSR North Western Regional Centre, Chandigarh, Indian Law Institute, Indian Social Institute, Delhi, Indian Statistical Institute, Calcutta, Indian Society of International Law, Institute of Public Finance and Policy, International Institute of Population Sciences, Bombay, Jayakar Library, Poona, K.K. Handique Library, Gauhati, Library of Geological Survey of India, Ministry of Agriculture, Ministry of Finance Library, Ministry of Industry, NIEPA, National Archives, (All Delhi), National Institute of Nutrition, Hyderabad, National Medical Library, Delhi, National Wasteland Development Board, Delhi, S.B. Art Library, Gulbarga, NISIET Library, Central Library, (Andhra Pradesh), USIS, Madras	1 each	0.6 each

No one disputes the best collection of the following libraries : JNU, ICWA, ANS Institute of Social Studies, Delhi University Library including Ratan Tata Library, Nehru Memorial Museum and Library, American Studies Research Center, Indian Council of Social Science Research Library (NASSDOC), National Library, Calcutta and Indian Institute of Public Administration. Well-known social science research libraries are : Gokhale Institute of Economics and Politics, Central Secretariat Library, Institute of Defence and Strategic Studies, Institute of Economic Growth, Administrative Staff College of India, and Indian Institute of Management, USIS post libraries and British libraries with their branches in big cities of India are also highly used by Indian scholars. These libraries are the best libraries because of their efficient service and management. There is a long list indicating the best libraries which have been ticked by more than one respondent.

Priority further proves that respondents have favoured university libraries as better equipped libraries than social science research libraries. Jawaharlal Nehru University Library tops the list. Social science research libraries and university libraries are found more useful to social science scholars for their research than the so-called National Library which has been considered as the best library by only 6 per cent social science scholars. The Department of Social Work Library, Delhi University, is used more than the National Library by social science scholars. One reason could be its location which hampers its utility.

9.3 *Reading Habits*

The reading habit of social science scholars is found to be stronger compared to science scholars. Science scholars devote their time in laboratories. For social science scholars, libraries are their laboratories. It is astonishing that 28.4 per cent scholars use libraries for less than 10 hours a week. Only 26.3 per cent scholars read more then 30 hours a week. Scholars who do not go to libraries are perhaps fresh scholars who are yet to be initiated into serious research. Libraries may not be that attractive as reflected in their critical comments. Scholars have complained about the higher learning libraries which are not well managed. They do not find primary and secondary sources at right places, and no one takes pains to help them know where and what are the tools available. Social science scholars have developed a kind of apathy towards the library staff.

TABLE 6.20: Hours spent in libraries

Hours	No. of Scholars	Percentage
Less than 10 hours	42	28.4
10 – 15	24	16.2
16 – 20	13	8.8
21 – 25	7	4.7
26 – 30	16	10.8
Above 30	39	26.3
Did not fill up the column	7	4.7
Total	148	100.0

Why scholars do not want to sit in libraries? Because we have yet to design and set libraries where facilities like carrel, xeroxing, availability of cool water and tea, air-conditioning, typing and prompt reference service are available. If these can be made available, reading habits of social science scholars will increase. Motivation of general reading habit needs to be examined more thoroughly.

Methods by which the reading habits of social science users can be improved could be: (1) Display of current journals including newspapers and popular magazines, (ii) Display of latest additions to the library at a prominent place, and (iii) Personalized reader's service. These measures will certainly help stimulate reading habits among social science scholars.[5]

9.4 The following are the comments and general suggestions made by the respondents:

(1) Now a days libraries are not being managed well. The staff of the libraries is irresponsible. They do not help the visitors. They have to have service motto.

(2) Trained professional library staff should be appointed to serve the users. It is a great help to research.

(3) Arrangement of ICSSR Library, Delhi, is not good.

(4) Existing bibliographical sources are not sufficient. A lot of improvement should be made.

(5) Reorganise university libraries from top to bottom. This is very important.

(6) All research scholars should be acquainted with the method of using bibliography. It should be a part of the training in research methodology.

(7) Subjectwise list of bibliography should be made available to all the researchers. This facilitates the job of the researchers.

(8) Scholars want specific bibliographies on their research topic, and on some topic, region or statewise. This helps to make a comparative study or analysis.

(9) The collection should be more specific and sub-groupwise (in a particular field). Accessibility must be widened.

(10) Try to implement the findings rather than merely collecting information. Libraries should have uptodate material on any subject. Library materials are often misplaced.

(11) Inclusion of microfilm for documentation should be made.

(12) If the library in-charge is well aware of the record the library possesses and is cordial to any reader, he is the ideal one. However, without maintaining proper chronological records

of the library materials, no library can render good service to a serious busy reader.

(13) Subjectwise bibliography is needed for scholars.

(14) Bibliography guide (employees) is to be provided in the libraries.

(15) There must be clippings on every subject.

(16) Libraries should receive bibliographical sources on standing orders so that these may go on pouring in the library. After a year, a hard-bound cumulative index should also be provided so that the missing issues are covered by one book.

(17) There should be a regular seminar on research methodology for freshers.

(18) Bibliographical information should be disseminated to the teachers in colleges also.

(19) University department should be supplied documentation lists regularly.

(20) Bibliographical index with annotation is more helpful to readers. Sometimes, the readers may not have the opportunity to go through all the documents, so unbiased and uptodated annotated bibliographical index may be more meaningful.

(21) Efforts should be made to uptodate the bibliographical list.

(22) Comprehensive bibliography is needed in anthropology.

(23) Libraries which have enough resources should go for computerization. Bibliographical services should be given a high priority in the computerized libraries so that minimum time is invested in preparing bibliographies for research. It would speed up the research work of scholars.

(24) Usually, abstracts prepared on the basis of Indian context are required more, but they are not sufficient.

(25) Bibliographical sources should be more systematic and comprehensive.

10. Conclusion

The survey reveals that the majority of the scholars engaged in research are aged 30 years. Next to this is the age group of 30—40. Social science subjects are quite popular among young scholars. Majority of the scholars are working for M.Phil. or Ph.D. degree followed by lecturers and readers. Scholars are more concerned with local, state and national issues than international as research problems undertaken by them are of immediate concern to the contemporary Indian society.

Many scholars say bibliographical control is necessary, but 32 per cent scholars saying "no" is surprising. These perhaps have little idea of the meaning of bibliographical control as 17 per cent scholars clearly accept that they are ignorant about the concept of bibliographical control.

The survey has revealed that the scholars depend on sources in the following order : subject bibliographies, abstracts, indexes, documentation list and union catalogues. It revealed that social science scholars consult bibliographical tools more for doing research than writing papers, dissertations and theses. They have suggested improvements in the arrangement of bibliographical tools. They want these to be designed user-oriented.

Scholars have felt that the bibliographical tools should be latest and uptodate. Few scholars felt that the services of librarians and reference librarians who are familiar with the use of bibliographical resources could be used. Few also felt that the bibliographical tools should be computerized, and they want that subject bibliographies should be made available on demand in view of the growing needs of social science scholars.

REFERENCES

1. Stephen Andrew Roberts, "Social Science Libraries and Collections." In *Encyclopaedia of Library and Information Science.* Allen Kent, Ed. Vol. 28 (New York : Marcel Dekker, 1980), pp. 60-62.
2. Eugene Garfield, "Mapping Science in the Third World." *Current Contents,* 5, 34 (22 October, 1983), pp. 5-16.
3. *University Grants Commission Annual Report,* 1968-69.
4. Information collected from South Asia Study Centre, University of Rajasthan, Jaipur.
5. Krishan Kumar, "Users" Survey of the Sapru House Library." *Library Herald,* 12, 4 (January, 1971), pp. 235-236.

7

NATIONAL INFORMATION SYSTEM FOR SOCIAL SCIENCES (NISSS)

Prospects

Introduction

Social science research has become important, and has gained ground in post-Independent India. India is listed among the first seven nations of the world which produce monographs, journals and serials in social sciences. There is proliferation of world social science knowledge and this could be measured by the fact that in 1820 the number of current serials in social sciences was only 22. In 1920, it rose to 694, in 1950 to 1,860 titles, in 1961 to 2,251 titles and in 1970 to 3,490 titles. This surely shows the growth of social science current titles. Let us now have a look at Ph.D degrees produced in Indian universities in social sciences. In 1968 only 266 doctoral degrees were awarded, and now it is estimated that 1,000 doctoral degrees are awarded every year in social sciences. This is a phenomenal growth of social science research in India.

Consequently there has been a rapidly increasing investment in social science research resulting in an enormous production of reports, articles, papers and other information carriers. Further, imprecision of social science vocabularies, proliferation of specialized terminologies and marked cultural and ideological contrasts in approaches to social, political and economic problems have also led to the growth of social science literature. The U.N. while reviewing the decade 1960-69 realized that due to lack of proper or systematic dissemination of information, the whole effort in bringing out research reports and other important social science information literature went waste. It is estimated that 60 per cent of the documents containing vital social science information are not generally available for dissemination or use. It is said that one-time solution of a particular problem does not guarantee solution of a particular problem for ever.[1] Hence new answers are always sought. Majority of researchers feel that had they known earlier about the research already done in the same area perhaps it would have made a difference in their teaching and research. It is realized that social science research is essential for the formulation of government policies. Further, in the absence of a national information system much of the research is leading to duplication as one does not know what the other is doing. It is felt that an information system at a national or international level is the only panacea for all the ills of lack of bibliographical control.

1. Use of Social Science Information

The use of social science information is as follows:

- (i) Educational purposes, teaching and research,
- (ii) Solution purposes, i.e. formulation of policies—at individual, group, corporation, national and international levels.

According to the Development Science Information System (DEVSIS) Study team, major categories of users for the information system are the following:

- (i) Policy-makers with respect to socio-economic development,
- (ii) Planners of socio-economic development projects and programmes,
- (iii) Managers of development projects and programmes in central authorities,
- (iv) Researchers and teachers of socio-economic development subjects and those involved in management of research projects and programmes,
- (v) Financiers who provide resources,
- (vi) Communicators who attempt to convey information about development policies, plans and projects,
- (vii) Personnel concerned with information analysis and products thereof (monographs, data compilations, trend reports, forecasts, etc.) as support to services to those involved in the type of work mentioned in (i) to (vi).[2]

2. Need for a National Information System

No single institution can perform the job of documentation centre, library databanks and information system to provide information services single-handed. Now information is regarded as "national resource" or a commodity and this awareness has led to indexing, abstracting and computer-based information services at national and international levels. Thus there is a need for a national network, and it is possible only if there exists a national social science information system.

ICSSR has already done much ground work in the form of compiling bibliographies, union lists, union catalogues of all the Indian States and bringing out indexing and abstracting journals since its inception. It also took a major stride in taking care of 240 periodicals of social science for indexing purposes up to 1970 for retrospective literature.

3. National Information System for Science and Technology (NISSAT) Model

In India the history of national information system is a recent phenomenon. The NISSAT could be considered as the first model of a national information system. At present NISSAT has five sectoral centres functioning in different parts of the country based on priorities of the Government besides having a separate National Science Library and Indian National Scientific Documentation Centre (INSDOC). If the same model plan is applied to social sciences it would become "National Information System for Social Sciences" (NISSS).

The Government of India had made an appeal to UNESCO for a short-term mission of a consultant to advise the INSDOC on the setting up of a national information system in the early seventies. UNESCO deputed Peter Lazar during March-April, 1972, who, after a thorough study, recommended the establishment of National Information System for Science and Technology (NISSAT) for India. Along with the recommendations of Peter Lazar, the Panel Group on the Information Sector of the National Committee on Science and Technology (NCST) of the Government of India (its report was prepared in 1973) also recommended the establishment of NISSAT under the Department of Science and Technology (DST) plan for

1974-79. A sum of Rs. 15 crores was proposed for the scheme during the plan period. As a result, the planning of NISSAT started in 1975 and was completed and approved by the Planning Commission and the Ministry of Finance for implementation in July, 1977. Thus it took more than five years to implement the recommendations of Peter Lazar.[3]

A seminar on "Towards the Evolution of Information System for National Development" was organized at the National Physical Laboratory in New Delhi in December, 1975, by INSDOC. This seminar could be considered historical as it was the first time in India that the importance and need of "information", "information system" and "national information system" was realized. The seminar felt an urgent need of information for development of science and technology in India, and this after a gap of 28 years. Papers on "DEVSIS", "national informations centre", "proposed plan of national agricultural system", a "national atomic energy system", "branch information system", etc., were presented in the seminar. The seminar could be considered historic as library and information scientists came to know about the existence of NISSAT.[4]

4. Concept of National Information System of Social Sciences (NISSS)

Launching of National Information System for Social Sciences (NISSS) is a prime need of the hour as whatever efforts towards building up a national information system were made have not fully materialized. Lacklustre functioning of NISSAT is an indication of its disastrous failure particularly from the point of view of social sciences.[5] Many years have gone waste due to lack of national information system for social sciences. In 1971 it was thought that as soon as NISSAT was launched, there would be a strong national network to meet the expanding needs of the scientists and researchers, and it would also take care of social sciences. Unfortunately, it did not happen. But now the Government of India should not delay it further, and should realize the importance of the role of social sciences in national development by launching NISSS.

It was a setback to social scientists, information scientists and information seekers when NISSAT failed to cover social sciences. However, interest is still being shown in the setting up of NISSS. NASSDOC has been raising the issue of establishing NISSS in conferences and seminars, and emphasizing strongly the need for it for the last one decade.

A national information system is based on the following objectives:

(i) to help in decision-making,
(ii) to help research,
(iii) to avoid waste of effort due to duplication of research,
(iv) to achieve directly or indirectly bibliographical control of social science literature, and
(v) to help international agencies like UNESCO, ILO, UNISIST and DEVSIS for providing national bibliographic data on social sciences.

Unfortunately the importance of information as a national resource was realized late after Independence. The Government is still groping in the dark. It needs a social and political will to act firm in implementing the recommendation provided by social scientists, librarians and information scientists.

ICSSR should be made a national focal point for coordination and cooperation for the network of information centres for which NISSS is to be developed. NISSS should then be in a position to provide precise, exhaustive, and within-reach information at the minimum cost to the users. Some ground work has already been done in this regard by NASSDOC. The Government of India should wake up now in order to strengthen the social sciences. Development of social science research does not mean that only a very high social science research with no national focus is to be encouraged.

5. Objectives of NISSS

The objectives of NISSS will remain the same as of NISSAT, DEVSIS and UNISIST. Wherever necessary a departure can be made to suit the information needs of Indian social scientists. The following are the objectives:

(i) Provision of national information service relevant to the present needs and capable of development to meet the future needs of social science scholars, researchers and common users of the social science information,

(ii) Optimum utilization of existing social science information services and systems and the development of new ones,

(iii) Promotion of national and international cooperation and liaison for exchange of social science information,

(iv) Support and active encouragement for the development and innovation in information science communication to enhance both efficiency of information services and quality of information provided by these services, and

(v) Support and promotion of research, development and innovation in information technology.[6]

Once NISSS starts functioning it will cater to the information needs of social science scholars and researchers. It will coordinate information activities, provide and receive information from national information and documentation centres, and exchange information with the international systems like DEVSIS, UNISIST, AGRIS, etc. As stated earlier, regional centres of ICSSR shall be directly governed by NISSS.

6. Participating Agencies

The following will be the participating agencies in NISSS:

6.1 *National Information Centres*

Effective bibliographical control of social sciences for rendering better social science information services to social scientists and interested users through NASSDOC was conceived and emphasized prior to 1969. NASSDOC is still a weak link in the ICSSR set-up and it lacks leadership in the field of social science information. In trying to do the job of three institutions (library, documentation centre and an information system) it is unable to bear the load, and in the process has failed to do a single job effectively.

6.2 *National Social Science Library (NSSL)*

At present the situation of NASSDOC is pathetic in the sense that it has neither grown as a National Social Science Library nor as a strong national social science documentation centre. The proposed NSSL will be developed initially by the Council as an institutional project to become a separate institution like the National Science Library separated from INSDOC. NSSL will try to avoid procuring duplicate material and rather will augment the national collection of social sciences through filling up the gaps and developing a sound logical policy of collection development. It will also assess the information resources already available in the country and identify the gaps. The main objective of NSSL would be to see that at least one copy of everything published all over the world in social sciences be made available. Though it seems a difficult task it should try to procure all the relevant material pertaining to social sciences.

6.3 *ICSSR Regional Centres*

ICSSR Regional Centres will be directly administered and funded under NISSS. The present condition of the ICSSR regional centres is not encouraging as these are merely reading rooms or at best could be considered as extension centres of the ICSSR/NASSDOC. Under the proposed NISSS, the regional centres will have to be handled independently. This is a step in right direction. Besides the existing six regional centres, the author proposes that there is need for four more regional centres which should be located at geographically convenient places throughout India. Jaipur, Bhopal, Patna and Madras should be given ideal. The new centres could function as ideal location centres based on the number of higher education libraries and social science research libraries in these cities (see Map 7.1). Setting up of regional centres in the big cities is incomplete unless other regions of India which were earlier uncovered are brought on the map. This is necessary keeping in view the size of the country and the social science manpower spread in these towns.

6.4 *Sectoral Centres*

Sectoral centres should be developed as a vital link in NISSS. It shall be developed from the most suitable research institution in the discipline concerned. The sectoral centres shall provide specialized services with a good amount of subject expertise and shall be looked after by subject specialists trained in information work. A centre which will be a leading centre in a particular field of social sciences along with other information will constitute a grid of its own, and take care of development of information resources and services.

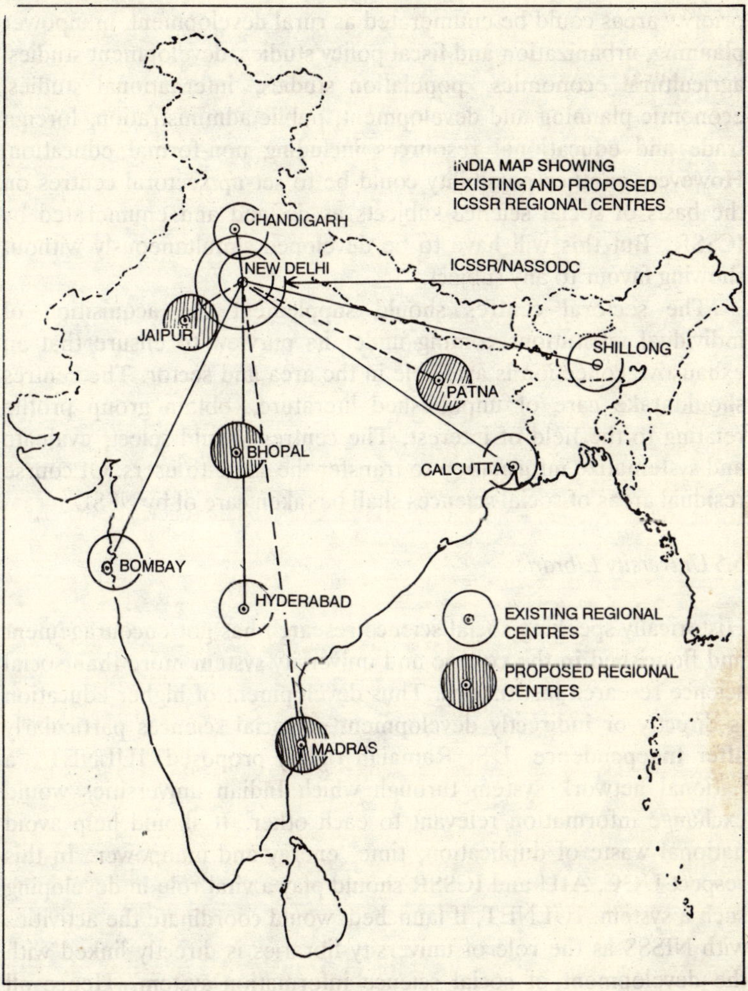

Map 7.1. India: Map showing existing and proposed ICSSR Regional Centres

The sectoral centres should be developed in major areas of social sciences on the basis of national relevance and priorities. These priority areas could be enumerated as rural development, manpower planning, urbanization and fiscal policy studies, development studies, agricultural economics, population studies, international studies, economic planning and development, public administration, foreign trade and educational resources including non-formal education. However, another possibility could be to set-up sectoral centres on the basis of social science subjects as defined and enumerated by ICSSR. But this will have to be developed simultaneously without showing favour to any subject.

The sectoral centres should supplement the acquisition of individual institutions coming under its purview to ensure that an exhaustive collection is available in the area and sector. The centres should take care of unpublished literature, obtain group profile relating to the field of interest. The centres should select, evaluate and systematize information to transfer the same to users. Of course residual areas of social sciences shall be taken care of by NSSL.[7]

6.5 *University Libraries*

Historically speaking social science research has got encouragement and flourished in the college and university system more than social science research institutions. Thus development of higher education is directly or indirectly development of social sciences particularly after Independence. L.S. Ramaiah rightly proposed "IULNET", a national network system through which Indian universities would exchange information relevant to each other. It should help avoid national waste of duplication, time, energy and manpower. In this respect UGC, AIU and ICSSR should play a vital role in developing such a system. IULNET, if launched, would coordinate the activities with NISSS as the role of university libraries is directly linked with the development of social science information system. Hence all university libraries should be linked with NISSS.[8]

6.6 *Information and Library Network (INFLIBNET)*

The leading role of the University Grants Commission (UGC) in the setting up of a national information network of all universities is laudable. It had appointed a Committee on National Network System for University Libraries in June 1988, to suggest measures for a network of libraries in the country with a view to sharing resources aimed at optimum utilization and avoiding duplication in holdings. The Committee constituted a Working Group to prepare a project report. The Group has recently submitted its report to UGC. A new name given to the network is *Information and Library Network* (INFLIBNET). A working document on the network system came out in December, 1988.[9]

6.7 *Subject Research Centres*

The concept of sectoral centres has already been discussed and will be developed depending upon the need and priorities of the Government. It is proposed that NISSS should develop subject research centres. Such centres should acquire, process and document information in almost all types of documents on a particular subject. This is essential because of specialization and development of research. Fig. 7.1 shows the six categories of subjects of social sciences.

NISSS shall also provide information to State agencies like State central libraries, city central libraries, State information centres, etc. Lastly, NISSS will be open to all social science scholars to use its referral facility.

6.8 *Manpower*

For managing the national information system different types of specialized skills will be required. Manpower development, therefore, is an immediate task on which depends the success of any information system. The national information system will meet diverse requirements of planners, policy-makers, business and industry, social scientists, academicians, etc. The institutions like libraries, documentation centres, data banks, clearing houses, translation centres, etc. will require skilled manpower to manage the different kinds of institutions. These organizations and their services will have planned development in computers, telecommunication networks and reprographic facilities. A national information system will be required to operate information services, carry out retrospective searches, bring out documentation lists, carry out statistical tests and compute correlations.

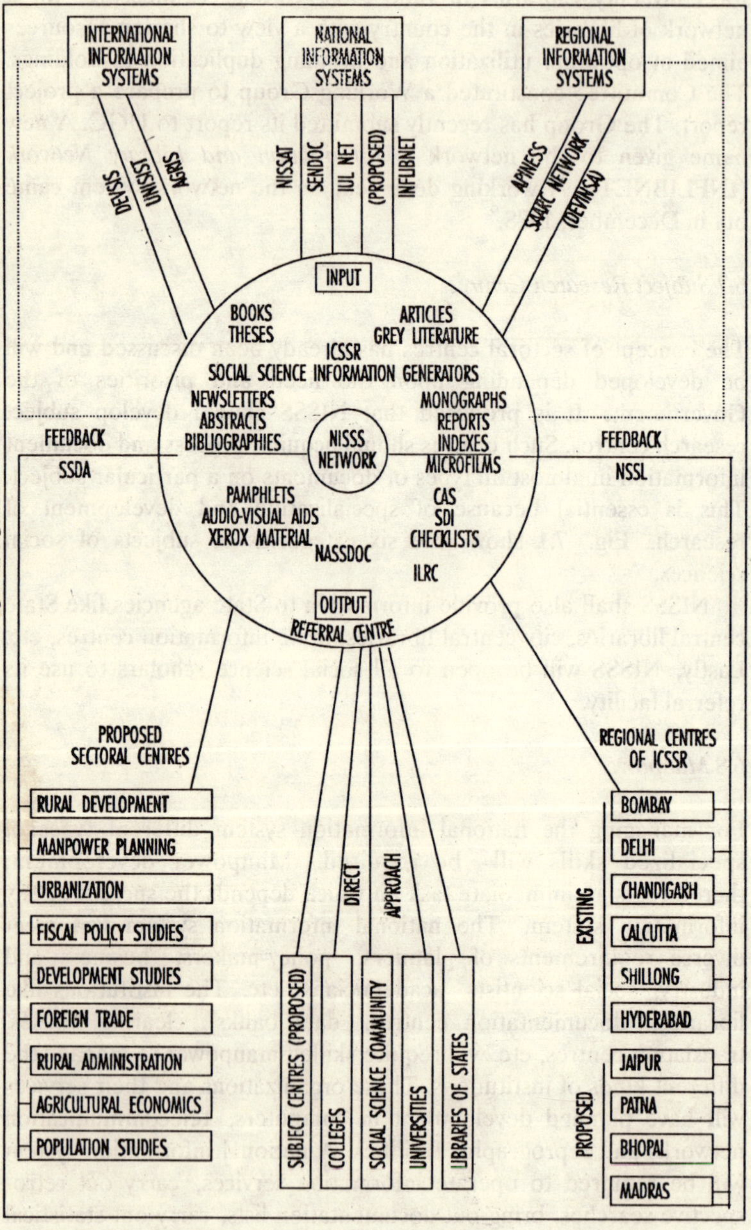

FIG. 7.1. National Information System for Social Sciences

Keeping in view the above development as wide variety of specialists are to be trained in order to strengthen the manpower force for national information system. The types of personnel required will be information scientists, librarians, computer specialists, system analysts, technical writers and editors, reprographic specialists, subject specialists, etc. The following types of personnel are required for:

(i) production and operation,
(ii) design and development, and
(iii) applied research.

Recently ICSSR decides to start a course on the lines of the INSDOC and DRTC to train social science information manpower. This course can be started any time as a policy decision has already been taken by the council. Manpower trained and prepared by the Council shall go a long way in creating big social science information manpower base to supply trained personnel to the different social science institutions including higher education libraries.

6.9 *Finance*

A national information system shall incur a heavy expenditure for which a budgetary provision has to be made in the Budget by the Government either on a planned or non-planned manner. It is to be noted that costwise the total outlay for the development of NISSS over a period of five years was estimated of Rs. 5.43 crores in 1980. If international inflationary trends is an indication, a rough estimate for developing NISSS would now be more than Rs. 10 crores, and if delayed further, an additional 10–15 per cent inflation margin should be kept in view. Incurring this heavy expenditure on NISSS could be justified if benefits can be achieved by systematizing bibliographical control measures.

It is a hoped that the Government will realize the importance of NISSS and make a budgetary provision in the Eighth Five Year Plan. If helped NISSS is quite capable to give a practical shape to the dreams of Indian information scientists/librarians and social scientists who have been advocating help for the last many years for social science scholars. Otherwise they have to waste much of their time in searching information, getting the material and using them.

7. International Information System

Development Science Information System (DEVSIS, 1975-) should be considered as an international information system of social sciences. Needless to say DEVSIS will be a detailed international information system. So far as the objectives of any information system are concerned they generally remain the same. Only the subject is different. The DEVSIS idea may look too big and there may be some initial problems, but it will be easier to get information through the regional, national and international system in due course.[10]

7.1 *Regional Information System*

The establishment of Asian Pacific Information Network in Social Sciences (APINESS) will help in disseminating information about the accumulated contribution to study and research of the social science scholars in the region and would ultimately enrich the pool of universal knowledge. The APINESS will link up the existing major social science libraries and documentation centres in the region to facilitate the exchange of knowledge. It will help in the development of new information centres and clearing houses and assist in improving bibliographical control by bringing out indexing and abstracting services, producing directories and computerization of the total information system. NASSDOC will (a) mail NASSDOC Research Information Series publications to National Contact Points, (b) Compile and update the directory of APINESS participants, (c) provide a regional dimension to the professional training courses which are planned to be started by NASSDOC, and (d) distribute them among Indian participating centres and other institutions.[11]

It is encouraging that APINESS has been launched, but surprisingly India has joined it without launching NISSS. In the absence of a national information system whether India would be able to successfully participate and how APINESS will function is difficult to answer. It would have been much better if, before joining the APINESS system, there were a thorough and loud discussion in the professional circles about the feasibility of such a regional information system.

India being the second largest country in Asia would be quite an active participant in the regional information system. Till NISSS is launched the country information will be provided by NASSDOC. With on-line facilities available NISSS will directly interact with the national and international data bases as and when necessary and convenient.

8. Conclusion

It has already been emphasized that launching of NISSS is the need of the hour, and if it is established it would certainly help Indian social science scholars, academicians, decision-makers and researchers to get the relevant social science information as quickly as possible. Library and information scientist will then have satisfaction that everything generated in social sciences in India is under full bibliographical control. A national information system of social sciences is to coordinate existing information institutions on priority, and not to create new institutions. An information system will ensure that the specific category of users receive the essential information and consulting services relevant to their needs. It is hoped that NISSS will try to detect the weak links and strengthen them, and if need arises, new institutions can be created.[12] All this is needed for achieving sound bibliographical control of social sciences. But the present position is not rosy. Everything done in this regard is only on paper. The Planning Commission has not included the NISSS plan in the Seventh Five Year Plan. It is hoped that it is included in the Eighth Plan. However, the need of NISSS will always be there to have a full bibliographical control of social sciences.

REFERENCES

1. N.K. Goil, "Need for Social Science Information System; Guideline for Modal for India." *Library Herald,* 17, 1-4 (April 1975—March 1979), pp. 70-93.
2. A. Nealameghan, "DEVSIS; Development Science Information System". In *Seminar on Towards the Evolution of Information System.* Organized by Insdoc, Delhi, INSDOC, 1975, p. B-2.2.
3. Girja Kumar, Thirtieth Presidential Address at *All India Library Conference Held at Jaipur.* (January 28-31, 1985). Presidential Address Brochure.
4. Seminar on Towards the Evolution of Information System for National Development. (December 8-9, 1975). Resolution.
5. Girja Kumar. Thirtieth Presidential Address at *All India Library Conference Held at Jaipur.* (January 28-31, 1985). Presidential Address Brochure.

6. *A Report of the Committee to Prepare Draft Plan for Development of Social Science Information System to the Country During the Next Plan Period.* Mimeographed Copy.
7. S.P. Agrawal, "National Information System for Social Sciences in India". In *Developing Horizons in Library and Information Science.* Edited by C.D. Sharma and Kailash Vyas. (Jaipur, Printwell, 1983), pp. 95-108.
8. L.S. Ramaiah, IULNET. *Deccan Chronicle* (October 19, 1986), p. 6.
9. INFLIBNET — Information and Library Network. Inter Agency Working Group Report. *University News.* (January 16, 1989), pp. 3-7.
10. A Nealameghan, pp. B-2.2.
11. S.P. Agrawal, *A Brief Write-up of APINESS* (The Information Network was initiated at the Regional Meeting of Experts to Develop an Asian — Pacific Network of Social Science Information and Documentation Centres, Bangkok, May 12-16, 1986. Brochure.
12. Unesco, *UNISIST: Guidelines on the Conduct of a National Inventory of Scientific and Technological Information and Documentation Facilities.* (Paris, Unesco, April, 1975.) Summary.

8

CONCLUSIONS

Introduction

Bibliographical control is a system of adequate recording of published/unpublished and audio-visual material by which one knows about their existence through bibliographical tools. It is necessary to have a complete check over the tremendous proliferation of publications so as to know their whereabouts and make its effective use. At international level attempts for bibliographical control have been made by UNESCO and IFLA by way of launching many programmes for achieving bibliographical control. The UNISIST programme inquired into the feasibility of a world science information system including social sciences. They have also encouraged national governments to improve and bring out current national bibliography. The last few decades have witnessed knowledge explosion in every branch of human endeavour. A large number of information generating agencies have become active in the field of social sciences also. This has resulted in an exponential growth of literature necessitating its bibliographical control.

1. Development of Social Sciences in India

Social sciences are now considered an important branch of knowledge pertaining to human activities and institutions. Social science subjects deal with human behaviour in its social and cultural aspects. Social sciences are generally viewed as relatively young in comparison to natural sciences. They have gained status after a long struggle of 200 years. Two tendencies visible in the development of social sciences are (1) to drive towards unification as one single master social science, and (2) diversification of social sciences. But it is the second tendency that has won with the result many disciplines and sub-disciplines have emerged today. Social sciences are a major contemporary influence though their growth has been slow and tortuous. Today, social sciences are as relevant to the poor nations as they are to the rich. Contemporary Indian society has all the identified problems of a developing society, wherein social scientists have acted an analysts. Development of social sciences can be attributed to number of factors like the growth of universities and university departments in social sciences with P.G. and research facilities, research institutions increasing number of doctorates in social sciences and establishment of RPC, UGC and ICSSR. A bibliography brought out by the Association of Indian Universities mentioned in Chapter 1) presents the development of social sciences in India. Now more than 1,000 doctoral theses are being submitted to the Indian universities every year. Under the chairmanship of D.R. Gadgil, ICSSR conducted research surveys in the early seventies in all the branches of social sciences to formulate priorities and significant programme to promote social science research. These surveys show the phenomenal growth of research literature in social sciences. This necessitates its bibliographical control.

2. Bibliographical Activities of Social Science Institutions

A survey of bibliographical activities of social science institutions including university libraries reveals that social science research is gaining ground as it is evident from the increasing financial support received from different quarters, viz. ICSSR, the Central and State Governments, UGC, etc. Documentation activities have been developing through the efforts of many social research institutions and higher education libraries. It is hoped that with cooperation and coordination among such institutions, the bibliographical control situation would further improve. This is based on the availability of increasing grants, growing collection and research output. Use of machine for information recording and dissemination will further speed up the services. Survey findings further reveal that cooperation among the institutions engaged in allied subjects is becoming popular. Few institutions are getting cooperation from foreign institutions. Linkage of such social science institutions with institutions of higher education will certainly help in improving the situation of bibliographical control. Though mutual linkage is there is shown in the Map 3.1 a network system does not exist. The findings reveal that a high percentage of social science institutions including university libraries have been feeling the need of bibliographical control because of the following reasons:

(i) Increased research output,
(ii) Increased research activities, and
(iii) More journals.

More than 50 per cent of the respondents have worked for bibliographical control in their own way. So far only manually produced bibliographical tools are in vogue and computerized social science information is yet to become the order of the day. In order to provide expeditious bibliographical and information services to social science scholars, ICSSR should launch "National Information System for Social Sciences" for an effective bibliographical control.

3. Documentation Activities in Social Sciences

Social sciences in India were a neglected sector till Independence. After Independence, the need for documentation services was realized. The Indian Council of Social Science Research (ICSSR) was established in 1969 and its SSDC (now NASSDOC) was started in 1970. Prior to this, documentation used to be a local activity. NASSDOC is doing a commendable job by providing documentation services to the social science community through its publications and activities. Study of documentation activities in the field of social sciences reveals that the various institutions engaged in such activities should work in coordination so as to avoid duplication of effort. This would help in reducing time lag and making their services uptodate and comprehensive. But due to some problems which are quite peculiar to the Indian situation most of the documentation activities do not continue for long. As a result of documentation activities, bibliographical tools are produced which proves the need for the cherished goal of achieving bibliographical control in social sciences. But unfortunately Indian bibliographical tools have a high mortality rate and incredibly high birth rate which is suicidal for the healthy growth of bibliographical control.

4. Major Bibliographical Tools

Emergence of secondary sources in social sciences was late in comparison to that of science and technology. Development of information services in social sciences does not reflect a planned and even growth. Low use of bibliographical tools is because of lack of awareness, and secondly, as pointed out by Bath Study as well as in the present survey (results recorded in Chapter 5) is that these bibliographical tools are not user-oriented. Social science research institutions and universities have emerged as the important centre of social science research after Independence. Social science scholars heavily depend upon the resources of the university libraries. Hence such libraries have taken lead in producing tools for bibliographical control. This activity got an impetus with the emergence of ICSSR/NASSDOC in the form of Union Catalogues, Indexes, Subject Bibliographies, etc. The major bibliographical tools have common problems like finance, manpower, technology, duplication, time lag and lack of awareness. Some problems are directly related to social sciences — lack of abstracting and citation machinery, grey literature, bibliographical control of retrospective literature, etc. However, underuse of Indian bibliographical tools is still surprising.

5. Information Needs and Expectations of Social Science Scholars and Researchers

Another survey reveals that majority of the scholars are in the age group of below 30, and next to them is the age group of 30–40. It shows that social sciences are quite popular among young scholars. Majority of the scholars are working either for M.Phil. or Ph.D. degree followed by the category of lecturers and readers. Further, majority of the scholars (51%) say bibliographical control is a necessity, but as many as 32 per cent scholars saying "no" is surprising. It seems that a few of them have failed to understand what bibliographical control means as 17 per cent scholars clearly accept that they are unaware of the concept of bibliographical control. The survey has revealed that subject bibliographies are heavily used by social science scholars. Next in order of use of bibliographical tools are abstracts, indexes and union catalogues. Social science scholars consult bibliographical tools mainly for doing research, writing papers and writing theses and dissertations. Scholars have suggested improvement in the arrangement of bibliographical tools. Some of them have suggested that bibliographical tools should be the latest and uptodate. Some scholars felt that they need the help of either librarian or reference librarian to be familiar with the use of bibliographical resources. Some felt that bibliographical tools should be computerized. Few even suggested that subject bibliography should be made available on demand in view of the growing needs of social science scholars.

6. Suggestion for Establishing National Information System for Social Sciences

In India social science institutions and universities have been generating social science information since Independence. A survey of social science institutions has revealed that social science research is gaining ground as is evident from the increasing financial support of the Government, ICSSR, UGC, etc. The survey further revealed that a high percentage of institutions have been feeling the need of bibliographical control.

Information services in social sciences do not reflect a planned and even growth. Low use of bibliographical tools is primarily because of lack of awareness, and secondly these are not user-oriented. Some common problems are: finance, manpower, technology, duplication, time lag and lack of awareness. Another survey revealed that a majority of social science scholars wanted bibliographical control. It further revealed that subject bibliographies are heavily used tools followed by abstracts, indexes and union catalogues in order of priority.

It is to be concluded that the bibliographical control of social science literature could be effective and achieved only through launching a "National Information System for Social Sciences". Hence it is suggested that a national information system should be immediately established by ICSSR. The information system will then coordinate the activities of existing institutions so that social science scholars receive the essential information relevant to their needs, which is the ultimate aim of bibliographical control.

APPENDICES

APPENDIX-A

Please return this complete questionnaire to Mr. S.D. Vyas, Assistant Librarian, American Studies Research Centre, Hyderabad-500 007.

QUESTIONNAIRE

A Survey of the Bibliographical Activities in Social Science Institutions in India

Name of the Institution ____________________

Year of Establishment ____________________

1. What disciplines or subjects are covered in your Institution/ Documentation centre? (Please tick)

   Anthropology, Commerce and Trade, Economics, Education, Geography, History, Industrial Psychology, Industrial Relations, International Relations, Law, Management Political Science, Psychology, Public Administration, Social Work, Sociology, Statistics, (if any other, please specify)

2. What is your total collection? Please mention the details as under:
   Books
   Bound Periodicals
   Current Periodicals
   Microforms
   Others (Please specify)

3. Who makes use of your resources? Please mention the number against concerned category
   Faculty Members

Research Scholars
Post Graduate Students
Administrative Staff
Others (Please specify)

4. Please tick the services offered by your Library/Documentation centre.
Lending Service, Reference/Reader's Advisory Service, Inter-Library Loan Service, Reprographic Service, Bibliographical Service, Any other (Please specify)

5. Do you feel any necessity for bibliographical control in the field of social sciences?

Yes/No

5.1 If yes, what has made it necessary? (Please tick)
Increased Research Activity, Increased Research Out put, More Journals, More Grants Available, Interest of the Government, Interest of Private Organisations/Commercial Houses

6. Have you ever attempted for bibliographical control? Yes/No

6.1 If yes, please mention in what way?
BY Compiling/Publishing Union Catalogue
BY Compiling/Publishing Subject Bibliographies
BY Bringing out Indexing Journal
BY Bringing out Abstracting Journal
BY Publishing Translations
In any other way (Please mention)

7. Please enlist the bibliographical publications of your institution :

Title	No. of Copies Published/ Circulated	Year of Publication of First Issue	Whether Continuing (Please mention the year of the current volume)

8. What kind of documents are included in your bibliographical publications? (Please tick)
Books, Conference, Proceedings, Government Publications, Newspapers, Pamphlets, Periodicals and Serials Reports, Theses and Dissertations, Unpublished Documents, Any other publications (Please specify)

9. Do you issue any checklist inviting suggestions from subscribers/users as to what improvements they would like to have as regards to format, contents and other features in your bibliographical service? Yes/No

9.1 If yes, at what intervals?

10. Are your using computer in bringing out bibliographical tools?

Yes/No

11. What are the problems generally faced in the publications of bibliographical tools? (Please tick)
Finance, Staff, Equipment, Cooperation from Staff/Authorities, Poor Response from Users/Subscribers, Any other. (Please mention)

12. Are you getting financial assistance from the government/other agency for bringing out your bibliographical publication (s)?

Yes/No

12.1 If yes, how much and from what source? (Please mention)

13. Are you familiar with the working and services of Social Science Documentation Centre (SSDC), New Delhi? Yes/No

13.1 If yes, have you ever made use of the services of SSDC? (Please tick). Frequently, Seldom, Never

13.2 If frequently, what kind of help you sought from SSDC? (Please mention)

14. Do you feel SSDC disseminates all the desired information for social science research? Yes/No

15. What is your general opinion about the bibliographical control of social science literature in India?

Satisfactory/Not Satisfactory

16. Have you used the bibliographical services from any other institution? Yes/No

16. If yes, please mention the names of such institutions

17. What are your perceptions and image of Indian Council of Social Science Research (ICSSR) and its documentation centre (SSDC)?

18. Any comments

APPENDIX-B

QUESTIONNAIRE

Information Needs and Expectations of Social Science Scholars and Researchers : A Survey

1. Name ____________________

2. Age group (Please tick) Below 30
   30-40
   41-50
   51-60
   Above 60

3. Qualifications (Please tick) M.A.
   M.Phil
   Ph.D.
   D.Litt.

4. Designation ____________________

5. Main fields of interest (Please mention subjects in order of priority)
   ____
   ____
   ____
   ____
   ____
   ____

6. Do you feel that there is a need to have a control of information explosion?
   Yes
   No
   Don't Know

6.1 Which of the following bibliographical sources do you use and the number of times used during one year?

	No. of times
(a) Abstracting Journals	☐
(b) Documentation List received from outside organization	☐
(c) Indexing Journals	☐
(d) Local Documentation List	☐
(e) Subject Bibliographies	☐
(f) Union Catalogue of Serials and Journals	☐

6.2 To what extent do you use the available bibliographical services ? (Please tick)

Regularly
Most often
Usually
Occasionally
Not at all

6.3 Have you been using the following bibliographical sources? If yes, please give order of merit by ticking 1,2,3, etc.

(a) *Accession List : South Asia*
(b) *Artha Suchi*
(c) *Documentation on Asia*
(d) *Guide to Indian Periodical Literature*
(e) *Index India*
(f) *Indian National Bibliography*
(g) *Suchika*

6.4 Any other bibliographical sources used by you? (Please mention the names)

6.5 In what connections are you using the bibliographical sources?

For Teaching
Doing Research

Writing Paper,
Writing Book,
Writing Report
Dissertation and Thesis, for presenting a paper in a seminar/conference/workshop
Guiding research
Any other purpose

6.6 How do you find the arrangement of the bibliographical sources?

Helpful
Helpful, but can be improved
Not helpful
Cannot say

6.7 Indicate how far these sources meet your Information needs?

Comprehensive
Limited
Cannot say

6.8 Whether the bibliographical sources used by you are uptodate and meet your requirements?

Yes
No
Cannot say

7. Please mention your valuable suggestions for the improvement of existing bibliographical sources.

8.1 Can you indicate the best bibliographical tool (any bibliography, index, abstract, etc.) of your subject?

8.2 In your opinion which are the best libraries where you find research material?

8.3 How many hours in a week do you spend in your library?

8.4 Any other Comments

9. Any suggestions.

Signature

Institution

APPENDIX-C

List of Social Science Institutions and Higher Education Libraries.

(* Institutions which have filled in the Questionnaire.)

1.* A.N. Sinha Institute of Social Studies, Patna.
2.* Administrative Staff College of India, Hyderabad.
3.* Agricultural Economic Research Centre, University of Delhi, Delhi.
4. Aligarh Muslim University Library, Aligarh.
5. All India Institute of Local Self-government, Bombay.
6. All India Management Association, Delhi.
7. Allahabad University Library, Allahabad.
8.* American Studies Research Centre, Hyderabad.
9.* Anthropological Survey of India, Calcutta.
10. Archaeological Survey of India, Delhi.
11. Asiatic Society of Bengal, Calcutta.
12.* Asiatic Society of Bombay, Bombay.
13. Association of Indian Universities, Delhi.
14. B.M. Institute of Mental Health, Ahmedabad.
15. Banaras Hindu University Library, Varanasi.
16. Bangalore University Library, Bangalore.
17.* Bhandarkar Oriental Research Institute, Pune.
18.* Bharat Itihas Samshodhak Mandal, Pune.
19. Bombay University Library, Bombay.
20.* Calcutta University Library, Calcutta.
21. Calicut University Library, Calicut.
22.* Central Arid Zone Research Institute, Jodhpur.
23. Central Institute of Education, Delhi.
24.* Central Institute of English and Foreign Languages, Hyderabad.
25.* Central Secretariat Library, Delhi.
26. Central Statistical Organization, Ministry of Planning, Delhi.
27. Centre for Development Studies, Trivandrum.
28.* Centre for Economic and Social Studies, Secundarabad.
29.* Centre for Policy Research, Delhi.

30.* Centre for Research in Rural and Industrial Development Chandigarh.
31. Centre for social Studies, South Gujarat University, Surat.
32.* Centre for Studies in Social Sciences, Calcutta.
33.* Centre for the Study of Developing Societies, Delhi.
34. Council for Social Development, Delhi.
35.* Council for Social Development, Hyderabad.
36. Directorate of Psychological Research, Ministry of Defence, Delhi.
37. Documentation Research and Training Centre, Bangalore.
38. Delhi Library Association, Delhi.
39.* Department of Social Work Library, University of Delhi, Delhi.
40. Economic and Statistical Organisation, Chandigarh.
41. Economic Development and Department of Statistics, Reserve Bank India, Bombay.
42. Film and Television Institute of India, Pune.
43. G.B. Pant Institute of Social Studies, Allahabad.
44. Institute of Gandhian Studies, Varanasi.
45.* Gauhati University Library, Gauhati.
46. Gandhigram Institute of Rural Health and Family Planning Gandhigram, Tamilnadu.
47. Geographical Society of India, Calcutta.
48.* Giri Institute of Development Studies, Lucknow.
49.* Gokhale Institute of Politics and Economics, Pune.
50.* Gokhale Institute of Public Affairs, Bangalore.
51. Gorakhpur University Library, Gorakhpur.
52. Gujarat Research Society, Bombay.
53.* Gujarat University Library, Ahmedabad.
54.* Guru Nanak Dev University Library, Amritsar.
55.* H.C.M. State Institute of Public Administration, Jaipur.
56. Heras Institute of Indian History and Culture, Bombay.
57. Himachal Pradesh University Library, Shimla.
58.* India International Centre, Delhi.
59. Indian Council for Social Science Research Regional Centre, Bombay.
60. Indian Council for Social Science Research Regional Centre, Calcutta.
61.* Indian Council for Social Science Research Regional

Centre, Chandigarh.

62. Indian Council for Social Science Research Regional Centre, Delhi.
63.* Indian Council for Social Science Research Regional Centre, Hyderabad.
64. Indian Council for Social Science Research Regional Centre, Shillong.
65.* Indian Association of Special Libraries & Information Centre, Calcutta.
66. Indian Bibliographic Bureau, Delhi.
67. Indian Council for Cultural Relations, Delhi.
68. Indian Council for World Affairs, Delhi.
69. Indian Documentation Service, Gurgaon.
70. Indian Econometric Society, Hyderabad.
71. Indian Economic Association, Bombay.
72. Indian Institute of Advance Studies, Shimla.
73. Indian Institute of Geography, Pune.
74. Indian Institute of Asian Studies, Bombay.
75. Indian Institute of Foreign Trade, Delhi.
76.* Indian Institute of Education, Pune.
77. Indian Institute of Management, Ahmedabad.
78.* Indian Institute of Management, Bangalore.
79. Indian Institute of Management, Calcutta.
80. Indian Institute of Mass Communication, Delhi.
81.* Indian Institute of Public Administration, Delhi.
82.* Indian Institute of Public Opinion, Delhi.
83. Indian Institute of Social Welfare and Business Management, Calcutta.
84. Indian Law Institute, Delhi.
85. Indian Library Association, Delhi.
86. Indian Management Association, Delhi.
87. Indian Political Science Association, Jodhpur.
88. Indian Psychological Association, Delhi.
89. Indian Social Institute, Delhi.
90. Indian Statistical Institute, Calcutta.
91. Indian Statistical Institute, Delhi.
92. Indore University Library, Indore.
93. Institute for Defence and Strategic Analysis, Delhi.
94.* Institute for Social and Economic Change, Bangalore.
95. Institute for Social Science and Research, Vellore.

96.* Institute of Applied Manpower Research, Delhi.
97. Institute of Constitutional and Parliamentary Studies, Delhi.
98.* Institute of Development Studies, Jaipur.
99.* Institute of Economic Growth, Delhi.
100.* Institute of Economic Research, Dharwar.
101.* Institute of Public Enterprise, Hyderabad.
102. Institute of Public Administration, Lucknow.
103.* International Institute of Population Studies. Bombay.
104. Jabalpur University Library, Jabalpur.
105.* Jawaharlal Nehru University Library, Delhi.
106. Jodhpur University Library, Jodhpur.
107.* Karnatak University Library, Dharwar.
108. Labour Bureau, Ministry of Labour, Delhi.
109. Linguistic Society of India, Pune.
110. Lucknow University Library, Lucknow.
111.* M.L. Sukhadia University Library, Udaipur.
112. Madras Institute of Development Studies, Madras.
113. Madras University Library, Madras.
114. Madurai Kamaraj University Library, Madurai.
115.* Management Development Institute, Delhi.
116.* Marathwada University Library, Aurangabad.
117. Mysore University Library, Mysore.
118. Nagpur University Library, Nagpur.
119. National Atlas Organization, Calcutta.
120. National Book Trust of India, Delhi.
121. National Centre for Science and Technology, Delhi.
122. National Council of Applied Economic Research, Delhi.
123. National Council of Educational Research and Training, Delhi.
124. National Geographical Society of India, Varanasi.
125.* National Institute of Educational Planning and Administration, Delhi.
126.* National Institute of Health and Family Welfare, Delhi.
127.* National Institute of Small Industry Extension Training, Hyderabad.
128.* National Institute of Mental Health and Neuro Sciences, Bangalore.
129.* National Institute of Nutrition, Hyderabad.
130.* National Institute of Rural Development, Hyderabad.
131. National Labour Institute, Delhi.

132. National Library, Calcutta.
133.* North Eastern Hill University Library, Shillong.
134. Nehru Memorial Museum and Library, Delhi.
135.* Osmania University Library, Hyderabad.
136. Panjab University Library, Chandigarh.
137.* Punjabi University Library, Patiala.
138. Planning Research and Action Institute, Lucknow.
139. Poona University Library, Pune.
140. Popular Prakashan, Bombay.
141. Prakasham Institute of Development Studies, Hyderabad.
142. Press Institute of India, Delhi.
143.* Rajasthan University Library, Jaipur.
144.* Ratan Tata Library, Delhi School of Economics, Delhi.
145.* SNDT University Library, Bombay.
146. Sardar Patel Institute of Economic and Social Research, Ahmedabad.
147. Saurashtra University Library, Rajkot.
148. School of Planning and Architecture, Delhi.
149. Shri Ram Centre for Industrial Relations and Human Resources, Delhi.
150. Shivaji University Library, Kolhapur.
151. Shri Venkateswara University Library, Tirupati.
152. Sterling Publishers, Delhi.
153. Survey of India, Hyderabad.
154.* Tata Energy Research Institute, Bombay.
155. Tata Institute of Social Sciences, Bombay.
156. Utkal University Library, Bhubaneshwar.
157.* Vaikunth Mehta National Institute of Cooperative Management, Pune.
158. Vidya Bhavan Rural Institute, Udaipur.
159. Vikram University Library, Ujjain.
160. Xavier Labour Relations Institute, Jamshedpur.

Note: See page 75 of 3rd Chapter.

BIBLIOGRAPHY

(A) **Books**

Adisheshiah, Malcolm. *Social Sciences in India.* 2 Vols. Delhi. ICSSR. n.d.

Agrawal, S.P. *Development of Documentation in India: Social Science Information*, Delhi, Concept, 1989.

Agrawal, S.P. *Social Science Information and Documentation Search for Relevance in India,* Delhi, Concept, 1987.

— *Library and Information Services in India : The Current Scenario*. New Delhi, Concept, 1987.

Altbach, Philip Geoffrey. *Publishing in India : An Analysis.* Delhi, Oxford, 1975.

Ashworth, Wilfred, ed. *Handbook of Special Librarianship and Information Work.* 3d. ed. London, Aslib. 1967.

Avicenni, Paul. Comp. *Bibliographical Services Throughout the World 1965-69.* Paris, Unesco, 1972.

Bath University. *Information Requirements of Researches in Social Sciences.* Bath, University of Bath, 1971. (INFROSS Research Report No.1)

Bath University. *Size, Growth and Composition of Social Science Literature.* Bath, University of Bath, 1975 (DISISS Research Reports. Series A. No. 2)

Beard, Charles A. *Nature of Social Sciences.* New York, Charles Scribner, 1934.

Bookstein, Abraham, Herman H. Fussler and Helen F. Schimierer, eds. *Prospects for Change in Bibliographic Control* : Proceedings of Thirty Eight Annual Conference of the Graduate Library School. November 8-9, 1976. Chicago, University of Chicago Press, 1977.

Brenni, Vito Joseph, ed. *Essays on Bibliography.* Metuchen, N.J., The Scarcrow Press, 1975.

Collison, Robert L. *Bibliographical Services Throughout the World 1950-1959.* Paris, Unesco, 1961.

Curti, Marle Eugene. *The Growth of American Thought,* 3d. ed. New York, Harper, 1964.

Davinson, D.E. *Bibliographic Control.* 2nd ed. London, Bingley, 1975.

FID. *Problems of Information Users' Needs.* 1973.

Freides, Thelma, *Literature and Bibliography of Social Sciences.* Los Angeles, Melville, 1973.

George, K.M. ed. *Indian Libraries : Trends and Perspectives.* Hyderabad, Orient Longmans, 1985.

Gidwani, N.N. *Comparature Librarianship : Essays in Honour of D.N. Marshall.* Delhi, Vikas, 1973.

Goode, Wilwam J. and Paul K. Hatt. *Methods in Social Research.* New York, Mcgraw Hill, 1952.

Gopal, M.H. *An Introduction to Research : Procedures in Social Sciences,* Bombay, Asia, 1964.

Guha, B. *Documentation and Information.* Calcutta, World Press, 1978.

Gupta, B.M. and Others ed. *Handbook of Libraries, and Archives and Information Centres in India,* Delhi, Information Industry Publication, 1984. 5 vols.

Gupta, Giri Raj., ed. *Contemporary India.* Delhi, Vikas, 1976.

Hale, B.M. *The Subject Bibliography of the Social Science and Humanities.* Oxford, Pergamon Press, 1970.

India. Lok Sabha. *Background to Evolving a National Information Policy.* 2nd. ed. Delhi, Government of India Press, 1987.

Institute of Economic Growth. *Relevance in Social Science Research : A Colloquium.* Delhi, Vikas, 1982.

Kaula, P.N. *National Library of India : A Critical Study.* Bombay, Somaiya, 1970.

Kesavan, B.S. *India's National Library,* Calcutta, National Library, 1961.

Kolby, Rober and Morris A. Geefend eds. *Access to the Literature of the Social Sciences and Humanities,* Flushing, N.Y. Queens College Press, 1974.

Krishan Kumar, *Research Libraries in the Developing Countries,* Delhi, Vikas, 1973.

Kumar, P.S.G. *Computerization of Indian Libraries,* Delhi, B.R. Publishing Corporation, 1987.

Linder, Le Roy Harold, *The Rise of Current Complete National Bibliography.* New York, Scarcrow Press, 1959.

Line, Maurice and Stephen Vickers. *Universal Availability of Publications : A Programme to Improve the National and International Provision and Supply of Publications.* IFLA Publications, 23, Munchen : K.G. Saur, 1983.

Loosjes, T.P. *On Documentation of Scientific Literature.* London, Butterworths, 1973.

Machlup, Fritz. *The Production and Distribution of Knowledge in the United States.* Princeton, N.J. Princeton University Press, 1962.

Mangla, P.B. ed. *Building Library Collections and National Policy for Library and Information Services.* Delhi, Indian Library Association, 30th All India Library Conference, Jaipur, 1985.

Mahendiratta, Pradeep R. *University Administration in India and the USA : A Comparative Study,* Delhi, Oxford IBH, 1984.

National Library and Raja Ram Mohan Roy Library Foundation. *Bibliographical Control in India : Working Papers.* A Seminar Held at Calcutta on 25th to 26th February 1984.

Needham, C.D. and E. Herman. eds. *Study of Subject Bibliography with Special Reference to the Social Sciences.*

Oleson, Alexandra and John Voss. *The Organization of Knowledge in Modern America,* 1860-1920. Baltimore, Johns Hopkins Univ. Press, 1979.

Penna, C.V. D.J. Foskett and P.H, Sewell. *National Library and Information Services : A Handbook for Planners,* London Butterworth, 1977.

Raben, J. and G. Marks eds. *Data bases in the Humanities and Social Sciences*, Amsterdam, North Holland, 1980.

Raichmann, Felix and Josephine M. Tharpe, with the Cooperation of Henriette Avram and Others. *Bibliographic Control of Microforms.* Westport, Conn., Greenwood, 1972.

Raju, K.A. and N.G. Satish. *Towards Understanding the Information : Needs of Development Scientists : A Case Study.* In Tenth Iaslic National Seminar, Kanpur, 1982.

Ranganathan, S.R. ed. *Documentation and Its Facets,* Bombay, Asia, 1963.

——. *Documentation : Genesis and Development,* Delhi, Vikas, 1973.

Rama Reddy, E. *Social Science Information : Some Indian Sources.* New Delhi, Affiliated East-West Press, 1985.

Roberts, N. ed. *Use of Social Sciences Literature.* London Butterworth, 1977.

Rosenberg, Paul. *The Urban Information Thesaurus : A Vocabulary for Social Documentation.* Westport, Greenwood, 1977.

Saha, J. *Special Libraries and Information Services in India and U.S.A.* Metuchen, N.J., Scarecrow Press, 1969.

Sharma, B.A.V., D. Ravindra Prasad and P. Satyanarayana, *Research Methods in Social Sciences.* New Delhi, Sterling (1985, c1983).

Sharma, C.D. *Use of Libraries : A Guide to Better use of Libraries and Their Resources.* New Delhi, Metropolitan, 1978.

Sharma, C.D. and Kailash Vyas. *Developing Horizons in Library and Information Science.* Jaipur, Printwell, 1983 2 Vols.

Shera, Jesse H. *Libraries and the Organization of Knowledge.* Hamden, Conn. Archon Books, 1965.

Shera, Jesse H. and Margaret E. Egan. *Bibliographic Organization.* Chicago, University of Chicago Press, 1950.

Seminar on Towards the Evolution of Information System for National Development. Organized by Insdoc, 8-9 December 1975.

Sogani, Kamal Chand and Vijai Narayan eds. *Master Motilal Sanmati Pustakalaya Souvenir,* Jaipur, Shri Sanmati Pustakalaya Trust, 1972.

Stokes, Roy. *Bibliographical Control and Service.* London, Andre Deutsch, 1965.

Stokes, Roy. *Function of Bibliography,* 2nd ed. Lexington Books, 1983.

Unesco. *ASCOBIC Manual on Bibliographic Control in Africa,* Prepared by Salion M'Baye. Paris, UNESCO; 1981.

Unesco. *Manual on Bibliographic Control.* Compiled by the IFLA International Office for UBC; 1983.

Unesco, *Guide to National Bibliographic Centres.* 3d. ed. Paris, UNESCO.

Unesco. *UNISIST : Guidelines on the Conduct of a National Inventory of Scientific and Technological Information and Documentation Facilities,* Paris, Unesco, 1975.

Unesco. *UNISIST : Synopsis of the Feasibility Study on a World Science Information System,* Paris, UNESCO, 1971.

Unesco/Library of Congress Bibliographical Survey; *Bibliographical Services: Their Present Stage and Possibilities.* Washington, 1950.

Vander Laan, A. and A.A. Winters, *The Use of Information in a Changing World.* Amesterdam, North-Holland, 1984.

Watson, Geogre. *The Literacy Thesis : A Guide to Research.* London, Longman, 1970.

White, Carl M. *Sources of Information in the Social Sciences : A Guide to Literature.* 3d. ed. Chicago, American Library Association, 1983.

Wilson, Patrick. *Two Kinds of Power : An Essay on Bibliographic Control.* Serkeley, University of California Press, 1968.

Wilson, T.C. and J. Stephenson. *Dissemination of Information.* 2d. ed. Hamden, CT. Shoe String, 1969.

Young, Heartsill. *The ALA Glossary of Library and Information Science.* Chicago, American Library Association, 1983.

(B) Journal Articles

Abrera, J.B. "Bibliographic Structure Possibility Set: A Quantitative Approach for Identifying Users' Bibliographic Information Needs." *Library Resources and Technical Service,* 26 (January 82), 21-36.

Adam, Ralph. "Putting the Minds of Social Scientist Together : Towards a World Social Science Information System." *International Social Science Journal,* 27, 3 (1975), 519-31.

Agrawal, S.P. "Social Science Research Institutions in India." *CLS Observer,* 2, 3-4 (July-Oct. 1985), 7-14.

——., "Asia-Pacific Information Network in Social Science." *India Book Industry,* 34, 4 (July 1986), 13-14.

——., "Indian Social Science Periodicals : Current Status." *Library Herald,* 22, 1 (April 1983), 30-46.

——., "Social Science Documentation Centre." *Library Herald,* 21, 1-2 (April 1982 September 1982), 46-53.

Alston, Ruth. "Hunger for the Poor? Some Observations on Information Provisions in India." *Journals of Information Science,* 6 (1983) 115-122.

Altbach, Philip G. "Knowledge Enigma : Copyright in the Third World." *Economic and Political Weekly,* 31, 37 (13 September 1986) 1643-1650.

Anderson, Dorothy. "The IFLA Programme of Universal Bibliographical Control." *Journal of Academic Librarianship,* 9, 2 (May 1983), 71-72.

——., "An International Framework for National Bibliographic Development : Achievement and Challenges." *Library Resources & Technical Services,* 30, 1 (Jan/March 1986), 13-22.

——. "Waiting for Technology : An Overview of Bibliographical Services in the Third World." *IFLA Journal,* 9, 4 (1983) 285-295.

Appel, John, S. and Gurr Ted. "Bibliographical Needs of Social and Behaviour Scientists." *American Behaviour Science,* 7 (June 1964) 51-54.

Ashworth, Wilfred. "Information Explosion," *Library Association Record,* 76 (April 1974), 63.

Balasubramaniam, A.S. "Publish and Perish." *Hindustan Times,* (11th December 1977).

Beandiques, Marcelli. "Retrospective Bibliographies in the Context of Universal Bibliographic Control." *IFLA Journal,* 9, 4 (1983) 309-316.

Bergen, Dan. "Bibliographic Organization in the Social Sciences." *Wilson Library Bulletin,* 40 (April, 1966) 751-58.

Black, John B. "Social Science Libraries and Documentation Centres in the North American Market Place." *International Forum on Information and Documentation,* 11, 1 (January 1986), 4-9.

Brittain, J.M. and S.A. Roberts. "Information Sources in the Social Sciences : Development and Rationalization". *International Social Science Journal,* 28, 4 (1976), 835-40.

Broadus, Robert N. "The Literature of Social Sciences. A Survey of Citation Studies." *International Social Science Journal,* 23, 2 (1971), 236-43.

Brock, Cligton, "Political Science." *Library Trends,* 15, 4 (April 1967). (Special Issue on "Bibliography").

Carter, Edward J. "UNESCO's Bibliographic Programs." *American Documentation.* 5 (January 1954), 1-7.

Case, M. "Scholarly Publishing in New Delhi." *Scholarly Publisher,* 12 (January 1981), 355-359.

Chaplin, A.H. "Basic Bibliographic Control." *Aslib Proceedings,* 27 (1975), 48-56.

Chitale, T.B. "Organization of Documentation Work in India." *Indian Librarian,* 25, 1 (June 1970), 25-46.

Coblans, Herbert, "Bibliographic Organization at the International Level." *Wilson Library Bulletin,* 40 (April 1966), 733-37.

Datta, Bhabatosh, "Social Science Research Universities and Autonomous Institutions." *Journal of Higher Education,* 6, 1-3 (1980-81), 15-24.

Dhawle, Anand S. and Amitabha Ghosh. "A Study of the Image of Indian Journal on Management and Social Sciences in the

International Academic Community." *Journal of Higher Education,* 4, 3 (Spring 1979), 313-26.

Earle, P. and B. Vickery. "Social Science Literature Use in the U.K. as Indicated by Citation." *Journal of Documentation,* 25 (1969), 123-41.

Egan, Margaret E. "Bibliographic Development in the Social Sciences." *American Documentation,* 2 (January 1951), 11-17.

Ferguson, A.W. "Bibliographical Control of Political Science Periodical Literature." *Teaching Political Science,* (7 July 1980), 439-64.

Fletchet, John. "Secondary Information Service in Economics." *International Social Science Journal,* 28, 3 (1973), 563-71.

Frieds, Thelma. "The State of Secondary Access Services : Social Sciences." *Journal of the American Society for Information Society,* 33, 3 (May 1982), 157-61.

Garfield, Eugene. "Mapping Science in the Third World." *Current Contents,* 5, 33 (15 August 1983), 6-15.

——., "Mapping Science in the Third World." *Current Contents,* 5, 34 (22 October 1983), 5-16.

Garg, B.S. "Natural Sciences and Social Sciences : A Comparative Study." *Library Herald,* 16, 1-2 (April-Sept. 1974), 48-62.

Gera, J.C. "Social Science Citation Index : Its Efficacy for Information Retrieval." *Library Herald,* 15, 3-4 (Oct. 1973 — March 1974), 132-145.

Ghai, O.P. "Indian Publishing : Yesterday, Today and Tomorrow, *Indian Book Industry,* 35, 6 (September 1986), 145-150.

Gibson, M.J. "United States of America National Bibliographical and Abstracting Services and Related Activities in 1976." *RQ,* 17, (Winter 1977), 101-127.

Girja Kumar. "National Library of Calcutta : A Critical Review." *Iaslic Bulletin,* 17, 2 & 3 (June & September 1974), 94 -

Girja Kumar and P.K. Jayaswal. "Social Science Periodicals in Libraries." *Library Herald,* 21, 1-2, (April-Sept. 1982), 1-27.

Girja Kumar and Others. "Note on the Proposed Establishment of the Indian National Social Science Documentation Centre." *Times Fellowship,* 3-4 (1966-67), 179-188.

Goil, N.K. "National Information System." *Library Herald* 16, 1-2 (April-Sept. 1974), 73-77.

——., "Need for a Social Science Information System : Guidelines for a Model for India." *Library Herald,* 17, 1-4 (April 1975 — March 1979), 70-93.

Gopal, M.H. "Criteria for Assessing Current Research in Social Sciences in India Universities." *Indian Economic Journal,* 32, 4 (April 75 – March 79), 70-93.

Gordon, Michael D. "Citation Ranking Versus Subjective Evaluation in the Determination of Journal Hierarchies in the Social Sciences." *Journal of the American Society for Information Sciences,* 33, 1 (January 1982), 55-57.

Gorman, G.E. and Maureen Mahoney. "Current National Bibliographies in Developing Countries of the Commonwealth." *Libri,* 33, 3 (September 1983), 177-189.

Grore, Pierce S. "Standards for the Bibliographic Control Non-print Media." *Bowkar Annual,* (1972), 203-06.

Guha, B. "The Origin, Objectives and Programmes of UNISIST." *Library Herald,* 16, 1-2 (April-Sept. 1974), 63-72.

——. "Bibliographical Tools in Sociology." *Library Herald.* 16, 1-2 (April-Sept. 1974), 63-72.

Gupta, Rama and Avinash Khurana. "Bibliographical Tools in Sociology, an Evaluation." *Library Herald,* 16, 3 (Oct. 74 — March, 75), 159-191.

Guttsman, W.L. "The Literature of the Social Science and Provision for Research in Them." *Journal of Documentation,* 22, 3 (September, 1966), 184-94.

Hussain, S. "Universal Availability of Publications : Problems and Prospects." *Iaslic Bulletin,* 28, (1983).

"IFLA Stresses Worldwide Bibliographic Control." *American Libraries,* 4 (1973), 603.

John, V.V. "Catalyst to Scholarship Catching up on Documentation" *Times of India,* Bombay (11th July 1969).

Johnson, D.C. "Bibliographical Heritage of the British Influenced Areas of Southern Asia." *Libri,* 23, 2 (1973), 109-123.

Joshi, P.C. "Founders of Lucknow School and their Legacy : Radhakamal Mukherji and D.P. Mukherji, Some Reflections." *Economic and Political Weekly,* 21-23 (August 16, 1986), 1455-1469.

——. "Social Science Research and the Institutes." *Journal of Higher Education,* 8, 2 (Autumn 1982), 155-165.

Kalia, D.R. "Library Services in India." *Bowkar Annual*, (1981), 377-383.

Kaltwasser, Frenz G. "The Quest for Universal Bibliographical Control." *Wilson Library Bulletin,* 46 (June 1972), 894-901.

Kapur, Shabad, etc. "Survey of Periodicals of Indian University Libraries." *Herald of Library Science,* 20, 3-4 (July-October 1981), 201-06.

Kaula, P.N. and S.N. Singh. "Characteristics of Information Material : A Bibliographic Investigation in the Field of Social Sciences in India." *Herald of Library Science,* 19, 3-4 (October 1980), 288-97.

Kesavan, B.S. "Documentation in India." *Library Trends,* 17, 3 (1969), 231-244.

——. "The Indian National Library," *Library World,* 63 (March 1982), 216-221.

Ketkar, N.M. "Indian Council of Social Science Research and Documentation." *ILA Bulletin,* 7,3 (July-September, 1971), 71-75.

Krishan Kumar, "Users' Survey of the Sapru House Library." *Library Herald,* 12, 4 (January 1971), 228-263.

Kumar, B.K. "A Comment on Bibliographical Control of Indian Publications in English." *ILA Bulletin,* 18, 3-4 (October 1982–March 1983), 59-61.

Kumar, R.P. "Origin and Development of Periodicals in English in India Before Independence." *International Library Review,* 16 (April 1984), 183-221.

Lancaster, F.W., and J.M. Neway. "Future of Indexing and Abstracting Services." *Journal of American Society of Information Science,* 33 (1982), 183-9.

Larson, Knud. "National Bibliographical Services." *Unesco Bulletin of Libraries,* 15, 6 (November-December 1961), 301-309.

Line, Maurice B. "The Information Uses and Needs of Social Scientists : An Overview of INFROSS." *Aslib Proceedings,* 23, (8 August 1971), 412-434.

——. "Universal Availability of Publications." *IFLA Journal,* 7, 2 (1980), 166-171.

——. "Universal Availability of Publications." *Journal of Academic Librarianship,* 9, 2 (March 1983), 73.

Madan, T.N. "For a Sociology of India." *Contributions to Indian Sociology* (New Series), 15, 1-2 (1981), 405-421.

Mangla, P.B. "Concept of National Library." *Journal of Library and Information Science,* 3 (1978), 12-13.

Mathew, R.M. "Marketing of Social Science Information and Documentation : The Challenge of the Third World Countries with Special Reference to India." *International Forum on Information and Documentation,* 11, 1 (1986), 19.

Moel, Peter, "Should the Third World Have Information Technology." *IFLA Journal,* 9, 4 (1983), 296-308.

Moore, Nicholas L. "Library Periodicals from Developing Countries, Coverage by Major Abstracting and Indexing Services." *Journal of Librarianship,* 13-1 (January 1981), 37-45.

Namjoshi, M.V. "Priorities in Social Science Research." *New Quest,* (March-April 1978), 83-93.

Neeley, James D. "The Management and Social Science Literature : An Interdisciplinary Cross-citation Analysis." *Journal of American Society for Information Science,* 32-3 (May 1981), 217-23.

Parekh, Harsha, "Social Science Literature, Size, Use Patterns and Bibliographical Services." *Economic and Political Weekly,* 17-35 (August 28, 1982), 1423-28.

Patterson, M.L.P. "Bibliographical Controls for South Asia." *Library Quarterly,* 4, 2 (April 1971), 95.

Raj, K.N. "Social Scientists and Social Revolution." *Mainstream,* (February 26, 1983), 9-10, 12.

Salman, L. "Information Needs of the Developing Countries : Analysis Case-Studies." *Unesco Journal of Information Science,* 3 (October 1981), 241-8.

Surdesai, D.B. "Social Science Data Archives : Emergence a New Institutions in India." *Artha Vijnana,* 15, 4 (December 1973), 383-90.

Scholberg, Henry. "The Indian National Bibliography (INB) : Its Origin, History and Accomplishments," *ILA Bulletin,* 14 (1978), 64-69.

Sethi, A.R. "Bibliographical Control of Indian Publications in English : An Assessment." *ILA Bulletin.* 18, 1-2 (April-Sept. 1982), 14-23.

—. "Bibliographical Control of Indian Publications in English." *ILA Bulletin,* 18, 1-2 (April-Sept, 1987), 14-23.

—. "Comments on Bibliographical Control of Indian Publications in India." A Reply *ILA Bulletin* 19, 4 (January-March, 1984), 149-150.

Sharma, C.L. "Development of the Social Sciences since 17th Century." *Libra.* 18 & 19 (1980-81 & 1981-82), 69-78.

Sharma, Jagdish, S. "India's Contribution in the Field of Bibliography." *Library Herald.* 16, 3 & 4 (Oct. 74–March 75), 87-138.

Skeleton, Barbara. "Scientists and Social Scientists as Information Users : A Comparison of Results of Science Users Studies with the Investigation into Information Requirements of the Social Sciences." *Journal of Librarianship.* 5, 2 (April 1973), 138-156.

Soper, Ellen and F. Benjamin. "Trends in Bibliographical Control : International Issues." *Library Trends.* 25, 3 (January 1977), 561-721.

Sriniwas, M.N. "Development of Sociology in India : An Overview." *Economic and Political Weekly,* 22, 4 (24 January 1987), 135-138.

Stevens, R.F. "The Study of the Research Use of Libraries. *Library Quarterly,* 26, 1, (1956), 41-51.

Stone, Sue. "Progress in Documentation : Humanities and Scholars; Information Needs and Uses." *Journal of Documentation.* 38, 4 (December 1982), 293-313.

Subrahmaniam, T.A. "Study of Information Seeking Behaviour of Doctoral Candidates in Social Sciences." *Herald of Library Science.* 22, 3-4 (January-October 1983), 189-200.

Vashistha, C.P. "Bibliographical Control of Newspaper Contents in India." *Library Herald.* (April 75 — March 76), 105-116.

Ved Bhushan and S.D.Vyas. "Social Science Information System," *Herald of Library Science.* 13, 2 (April 1974), 116-123.

Vishwanathan, C.G. "What Ails the Indian National Bibliography," *Library Association Record,* 81 (January 1979), 333.

Vyas, S.D. and D. Sudarsana Reddy. Users' Survey of the American Studies Research Centre (ASRC) Hyderabad with a special reference to use of Periodicals : A User Study. *ILA Bulletin,* 19, 1-3 (1983) 61-84.

Wood, D.N. and C.N. Bower. "The Use of Social Science Literature." *Journal of Documentation.* 25, 2 (June 1969), 69.

Weiner, Myron. "Social Science Research and Public Policy in India," *Economic and Political Weekly,* 14, 37 (15 Sept. 1979), 1579-87.

—. "Social Science Research and Public Policy in India," *Economic and Political Weekly,* 14, 38 (22 Sept, 1979), 1622-28.

(C) **ICSSR Surveys of Research**

Rao, M.S.A. *ICSSR Survey in Sociology and Social Anthropology.* A Project Sponsored by the ICSSR. Bombay, Popular Prakashan, 1974.

Lakdawala, D.T. *ICSSR : A Survey of Research in Economic,* Bombay, Allied, 1977.

Desai, P.B. *A Survey of Research in Demography* : A Project Sponsored by the ICSSR. Bombay, Popular Prakashan, 1975.

ICSSR. *A Survey of Research in Political Science,* New Delhi, Allied, 1979.

ICSSR. *A Survey of Research in Public Administration,* Bombay, Allied, 1973.

ICSSR. *A Survey of Research in Management,* Delhi, Vikas, 1973.

Mitra, S.K. *Psychological Research in India.* A Project Sponsored by the ICSSR. Bombay, Popular Prakashan, 1972.

Raza, Moonis. *Geography as a Social Science.* A Project Sponsored by the ICSSR. Bombay, Popular Prakashan, 1977.

(D) **ICSSR, UGC and Government Reports**

ICSSR. *Indian Council of Social Science Research : Annual Report, 1970-71.*

ICSSR. *Indian Council of Social Science Research : Annual Report, 1984-85.*

ICSSR Review Committee on Social Sciences in India. *Retrospective and Prospective : A Report.* New Delhi, ICSSR, 1978.

ICSSR. *Report of the Committee to Prepare Draft Plan for Development of Social Science Information System in the Country During the Next Plan Period,* Delhi, ICSSR, n.d. (Mimeographed)

Press in India, 1980 : Twenty Fourth Report of the Registrar General of Newspaper for India Under the Press and Registration of Books Act. 2 Pts. New Delhi, Ministry of Information and Broadcasting, 1981.

University Grants Commission, *University and College Libraries : Containing the Report of the Library Committee of the University Grants Commission and the Proceedings of the Seminar on From Publisher to Reader.* March 4-7, 1959, New Delhi, 1965.

(E) Theses and Dissertations

Kumar, R.P. *Research Periodicals of Colonial India* 1780-1947. Delhi, Academic Publications, 1985. (Published Ph.D. Thesis).

Kumar, P.S.C. *Computerization of Indian Libraries,* Delhi : B.R. Publishing Corporation. 1987 (Published Ph.D. Thesis).

Linder, Le Roy Harold. *Rise of Current Complete National Bibliography.* New York, Scarecrow, 1959. (Published Ph.D. Thesis).

Ojha, Dinesh. *Technology Transfer of Centre for Arid Zone and Semi Arid Zone Research : A Critical Study,* 1987, Jaipur, University of Rajasthan. (Ph.D. Thesis).

Satish Chander. *To Prepare a Manual of Different Set of Operations Involved in the Preparation Involved in the Preparation of "Guide to Indian Periodical Literature" : Social Sciences and Humanities.* 1973. Delhi. (M. Lib.Sc Dissertation).

Sharma, Chandra Dhar. *Libraries and Librarianship in Modern India, 1857-1972.* 1981. Varanasi, Banaras Hindu University (Ph.D. Thesis).

Shambhu Narayan Singh. *Use of Social Science Literature in India 1984.* Varanasi, Banaras Hindu University. (Ph.D. Thesis).

Sohanlal, *Growth of Periodical Literature in the Field of Sociology in India During Last Ten Years.* 1979. Delhi (M. Lib.Sc. Dissertation).

Suri, Balraj Kumar. *Bibliography of Selected Reference Tools on Economic Published in India,* Delhi, 1971. (M. Lib.Sc. Dissertation).

Talukdar, Ajit Kumar. *Growth and Development of Periodical Literature in India in the Field of Economics with Reference to Post Independence Period*. 1974, Delhi. (M. Lib. Sc. Dissertation).

Wanchoo, Asha. *Growth and Development of Periodical Literature in Law in India.* 1976, Delhi (M. Lib. Sc. Dissertation).

(F) Bibliographies

Inter University Board of India, New Delhi. *Social Sciences : A Bibliography of Doctoral Dissertations Accepted by Indian Universities, 1857-1970.* Delhi, 1974.

Mohinder Singh. *State Governments Publication in India, 1947-1982.* Delhi, Academic Publications, 1985.

Pathak, Vijay and L.S. Ramaiah, *Bibliography of Research in Library and Information Science in India,* Gurgaon, Indian Documentation Service. 1986

Skagen, Kibi, Comp. *Bibliographical Resources About India: An Annotated List of English-Language Reference Works Published in India, 1965-70,* Washington, D.C. Department of Health Education, U.S. Government Printing Office, 1972.

(G) Directories

Gidwani, N.N., and Navlani, K. *Indian Periodicals : An Annotated Guide.* Jaipur, Rajasthan University Press, 1969.

Joginder Singh and A.R. Sethi, *Indian Library Directory,* 4th ed. Delhi, Indian Library Association, 1985.

Mohinder Singh. *Learned Societies and Institutions in India : Activities and Publications Including Over 4000 Research Oriented Titles.* Delhi, Metropolitan, 1985.

(H) Indexes

Bibliographia Asiatica : A Monthly Documentation List on Asia of Material in English. Calcutta, K.K. Roy, 1968.

Dissertation Abstract International, Ann Arbor, Mich. University Microfilms.

Documentation Indian National Affairs, Abstracts and Index, Chandigarh, Gian Publishers, 1986.

Documentation on Asia. Delhi, Vikas.

Guide to Indian Periodical Literature. 1986. *Journal Index List.* Gurgaon, Indian Documentation Service, 1986.

Index India. 1984. *Journal Index List.* Jaipur, Rajasthan University Library. 1984.

Indian National Bibliography. Calcutta, Central Reference Library.

Library Literature. New York, H.W. Wilson.

INDEX

CICIL LIST

CONCEPTS IN COMMUNICATION, INFORMATICS & LIBRARIANSHIP

(CICIL)

General Editor: **S.P. AGRAWAL**

CICIL-1 Development of Library Services in India: Social Science Information
S.P. Agrawal Rs. 150

CICIL-2 Development of Documentation in India: Social Science Information
S.P. Agrawal Rs. 250

CICIL-3 UNESCO and Social Sciences: Retrospect and Prospect
S.P. Agrawal and J.C. Aggarwal Rs. 250

CICIL-4 INDIANA : A Bibliography of Bibliographical Sources
M.K. Jain Rs. 200

CICIL-5 Dimensions of Library and Information Science: Kaula Festschrift
V. Venkatappaiah (Eds.) Rs. 600

CICIL-6 Book Numbers: Some Indian Methods
M.P. Satija and S.P. Agrawal Rs. 100

CICIL-7 National Policy for University Libraries in India: Problem and Perspectives
N.B. Inamdar and L.S. Ramaiah (Ed.) Rs. 250

CICIL-8 Media Utilisation for the Development of Women and Children
B.S. Thakur and Binod C. Agrawal Rs. 150

CICIL-9 Terrorism: An Annotated Bibliography
Susheela Bhan (Ed.) Rs. 275

CICIL-10 Transnational Library Relations: The Indo-American Experience
M.B. Konnur Rs. 175

CICIL-11 Geography of Marketing and Commercial Activities in India (Documentation on Research Information)
R.S. Dixit Rs. 130

CICIL-12 Information India 1988: Global View
S.P. Agrawal and J.C. Aggarwal Rs. 200

CICIL-13 Women's Education in India: Historical Review, Present Status and Perspective Plan
S.P. Agrawal and J.C. Aggarwal Rs. 360

CICIL-14 Cultural Communication in India: Role and Impact of Phonograms
J.M. Ojha Rs. 220

CICIL-15 Second Historical Survey of Educational Development in India: Select Documents 1985-1989
S.P. Agrawal and J.C. Aggarwal Rs. 490

CICIL-16 Documentation Encyclopaedia of UNESCO and Education
J.C. Aggarwal and S.P. Agrawal Rs. 800 (set of 2 parts)

CICIL-17 Attitude Towards Information: A Study of Post-Graduate Teachers and Researchers in Social Sciences
N.G. Satish (in press)

CICIL-18 Librarianship and Bureaucratic Organisation: A Study in the Sociology of Library Profession in India
P.K. Jayaswal Rs. 175

CICIL-19 Literature Search
K.A. Isaac Rs. 150

CICIL-20 Child Education in India: Index to Scholarly Writings in Indian Educational Journals and Newspapers since independence
S.P. Agrawal and Naresh Kanta Rs. 100

CICIL-21 Lok Sabha and Vidhan Sabha Elections in India 1989 & 1990: Process and Results with Comparative Study of Manifestos
S.P. Agrawal and J.C. Aggarwal Rs. 250

CICIL-22 Islamic Studies in India: A Survey of Human, Institutional and Documentary Sources
Mohamed Taher Rs. 180

CICIL-23 Panchayati Raj: An Annotated Bibliography
N.B. Inamdar, N.G. Satish and Anil Takalkar 290

CICIL-24 Information India 1989-90: Global View
S.P. Agrawal and J.C. Aggarwal Rs. 500

CICIL-25 First Handbook of Psychological and Social Instruments
Udai Pareek and T. Venkateswara Rao Rs. 500

CICIL-26 Educational and Social Uplift of Backward Classes: At What Cost and How? Mandal Commission and After
S.P. Agrawal and J.C. Aggarwal Rs. 275

CICIL-27 Mass Media and New Horizons: Impact of TV & Video an Urban Milieu
H.R. Trivedi Rs. 180

CICIL-28 Indian Writings on Education : An Indicator to Indian Educational Journals Grouped by Subject Deseriptors 1979 to 1986 (in two parts)
S.P. Agarwal Rs. 900 (per set)

CICIL-29 Nation in Crisis
S.P. Agrawal and J.C. Aggarwal Rs. 200

CICIL-30 Information India 1990-91: Global View
S.P. Agrawal and J.C. Aggarwal Rs. 500

CICIL-31 Development of University Libraries in India After Independence
O.P. Gupta Rs. 270

CICIL-32 Handbook on Child : With Historical Background
Pramila Pandit Barooah Rs. 320

CICIL-33 Weaker Section in Indian Society : Undiscovered Past, Uncertain Present and Unpredictable Future Index to Writings in Indian Scholarly Journals and 10 National Newspapers Classified under 1500 Descriptors 1886-1990
S.P. Agrawal and Rajeev Kumar Sharma Rs. 600

CICIL-34 Communication Informatics and Librarianship in India : An Introductory Guide to Publications Based on a Survey of Libraries in Capital of City India
S.P. Agrawal and Pushpa Rani Sharma Rs. 720

CICIL-35 Problems of Collection Development in Special Libraries
M.S. Sridhar Rs. 225

CICIL-36 National Information Resources for Social Sciences in India : Mobilisation, Dispersal and International Enhancement
S.P. Agrawal Rs. 225

CICIL-37 Modern History of Punjab : A Look Back into Ancient Peaceful Punjab Focusing Confrontation and Failures Leading to Present Punjab Problem, and a Peep Ahead : Relevant Select Documents
J.C. Aggarwal and S.P. Agrawal Rs. 400

CICIL-38 India Information Sources : Economics and Business
Kyllikki Ruokonen and Manohar Lal Rs.

CICIL-39 Educational Planning in India : With a Slant to Educational Financing and Administration, Vol. 1, Reports of Committees and Commissions, Five Year Plans, Statistical Tables
J.C. Aggarwal and S.P. Agrawal Rs. 650

CICIL-40 Integrated Library System : Two Case Studies : Latin America and India
Maria Luiza Rigo Pasquarelli, Rosaly Favero Krzyanowski, Ines Maria M. Imperatriz and S.P. Agrawal Rs. 160

CICIL-41 Social Science Information in India: Effort towards Bibliographical Control
S.D. Vyas Rs. 300

CICIL-42 Higher Education in India Since Independence: U.G.C. and its Approach
O.P. Gupta Rs. 360